PUBLISHED

Jane Austen: *Emma* DAVID LODGE
Jane Austen: *'Northanger Abbey' and 'Persuasion'* B.C. SOUTHAM
Jane Austen: *'Sense and Sensibility', 'Pride and Prejudice' and 'Mansfield Park'* B.C.
SOUTHAM
William Blake: *Songs of Innocence and Experience* MARGARET BOTTRALL
Charlotte Brontë: *'Jane Eyre' and 'Villette'* MIRIAM ALLOTT
Emily Brontë: *Wuthering Heights* MIRIAM ALLOTT
Browning: *'Men and Women' and Other Poems* J.R. WATSON
Bunyan: *The Pilgrim's Progress* ROGER SHARROCK
Byron: *'Childe Harold's Pilgrimage' and 'Don Juan'* JOHN JUMP
Chaucer: *Canterbury Tales* J.J. ANDERSON
Coleridge: *'The Ancient Mariner' and Other Poems* ALUN R. JONES AND WILLIAM TYDEMAN
Congreve: *'Love for Love' and 'The Way of the World'* PATRICK LYONS
Conrad: *'Heart of Darkness', 'Nostromo' and 'Under Western Eyes'* C.B. COX
Conrad: *The Secret Agent* IAN WATT
Dickens: *Bleak House* A.E. DYSON.
Dickens: *'Hard Times', 'Great Expectations' and 'Our Mutual Friend'* NORMAN PAGE
Donne: *Songs and Sonets* JULIAN LOVELOCK
George Eliot: *Middlemarch* PATRICK SWINDEN
George Eliot: *'The Mill on the Floss' and 'Silas Marner'* R.P. DRAPER
T.S. Eliot: *Four Quartets* BERNARD BERGONZI
T.S. Eliot: *'Prufrock', 'Gerontion', 'Ash Wednesday' and Other Shorter Poems* B.C. SOUTHAM
T.S. Eliot: *The Waste Land* C.B. COX AND ARNOLD P. HINCHLIFFE
Farquhar: *'The Recruiting Officer' and 'The Beaux' Stratagem'* RAYMOND A. ANSELMENT
Henry Fielding: *Tom Jones* NEIL COMPTON
E.M. Forster: *A Passage to India* MALCOLM BRADBURY
Hardy: *The Tragic Novels* R.P. DRAPER
Hardy: *Poems* JAMES GIBSON AND TREVOR JOHNSON
Gerard Manley Hopkins: *Poems* MARGARET BOTTRALL
Jonson: *Volpone* JONAS A. BARISH
Jonson: *'Every Man in His Humour' and 'The Alchemist'* R.V. HOLDSWORTH
James Joyce: *'Dubliners' and 'A Portrait of the Artist as a Young Man'* MORRIS BEJA.
John Keats: *Odes* G.S. FRASER
D.H. Lawrence: *Sons and Lovers* GAMINI SALGADO
D.H. Lawrence: *'The Rainbow' and 'Women in Love'* COLIN CLARKE
Marlowe: *Doctor Faustus* JOHN JUMP
Marlowe: *'Tamburlaine the Great', 'Edward the Second' and 'The Jew of Malta'* JOHN
RUSSELL BROWN
Marvell: *Poems* ARTHUR POLLARD
The Metaphysical Poets GERALD HAMMOND
Milton: *'Comus' and 'Samson Agonistes'* JULIAN LOVELOCK
Milton: *Paradise Lost* A.E. DYSON AND JULIAN LOVELOCK
John Osborne: *Look Back in Anger* JOHN RUSSELL TAYLOR
Peacock: *The Satirical Novels* LORNA SAGE
Pope: *The Rape of the Lock* JOHN DIXON HUNT
Shakespeare: *Antony and Cleopatra* JOHN RUSSELL BROWN
Shakespeare: *Coriolanus* B.A. BROCKMAN
Shakespeare: *Hamlet* JOHN JUMP

Shakespeare: *Henry IV Parts I and II* G..K. HUNTER
Shakespeare: *Henry V* MICHAEL QUINN
Shakespeare: *Julius Caesar* PETER URE
Shakespeare: *King Lear* FRANK KERMODE
Shakespeare: *Macbeth* JOHN WAIN
Shakespeare: *Measure for Measure* G.K. STEAD
Shakespeare: *The Merchant of Venice* JOHN WILDERS
Shakespeare: *'Much Ado About Nothing' and 'As You Like It'* JOHN RUSSELL BROWN
Shakespeare: *Othello* JOHN WAIN
Shakespeare: *Richard II* NICHOLAS BROOKE
Shakespeare: *The Sonnets* PETER JONES
Shakespeare: *The Tempest* D.J. PALMER
Shakespeare: *Troilus and Cressida* PRISCILLA MARTIN
Shakespeare: *Twelfth Night* D.J. PALMER
Shakespeare: *The Winter's Tale* KENNETH MUIR
Shelley: *Shorter Poems and Lyrics* PATRICK SWINDEN
Spenser: *The Faerie Queene* PETER BAYLEY
Swift: *Gulliver's Travels* RICHARD GRAVIL
Tennyson: *In Memoriam* JOHN DIXON HUNT
Thackeray: *Vanity Fair* ARTHUR POLLARD
Webster: *'The White Devil' and 'The Duchess of Malfi'* R.V. HOLDSWORTH
Wilde: *Comedies* WILLIAM TYDEMAN
Virginia Woolf: *To the Lighthouse* MORRIS BEJA
Wordsworth: *Lyrical Ballads* ALUN R. JONES AND WILLIAM TYDEMAN
Wordsworth: *The Prelude* W.J. HARVEY AND RICHARD GRAVIL
Yeats: *Last Poems* JON STALLWORTHY

Drama Criticism: Developments since Ibsen ARNOLD P. HINCHLIFFE
Poetry of the First World War DOMINIC HIBBERD
Tragedy: Developments in Criticism R.P. DRAPER
The English Novel: Developments in Criticism since Henry James STEPHEN HAZELL
The Romantic Imagination JOHN SPENCER HILL

TITLES IN PREPARATION INCLUDE

Defoe: *'Robinson Crusoe' and 'Moll Flanders'* PATRICK LYONS
T.S. Eliot: *Plays* ARNOLD P. HINCHLIFFE
Henry James: *'Washington Square' and 'Portrait of a Lady'* ALAN SHELSTON
O'Casey: *'Juno and the Paycock', 'The Plough and the Stars' & 'The Shadow of a Gunman'*
    RONALD AYLING
Trollope: *The Barsetshire Novels* T. BAREHAM
Keats: *Narrative Poems* JOHN SPENCER HILL
Shakespeare: *A Midsummer Night's Dream* ANTONY W. PRICE
Yeats: *Poems, 1919–35* ELIZABETH CULLINGFORD
The 'Auden Group' Poets RONALD CARTER
Post-Fifties Poets: Gunn, Hughes, Larkin & R.S. Thomas A.E. DYSON

Poetry Criticism: Developments since the Symbolists A.E. DYSON
Comedy: Developments in Criticism DAVID PALMER
The Language of Literature NORMAN PAGE
Medieval English Drama PETER HAPPÉ
Elizabethan Lyric and Narrative Poetry GERALD HAMMOND
The Pastoral Mode BRYAN LOUGHREY
The Gothick Novel VICTOR SAGE

Shakespeare
Henry V

A CASEBOOK

EDITED BY

MICHAEL QUINN

M

First edition 1969
Reprinted (with revision) 1980, 1983

Published by
THE MACMILLAN PRESS LTD
London and Basingstoke
Associated companies in Delhi Dublin
Hong Kong Johannesburg Lagos Melbourne
New York Singapore and Tokyo

Printed in Hong Kong

ISBN 0 333 04185 2 (pbk)

CONTENTS

ACKNOWLEDGEMENTS

Barrett Wendell, *William Shakespeare: A Study in Elizabethan Literature* (J. M. Dent & Sons Ltd and Charles Scribner's Sons); W. B. Yeats, 'At Stratford-on-Avon', from *Essays and Introductions* (Mr M. B. Yeats); George Bernard Shaw, *Dramatic Opinions and Essays*, vol. 1 (The Public Trustee and The Society of Authors); *Henry V*, ed. Sir Sidney Lee, in the Renaissance edition of Shakespeare 1908 (the Trustees and Guardians of Shakespeare's Birthplace); *William Shakespeare* (The Society of Authors for the Estate of John Masefield, and The Macmillan Company); Harley Granville-Barker, 'From *Henry V* to *Hamlet*', from *Studies in Shakespeare: British Academy Lectures* (Oxford University Press); H. B. Charlton, *Shakespeare, Politics and Politicians* (Mrs E. F. Charlton); William Empson, *Seven Types of Ambiguity* (Chatto & Windus Ltd and New Directions Publishing Corp.); E. M. W. Tillyard, *Shakespeare's History Plays* (Mr Stephen Tillyard, Chatto & Windus Ltd and Barnes & Noble Inc.); J. I. M. Stewart, *Character and Motive in Shakespeare* (Longmans, Green & Co. Ltd); Arthur Sewell, *Character and Society in Shakespeare* (The Clarendon Press); G. Wilson Knight, *The Sovereign Flower* (Methuen & Co. Ltd); Anne Righter, *Shakespeare and the Idea of the Play* (Chatto & Windus Ltd); Gerald Gould, 'A New Reading of *Henry V*', from *English Review* (1919) (Eyre & Spottiswoode (Publishers) Ltd); E. E. Stoll, '*Henry V*', from *Poets and Playwrights*, University of Minnesota Press, Minneapolis; © 1930, University of Minnesota; © renewed 1958 by Elmer E. Stoll. Charles Williams, 'The Honour of King Henry V', from *Shakespeare Criticism*, ed. Anne Bradby (The Clarendon Press); *Shakespeare* (Holt, Rinehart & Winston Inc.; © Mark van Doren 1939, 1967); Una Ellis-Fermor, *The Frontiers of Drama* (Methuen & Co. Ltd); *King Henry V*, ed. J. H. Walter, in the Arden Shakespeare series (Methuen & Co. Ltd and Harvard University Press); Derek A. Traversi, *An Approach to Shakespeare* (The Bodley Head); 'The Formalism of *Henry V*', from *Shakespeare Encomium*, ed. Anne Paolucci (City College Papers 1) (Miss Rose A. Zimbardo and The City College of the City University of New York; © The City College 1964); Zdeněk Stříbrný, '*Henry V* and History', from *Shakespeare in a Changing World*, ed. Arnold Kettle (Lawrence & Wishart Ltd and International Publishers, New York); Professor A. C. Sprague, *Shakespeare's Histories: plays for the stage*; Honor Matthews, *Character and Symbol in Shakespeare's Plays* (Chatto & Windus Ltd and Schocken Books Inc.); 'Shakespeare's Politics: with Some Reflections on the Nature of Tradition', from *Further Explorations* (Chatto & Windus Ltd and Stanford University Press; © L. C. Knights 1965).

GENERAL EDITOR'S PREFACE

EACH of this series of Casebooks concerns either one well-known and influential work of literature or two or three closely linked works. The main section consists of critical readings, mostly modern, brought together from journals and books. A selection of reviews and comments by the author's contemporaries is also included, and sometimes comments from the author himself. The Editor's Introduction charts the reputation of the work from its first appearance until the present time.

What is the purpose of such a collection? Chiefly, to assist reading. Our first response to literature may be, or seem to be, 'personal'. Certain qualities of vigour, profundity, beauty or 'truth to experience' strike us, and the work gains a foothold in our mind. Later, an isolated phrase or passage may return to haunt or illuminate. Where did we hear that? we wonder – it could scarcely be better put.

In these and similar ways appreciation begins, but major literature prompts to very much more. There are certain facts we need to know if we are to understand properly. Who were the author's original readers, and what assumptions did he share with them? What was his theory of literature? Was he committed to a particular historical situation, or a set of beliefs? We need historians as well as critics to help us with this. But there are also more purely literary factors to take account of: the work's structure and rhetoric; its symbols and archetypes; its tone, genre and texture; its use of language; the words on the page. In all these matters critics can inform and enrich our individual responses by offering imaginative recreations of their own.

For the life of a book is not, after all, merely 'personal'; it is more like a tripartite dialogue, between a writer living 'then', a reader living 'now', and whatever forces of survival and honour link the two. Criticism is the public manifestation of this dialogue, a witness to the continuing power of literature to arouse and excite. It illuminates the possibilities and rewards of the dialogue, pushing 'interpretation' as far forward as it can go.

And here, indeed, is the rub: how far can it go? Where does 'interpretation' end, and nonsense begin? Why is one interpretation superior to another, and why does each age need to interpret for itself? The critic knows that his insights have value only in so far as they serve the text, and that he must take account of views differing sharply from his own. He knows that his own writing will be judged as well as the work he writes about, so that he cannot simply assert inner illumination or a differing taste.

The critical forum is a place of vigorous conflict and disagreement, but there is nothing in this to cause dismay. What is attested is the complexity of human experience and the richness of literature, not any chaos or relativity of taste. A critic is better seen, no doubt, as an explorer than as an 'authority', but explorers ought to be, and usually are, well equipped. The effect of good criticism is to convince us of what C. S. Lewis called 'the enormous extension of our being which we owe to authors'. This Casebook will be justified only if it helps to promote the same end.

A single volume can represent no more than a small selection of critical opinions. Some critics have been excluded for reasons of space, and it is hoped that readers will follow up the further suggestions in the Select Bibliography. Other contributions have been severed from their original context, to which some readers may wish to return. Indeed, if they take a hint from the critics represented here, they certainly will.

A. E. DYSON

INTRODUCTION

Henry V is one of the few plays of Shakespeare that can be dated with some precision, mainly because of a remarkable topical reference to the Earl of Essex which occurs in the fifth Chorus: this establishes with a fair degree of certainty that the play was completed and probably performed some time in the late spring or early summer of 1599.[1] It was thus the last of the nine English history plays that Shakespeare wrote in the 1590s. With *Richard II* and two parts of *Henry IV*, it composes a cycle of four plays dealing with the deposition of Richard II and the establishment of the House of Lancaster on the English throne, and it provides a link with Shakespeare's earlier cycle of four plays that tells the story of the civil wars between the Houses of York and Lancaster, the triumph of the monstrous Yorkist Richard III, and the final union of the warring houses and the restoration of peace to England by the first Tudor, Henry VII.

These eight plays, with *King John* and *Henry VIII*, were grouped together by the editors of the First Folio under the general heading of 'Histories'. Whether these and other comparable contemporary plays can properly be regarded as constituting a distinct dramatic genre remains an open and complex critical question: important contributions to the discussion will be found in the works by Ribner, Tillyard and Reese listed on pp. 239–40. As the following selection of criticism on *Henry V* shows, the question is important because one's response to a play is very likely to be different if one regards it as, say, primarily historical

[1] For a detailed consideration of dating and sources, see any good critical edition, such as those of Wilson and Walter listed on p. 239; for sources, see also *Narrative and Dramatic Sources of Shakespeare*, ed. G. Bullough, IV (London and New York, 1962).

in intention, rather than political or tragic or comic or epic. But Shakespeare's ten English history-plays do have certain common characteristics of which the most obvious is that they were based on the chronicles of English history, such as those of Hall (1547) and Holinshed (1577, 1587): for *Henry V*, for instance, Shakespeare read both of these chronicles, although he also seems to have had knowledge of other, less well-known chronicles and of an earlier play on the same subject. Although playwrights using chronicle material were undoubtedly concerned to cater for the growing appetite of the new middle-class for 'useful knowledge', it is unlikely that their main impulse was simple didacticism. The rapid expansion of demand for plays, following the heavy investment of capital in the theatre in the late 1570s and 1580s, produced a somewhat desperate search for narrative material suitable for adaptation to the stage, and the chronicles proved a magnificent storehouse of dramatic material. They provided almost unlimited scope for the kind of spectacle and violent action demanded by a popular audience: robes (royal, noble, ecclesiastical), armour, swords and spears, cannons, flags and pennants, hautboys and trumpets; sword-fights, brutal killings, riots, battles and sieges; characters with strongly outlined motives and violent passions. Only comedy was lacking to satisfy the popular taste and, as the early chronicle plays demonstrate clearly enough, there was little difficulty in infiltrating comic matter into an historical story: even *Tamburlaine*, it seems, included in its stage performances 'some fond and frivolous Iestures'.

Although other playwrights, such as Marlowe, had already based plays on the chronicles, Shakespeare may have been the first to use English chronicle material on the popular stage and the the whole 'feel' of his histories is radically different from those dramatizing the stories of continental and oriental figures such as Tamburlaine, Selimus and Alphonsus of Aragon. The proximity of time and place, and especially the use of English names of people and places, inevitably charge the stories with qualities of intimate involvement. Moreover, and much more important, since eight of the nine histories written by Shakespeare in the 1590s are devoted to the hundred years leading up to the Battle of Bosworth and the establishment of the Tudors on the English throne, they represent an extended study of the origins of the political situation in which their Elizabethan spectators found themselves. Whether or not these plays were deliberately intended to reflect directly contemporary situations in the way Lily B. Campbell has suggested (and the undeniable and harsh fact of censorship may make us hesitate to go all the way with her), there can be little doubt that the best of them were conceived by their authors and understood by their more thoughtful spectators as relevant to their own situation, as reminding them of present social and political problems.

Not all Elizabethan chronicle plays, however, reveal the serious concern for the contemporary situation that we find in Shakespeare. Some of them are little more than dramatizations of episodes selected from the chronicles mainly for their qualities of spectacle, sensation or crude morality. But Shakespeare seems to have read his chronicles with the serious mind of a moralizing historian as well as with the lively mind of a practising dramatic entertainer. Renaissance historians were in no doubt about the didactic value of their subject: by revealing patterns of conduct in the past which could be expected to recur in the present, it provided the reader with the benefits of experience without actually submitting him to that 'schoolemistresse of fooles'. History

not only maketh things past present; but inableth one to make a rationall conjecture of things to come. For this world affordeth no new accidents ... Old actions return again, furbished ouer with some new and different circumstances.[1]

Because history repeated itself, the historian could demonstrate the virtues and vices of kings and statesmen of the past, provide illustrations of the truth or falsity of political theories, demonstrate the glory of the nation, and, not least important, reveal that there was a rational and moral plan in human affairs. And in all this Hall and his echo Holinshed were as good examples of the Renaissance historian as could be found writing in English, and Shakespeare took over much of their attitude to history.

[1] Thomas Fuller, *Historie of the Holie Warre* (1638) sig. 4ʳ.

Hall, following Polydore Vergil, had seen in the agonies of fifteenth-century English history a unifying theme that made some sense of the apparent anarchy. The bitter enmity of the Houses of York and Lancaster that issued in the Wars of the Roses had its origin in the deposition and murder of the last Plantagenet king, Richard II; and the chain of killing and revenge that followed that 'original crime' was in fact a working-out of the evil under the guiding control of Divine Providence, until at last unity and order were restored under Henry VII. Shakespeare took over from his sources both this reading of fifteenth-century English history and the view that the accession of the Tudors was an unmitigated blessing for England. But he brought out much more strongly a deep horror of a world given over to anarchy, a world in which right values were continually being inverted and which seemed to be regressing to presocial chaos.

As Tillyard and many others have demonstrated, Elizabethan thinkers were much concerned with the concept of 'Order', of obedience to law.[1] The state was regarded not merely as a political structure but also, through analogies with the celestial hierarchy, the universe, and especially with the human body, as a living organism. The soul of this organism was civil order or 'proportion', 'the iust, right, and naturall measure of thinges, directed to theyr originall and first creation',[2] and this idea of harmony governed the treatment of all the consequences of disruptive activity. If any part of the organism failed to function properly, then the whole would necessarily suffer, for 'by order all things are preserued and maintayned, and without order all things come to ruine and confusion'.[3] Shakespeare's histories present an elaborate vision of just such 'ruine and confusion' and, the longer he contemplated the problem, the more Shakespeare seems to have come to the conclusion that order depended primarily on the exercise of authority and that 'the great image of authority' was the absolute ruler.

[1] See the works by Tillyard listed on p. 239; Theodore Spencer, *Shakespeare and the Nature of Man* (New York, 1942).
[2] William Blandy, *The Castle, or picture of pollicy* (1581) fo. 4^r.
[3] Richard Crompton, *The Mansion of Magnanimitie* (1599) sig. A3^r.

Whether or not Shakespeare was as ardently royalist as is sometimes suggested, characters in the plays frequently express fairly
extreme views of kingship: the King is 'God's substitute, His
deputy anointed in His sight', 'the figure of God's majesty', even
'a god on earth'. But he also retains much of the medieval view
of kingship that stressed the moral responsibility of the ruler to
the body politic of which he was the head. When Shakespeare's
Henry V, ascending the throne, insists that he is no Turkish
Amurath but an English Harry (2 *Henry IV*, v ii 47–9), or,
later, that he is 'no tyrant, but a Christian king' (*Henry V*, I ii
241), he is making the contrast, a commonplace of Elizabethan
political writing, between the Good Prince and the Tyrant. (See
Walter, below, pp. 132–4.) Good order depended on a good
prince.

In the fifteenth century, however, the nature of every English
king, with (for the Elizabethans anyway) the outstanding exception of Henry V, was marred by a fatal flaw: either they were
weak or wicked, or their title to the throne was dubious. That the
king's title should be so important may seem somewhat odd to us
today but for the Elizabethans, when Richard II was deposed,
the legitimate succession to the throne was broken, the 'good and
necessary order' of the state was shattered, the integration of
human social relationships into the cosmic harmony designed by
God was lost. The situation was analogous to that produced by
the religious divisions in the sixteenth century: if one knew
where truth reposed, one might discover God's will and possibly
follow it; in the political sphere, if one knew who embodied the
'image of authority', then one might obey. In *Henry IV* the
question of divine right, which had figured so prominently in
Richard II, is no longer an issue: human force, not divine
ordinance, has laid the basis of this state. Because Henry IV
rules by power and not by right, he depends on the support of
those who helped him to the throne; but

> The love of wicked men converts to fear;
> That fear to hate; and hate turns one or both
> To worthy danger and deserved death.
> (*Richard II*, v i 66–8)

The authority of a king *de facto* may be challenged by one who claims a better title and, more important, proves more capable of wielding effective power. In the *Henry VI* plays, although the search to discover which of the rival houses has the better claim to the throne seems hopeless, the historical action moves inevitably, if erratically, under the guidance of Divine Providence towards the Tudor restoration of order. In *Henry IV*, however, this consummation, this 'second coming' of divinely ordained kingship, is still far away.

This is the situation in which Prince Hal, son of the usurping Henry IV, declares his intention to 'redeem the time', because, as the Epistle to the Ephesians puts it, 'the days are evil'. In a corrupt and power-ridden world, what kind of order may be achieved and what kind of man may effectively and justly exercise authority? The popular legend of Hal's dissolute youth was specially suited to a consideration of such a problem because it suggested something of the struggle of fallen man towards a more moral and responsible attitude. Hal's reform was exploited in the anonymous play, *The Famous Victories of Henry V*, which was probably, in some sense, a source for *Henry IV* and *Henry V*; and many modern critics have seen these three plays as presenting this progress from irresponsible madcap to responsible king.

But in popular esteem Hal was more than the reformed rake: as King Henry V, the glorious victor of Agincourt, he was regarded by the Elizabethans as an exemplar of the Good Prince, on a par with Edward III and the mythical Alexander Severus. Holinshed's praise of him is wholly unequivocal:

This Henrie was a king, of life without spot; a prince whome all men loved, and of none disdained; a capteine against whome fortune never frowned, nor mischance once spurned; whose people him so severe a iusticer both loved and obeied, (and so humane withall,) that he left no offense unpunished, nor freendship unrewarded ... a paterne in princehood, a lode-starre in honour, and mirrour of magnificence ...[1]

And most critics accept that Shakespeare, having treated the reform of the Prince in *Henry IV*, intended to present in *Henry V*

[1] *Sources of Shakespeare*, ed. Bullough, pp. 406–8.

the popular hero-king: the opening panegyric of the churchmen, the praise of the king put in the mouth of such a wide variety of characters, above all the way in which the Chorus continually nudges the audience's responses into the channels of approbation and admiration, all have been seen as confirming beyond doubt such an intention. What is not agreed is whether Shakespeare in fact succeeded in this overt purpose or whether he did not have a covert intention more ambiguous or complex.

We have no means of knowing for sure how *Henry V* was received by its first audiences. Dover Wilson, however, has little doubt, not only that the play was peculiarly apt for the feeling of the country in 1599, but also that its subject-matter, the theme and the occasion all combined to call forth the best of Shakespeare's endeavours:

The national emergency, the height of his great argument, the urge to equal if not surpass his earlier successes in historical drama, the quickened pulse of his own heart at the thought of England at war; all these would stimulate him to put forth his utmost strength.[1]

Nevertheless there do not appear to have been many revivals of the play through the seventeenth century and it was not until after 1730 that it really regained its place in the theatre repertory. Nor were eighteenth-century critics generally very enthusiastic about it, most of them inclining to Dr Johnson's implied view of the play as something of a 'pot-boiler' (see below, pp. 32–4): a view that recurs sporadically in the following centuries, finding its fullest and most damaging statement from Mark Van Doren, some of whose criticisms of the play would still seem to require satisfactory answers. (See below, pp. 116–24.)

The debate on the quality of the play goes on, as one would expect, but in the last hundred years or so it has been complicated by an extraordinary split in critical responses. For the greater part of the nineteenth century there was little serious doubt that the play presented, more or less successfully, the hero-king. Hazlitt's virulent and brilliant abuse of Henry, being politically

[1] *King Henry V*, ed. J. Dover Wilson (Cambridge, 1968) p. xi.

inspired, need not be taken too seriously and it did not prevent him from admiring the king, even if only as an 'amiable monster'. But Schlegel, who was critical of the artistic integrity of the play, saw Henry as 'manifestly Shakespeare's favourite hero in English history ... endowed with every chivalrous and kingly virtue' (see below, p. 34). And Carlyle, Knight, Gervinus, Dowden, Moulton and Lee generally carry on this traditional view. But some uneasiness about the character of the king begins to stir in the comments of Knight and Kenny, while Dowden, a very balanced and influential critic, having eulogized the king with all the gusto of Victorian patriotism, finds it necessary to introduce a sharp limitation: Henry is 'Shakespeare's ideal of the *practical* hero' but is not Shakespeare's highest ideal, this being represented by the spiritually more developed but temporally less successful heroes of the following tragedies. Moulton maintains a scholarly impartiality but, as Jorgensen notes in his useful brief survey of criticism of the play, he lets his mask slip in 'one sentence bright with irony';[1] the conspirators, uncovered and condemned by the king,

have grace enough to long for their death; and Henry, who has no weakness, not even the weakness of mercy, dismisses them to their fate. (See below, p. 50.)

After Moulton the concealed dislike of Henry's practical efficiency and success becomes explicit in the comments of Shaw, Yeats, Bradley and Masefield. The king is now seen as 'an able young Philistine', a 'vessel of clay' with 'gross vices' and 'coarse nerves', a 'commonplace man', and (in Bradley's more subtle assessment) as a national hero whose 'nature is limited', whose religion is 'superstitious', who is ready 'to use other people as means to his own ends' and who is incapable of 'strong affection'. Gould, writing – significantly – in 1919, launches the first full-scale assault on the traditional reading of the play and thereafter even the unequivocal admirers of Henry have an air of being on the defensive.

[1] Paul A. Jorgensen, 'Accidental Judgements, Casual Slaughters, and Purposes Mistook: Critical Reactions to Shakspere's *Henry the Fifth*', in *Shakespeare Association Bulletin*, XXII (1947) p. 56.

How can we explain this remarkable revulsion of feeling from the hero of the Elizabethans and even of the Victorians? Some of it is undoubtedly carried over from Bradley's reading of *Henry IV* that sees Hal's dismissal of Falstaff at the end of Part II as the rejection of all that is warm, lovable and human in favour of cold, ruthless, calculating expediency. Since *Henry V* was clearly conceived as a continuation of *Henry IV* (the report of Falstaff's death, the inclusion of his old friends, the numerous references to Hal's 'misspent youth' and to the political difficulties of Henry IV, the episode of the conspirators, and above all the whole conception of Henry as redeeming the country from the corruption engendered at the deposition of Richard II, put this beyond doubt), the king is identified with the prince in *Henry IV* and the objections to Hal then find reinforcement in various aspects of the king's behaviour in *Henry V*. So, for many critics, the large shadow of Falstaff haunts the king even in the play in which he does not appear. Why *did* Shakespeare omit Falstaff from *Henry V*? The Epilogue to *2 Henry IV* had promised that he would appear:

If you be not too much cloy'd with fat meat, our humble author will continue the story, with Sir John in it, and make you merry with fair Katherine of France; where, for anything I know, Falstaff shall die of a sweat, unless already 'a be killed with your hard opinions . . .

Dover Wilson has argued persuasively that Falstaff was in the first draft of the play but that Shakespeare had to remove him, probably because of 'the desertion or expulsion of Will Kempe', who played the part, from the company.[1] But another frequent and more fundamental explanation is that the presence of the cynical and realistic old reprobate would have deflated disastrously the heroism of the warrior-king. Even his presence by report, in the account of his death in Act II, is felt by some critics to convey a most telling criticism of the king, coming at is does immediately after Henry's own sermon to Scroop on the requirements of friendship. In other words, the very absence of Falstaff

[1] *Henry V*, ed. Wilson, pp. xlv, 113–16; see also his *The Fortunes of Falstaff* (Cambridge, 1943) pp. 124–5.

from *Henry V* is seen as pointing to deficiencies in the character of its hero.

However, even if we allow that some of the dislike of the king is inherited from *Henry IV*, it does seem that often the reformed and triumphant King Henry is found to be even less likeable than the prince of *Henry IV*. Can it be that the growth of democracy has made the modern audience antipathetic to Henry V's autocracy? This seems unlikely. Hazlitt could hardly have been more violently opposed to autocracy but even he could recognize that

The behaviour of the king, in the difficult and doubtful circumstances in which he was placed, is as patient and modest as it is spirited and lofty in his prosperous fortune. (See below, p. 38.)

Moreover, Henry's autocracy is hardly stressed in the play: rather, as we have said, he is presented as an image of the Good Prince, the reverse of the wilful tyrant, one who is, as far as possible, identified with his people. The whole emphasis of the portrait is that of an ordinary man called to an extraordinary office and fulfilling it magnificently, and so becoming himself extraordinary. Such a conception of a national leader, not so very different from a successful American President or British Prime Minister (especially a wartime leader such as Churchill), does not seem to offer very obvious grounds for rejection by a modern audience.

Perhaps a more satisfying explanation is that our attitude to war has changed: that the experience of two world wars and innumerable other wars, involving innocent civilians as well as fighting men, has made us less nationalistic and even less patriotic, and certainly more pacifist and far less inclined to be enthusiastic about wars of aggression. Schlegel was, I think, the first to draw attention to the dubiousness of Henry's reasons for the expedition into France and several later critics have made much of the issue, seeing the invasion as simply aggression, with no justification other than as a means of keeping Henry secure on his throne and satisfying his lust for personal glory. Sometimes the blame is placed mainly on the bishops in the first scene who plot to encourage the king to attack France in order to distract him from the proposal to confiscate church lands. Other critics, such as John Palmer, place the blame directly on Henry himself by pointing out that he had issued his ultimatum to the French *before* conferring with his ecclesiastical advisers, so that in fact he 'was not seeking spiritual or legal advice' but merely 'inviting moral approbation for a *fait accompli*'.[1] The difficulty with all these objections that centre on the politic, self-preserving casuistry of the churchmen or the timing of Henry's ultimatum is that they depend on a precise hearing and understanding of a few sentences or even phrases, and on the drawing of fairly extensive logical conclusions from them. Will such deductions stand against what would seem to be the main intention and impression of the second scene of the play: that Henry is carefully weighing the justice of his claim to the French throne, with a full awareness of the implications of his decision and with a firm control over his personal passions?

The king's threatening speech before Harfleur (III iii) raises more serious difficulties. His words have been described as 'ravings, almost incredible in their mingled brutality and hypocrisy' (p. 91 below), as presenting a combination of triumphant warrior with 'a ruthless and inhuman engine of destruction' (p. 154 below). The savagery of the speech is such that even the pro-Henry Stoll is moved to remark, 'his bark is worse than his bite, *we trust*', and, seemingly somewhat puzzled, notes that Shakespeare's Henry before Harfleur is more savage than Holinshed's (p. 100 below). This view of the king's character as revealing a strain of ruthless brutality is sustained by integrating it with the view of the French war as mere aggression and with later episodes, especially the massacre of the French prisoners and the execution of Bardolph. But is this how we are meant to respond to this speech? It can be argued that here we have an example of a kind of 'depersonalisation' where the playwright is more concerned with the content of the speech than with the attitudes or feelings of the speaker; in which case the speech might be read, not as a revelation of Henry's bloodthirstiness and innate cruelty, but as an objective description of the horrors that are likely to

[1] *The Political Characters of Shakespeare* (1945) p. 224.

follow the taking of a besieged town in the fifteenth century, establishing for the audience the hideous realities of war. Henry might be seen as speaking here *ex officio*, as a king and a military commander conducting a siege with a small army that will soon be in desperate danger. And Henry's other speeches might stand as objective statements on the morality of declaring war, the obligations of loyalty and friendship, the demands of courage in the face of danger, the dreadful responsibility resting on a king who has to exercise justice on malefactors and to lead his people into war. Our reading of the character of the king in *Henry V* may then vary according to whether we are more concerned with the problems he faces or with the nature of the man facing them.

Such questions lead on to a consideration of what kind of play *Henry V* is supposed to be. Shakespeare's English history-plays, although they share many common characteristics, are often very clearly distinguishable from each other in dramatic technique and total effect. *Henry V* is very different from its predecessors and one of the earliest explanations of its supposed failure was that in this instance the material and theme proved unsuitable for the kind of dramatic treatment Shakespeare had used in his previous histories. The reiterated apologies of the Chorus for the inadequacy of the stage are taken as implying a recognition that the matter was not truly dramatic but rather epic in nature. Schlegel, whose comments on the difference between epic and drama are particularly interesting (below, p. 35), Walter (pp. 131–3), Zimbardo (pp. 163–70), and J. Dover Wilson, in his introduction to the New Cambridge edition of the play, all develop this idea. If we accept this explanation of the play's construction and intention, it seems reasonable to assume that epic drama of this kind will demand a different kind of response from that we give to other kinds of drama: here our experience of Brechtian epic drama may help us.

Such drama would seem to belong to what Robert Langbaum has called a pre-Enlightenment

literature of external action in which the events derive meaning from their relation to a publicly acknowledged morality.

Langbaum distinguishes this literature from a romantic and post-romantic

literature of experience, in which the events have meaning inasmuch as they provide the central character with an occasion for experience – for self-expression and self-discovery.[1]

In such a 'literature of external action' the 'publicly acknowledged morality' will obviously be of central importance and, when time brings that morality into question or even disrepute, the spectators and readers of a later age may be expected to have difficulty with the work. As we have suggested, this appears to be an important element in the critical debate on *Henry V*. But there are innumerable literary works the events of which derive their meaning from a morality that many modern readers find difficult to accept and to which they nevertheless respond satisfactorily. We need to distinguish two questions. First, to what extent do we find the 'publicly acknowledged morality' presented in *Henry V* repugnant to us and how does this affect our response to the play? And secondly, did Shakespeare himself, as he was writing the play, come to feel that the values that he set out to promulgate were in fact inadequate? This latter question, answered with a convinced affirmative by several critics, involves political considerations of the kind raised by L. C. Knights in the last essay in this book. Viewing *Henry V* not simply as the conclusion of the English history-plays of the 1590s but also as an immediate precursor of *Julius Caesar, Hamlet,* the Dark Comedies and the later tragedies, Knights sees the play as part of 'a continuous exploration and assessment of experience', moving towards the conviction that 'the political problem, purely on the level of politics and the political man, is insoluble', 'that a wholesome political order is not something arbitrary and imposed, but an expression of relationships between particular persons within an organic society'.

There is, however, a further question that may be asked. Even if we grant that as Shakespeare worked on the task of presenting his hero-king his admiration began to go sour, does this radically

[1] Robert Langbaum, *The Poetry of Experience* (New York, 1957), p. 160.

alter the effect of the play as a whole? The play was written for a
popular theatre and presumably succeeded there; it has continued
to be played in popular theatres and usually successfully. Does
the play's popular success spring from the audience's recognition
of the tension between the 'publicly acknowledged morality' of
the play, its presentation of a patriotic, even chauvinistic image of
a national warrior-hero, and Shakespeare's subtle criticism of this
morality? Or does it spring from an unsubtle, uninhibited enjoy-
ment of the first element only ? The popular success of Olivier's
film version of the play suggested to Jorgensen

that dislike of the king might be almost confined to poets,
scholars, and other intellectuals who have not witnessed or conceived the play as a dynamic spectacle. Furthermore, the popular
audiences of today, particularly in America, are not, like intellec-
tuals, alienated by low-comedy courtship scenes, practical jokes,
successful business men, and happy endings.[1]

Certainly Sprague, after his careful review of the productions of
two centuries, has little doubt that the play is 'no more a scholar's
play than it is a giddy one', that it is 'on the whole a clear, straight-
forward history', and that 'a soundly conceived interpretation of
the character' of the king must be based on the cry, 'Praise and
glory on his head'. (See below, pp. 189, 199.)

Nevertheless, the argument from the stage or screen success of
the play needs to be handled carefully, since often one cannot be
wholly sure that the 'dynamic spectacle' witnessed was in fact
Shakespeare's play. It is not simply a matter of the various spec-
tacular additions that must inevitably have modified in performance the effect of the whole. Modification can involve a good
deal more than theatrical elaboration. For instance, if my memory
and notes serve me, the text for Olivier's film version of 1945,
frequently quoted as an example of successful performance, was
in fact trimmed with consistent and ruthless purpose: the conspirators' scene is omitted, so that we do not see Henry con-
demning an erstwhile friend nor can we make any unfavourable
comparisons between Scroop's treatment of his friend Hal and
Hal's treatment of his friend Falstaff; there is no reference to

[1] Loc. cit. pp. 59–60.

Richard II so that the dubiousness of Henry's title is never raised; the disturbing Harfleur speech, Williams's challenge to the king concerning responsibility for the war, the report of the execution of Bardolph, all are cut; Henry's order to kill the French prisoners is cut, although the French attack on the English camp-boys is not only retained but is translated from mere report to vivid enactment; and, finally, the reference in the Epilogue to Henry VI who, as Schlegel puts it, 'miserably lost all', is also missing. In other words, a considerable number of the points in the text which critics have seized upon as reflecting badly on the king and on the patriotic ideal have been silently removed so that nothing shall tarnish the image of the English warrior-king and the film justify its dedication to the British commandos and air-borne troops in the Second World War. To argue that the popular success of such a version answers the objections of the critics would scarcely seem to be convincing.

This does not mean, of course, that only a heavily cut or modified version of the text can succeed with a popular audience, Whether or not Jorgensen is right in his assertion that 'intellec-tuals' are 'alienated by low-comedy scenes, practical jokes, suc-cessful business men, and happy endings', it does not follow that, because popular audiences enjoy such elements in a play, they are therefore incapable of responding to subtle and complex ironies and ambiguities. S. L. Bethell argued that the dominant character-istic of a popular audience was its ability 'to respond spontane-ously and unconsciously on more than one plane of attention at the same time', and that this 'multi-consciousness' allowed them to find a character such as Falstaff both amusing and morally reprehensible without experiencing any sense of intolerable contradiction.[1] Such an audience might recognize Henry V as ruthless, calculating, sanctimonious, even hypocritical, and still find him wholly admirable as king and military leader. But it may be that the very sophistication of the literary critic makes it difficult for him to entertain such contradictions; that, paradoxi-cally more simple than the groundling, he feels obliged to love where he admires.

[1] *Shakespeare and the Popular Dramatic Tradition* (1944), p. 29.

A NOTE ON THE TEXT OF
HENRY V

Although two early versions of *Henry V* have survived, the text does not present any great difficulty. The play was first published as a quarto in 1600 (Q1), with the title:

The Chronicle History of Henry the fift, With his battel fought at Agin Court in France. Togither with Auntient Pistoll. As it hath bene sundry times playd by the Right honorable the Lord Chamberlaine his seruants ...

This version was reprinted, with minor corrections, in 1602 (Q2) and in 1619 (Q3: falsely dated 1608). It is now generally agreed by scholars that this text is a 'bad quarto', a corrupt text probably reconstructed from memory by two or three actors who had played (possibly the parts of Gower and Exeter) in a shortened form of the play while on tour in the provinces.

The second version is that published in the First Folio of 1623. This is generally considered to have been printed from Shakespeare's own manuscript or 'foul papers' and may represent the text before it was prepared for the theatre by the Company's prompter. It has been argued that the Folio was set up from a copy of the quarto, probably Q3, which had been corrected from a superior manuscript; this argument, which would seem to involve a rather less respectful attitude to the Folio text, is disputed, however. But no textual discussion or discovery is likely to alter the view that the only authoritative copy-text for *Henry V* is that of the First Folio. And, compared with other Shakespeare texts, it is a good one; the punctuation has been described by Dover Wilson as 'quite surprisingly good', suggesting to him that Shakespeare composed the play in a 'deliberate' mood.

The play as we read it in most modern editions contains what is undoubtedly the most famous emendation in Shakespeare. Lewis Theobald, in his edition of 1733, emended the Folio reading of II iii 17 (in the Hostess's description of the death of Falstaff) from 'and a Table of green fields' to 'and a' babbled of green fields'. Later eighteenth-century editors tended to ridicule Theobald's emendation but it established itself as the accepted reading, mainly on aesthetic grounds. In the last fifty years or so, the question has been reopened: support for Theobald has come from scholars expert in Renaissance handwriting and printing techniques and on other grounds, while a variety of arguments have been put forward for a return to a reading nearer that of the Folio; the simplest and perhaps the most impressive of the latter suggests that 'Table' is simple a misprint for 'Talk'd'. A useful survey of the debate and a strong argument against Theobald will be found in E. G. Fogel, ' "A Table of Green Fields": A Defense of the Folio Reading', *Shakespeare Quarterly*, IX (1958), pp. 485–92; and the matter is of course considered in most good editions of the play. It does not seem likely, however, that Theobald's brilliant emendation will be unseated, at least not for many years to come.

Article-titles. In the case of one or two of the extracts reprinted in this volume it has been found necessary to provide an *ad hoc* title. The source of the extract is, however, always clearly indicated.

MICHAEL QUINN

PART ONE
Shorter Critical Extracts

CHARLES GILDON

THE Prologue to this Play is as remarkable as any thing in *Shakespear*, and is a Proof that he was extremely sensible of the Absurdity which then possess'd the Stage, in bringing in whole Kingdoms, and Lives, and various Actions in one Piece; for he apologizes for it, and desires the Audience to persuade their Imaginations to help him out, and promises a Chorus to help their Imagination.

For 'tis your Thoughts [says he] that now must deck our Kings,
Carry them here and there, jumping o'er Times;
Turning the Accomplishments of many Years
Into an Hour-glass; for the which Supply
Admit me *Chorus* to this History, &c.

He here and in the foregoing Lines expresses how preposterous and unnatural it seem'd to him to huddle so many Actions, so many Places, and so many Years into one Play, one Stage, and two Hours. So that it is not to be doubted, but that he would have given us far more noble Plays, if he had had the good Fortune to have seen but any one regular Performance of this nature. The Beauty of Order would have struck him immediately, and at once have made him more correct, and more excellent . . .

The Character of *Hen. V* given by the Bishop of *Canterbury*, is very noble. His Discourse of the Salique Law, is a Proof that *Shakespear* was well acquainted with the History of modern Times; and that very Controversy, which was an Argument of his Application to reading, will not let me think, that having some Foundation of *Latin*, he should totally neglect that.

Obedience and Order
Therefore doth Heaven divide
The State of Man to divers Functions, &c.

The fine Description of the State of the Bees, is worth a careful Observation in this same Speech. The King's Answer to the *French* Ambassadors, on the *Dauphin*'s Present, is not only fine, but shews that *Shakespear* understood Tennis very well, and is perfect in the Terms of the Art. . . .

The Character of *Fluellen* is extremely comical, and yet so very happily touch'd, that at the same time when he makes us laugh, he makes us value his Character. The Scene of Love betwixt *Henry* V and *Catharine* is extravagantly silly and unnatural; for why he should not allow her to speak in *English* as well as all the other *French*, I cannot imagine; since it adds no Beauty, but gives a patch'd and pye-bald Dialogue of no Beauty or Force.

(from *Remarks on the Plays of Shakespeare.*
Works of Shakespeare, IX, 1714)

SAMUEL JOHNSON

ACT II. SCENE iv. (II iii 27–8)   *Cold as any stone.*
SUCH is the end of *Falstaff*, from whom *Shakespeare* had promised us in his epilogue to *Henry IV* that we should receive more entertainment. It happened to *Shakespeare* as to other writers, to have his imagination crowded with a tumultuary confusion of images, which, while they were yet unsorted and unexamined, seemed sufficient to furnish a long train of incidents, and a new variety of merriment, but which, when he was to produce them to view, shrunk suddenly from him, or could not be accommodated to his general design. That he once designed to have brought *Falstaff* on the scene again, we know from himself; but whether he could contrive no train of adventures suitable to his character, or could match him with no companions likely to quicken his humour, or could open no new vein of pleasantry, and was afraid to continue the same strain lest it should not find the same reception, he has here for ever discarded him, and made haste to dispatch him, perhaps for the same reason for which *Addison* killed Sir *Roger*, that no other hand might attempt to exhibit him.

Let meaner authours learn from this example, that it is dangerous to sell the bear which is yet not hunted, to promise to the publick what they have not written.

ACT IV. SCENE xiv. (IV vii 51–2)

The fat Knight with the great belly-doublet.

This is the last time that *Falstaff* can make sport. The poet
was loath to part with him, and has continued his memory as
long as he could.

ACT V. SCENE ii. (V i 94)   *Exit* Pistol.

The comick scenes of the history of *Henry* the fourth and fifth
are now at an end, and all the comick personages are now dis-
missed. *Falstaff* and Mrs. *Quickly* are dead; *Nym* and *Bardolph*
are. hanged; *Gadshill* was lost immediately after the robbery;
Poins and *Peto* have vanished since, one knows not how; and
Pistol is now beaten into obscurity. I believe every reader
regrets their departure.

ACT V. SCENE iv. (V ii 125 foll.)

KING HENRY.   *I'faith*, Kate, *thou wouldst find me such a plain
King*, &c.

I know not why *Shakespeare* now gives the king nearly such
a character as he made him formerly ridicule in *Percy*. This military grossness and unskilfulness in all the softer arts, does not
suit very well with the gaieties of his youth, with the general
knowledge ascribed to him at his accession, or with the contemptuous message sent him by the *Dauphin*, who represents him as
fitter for the ball room than the field, and tells him that he is not
to revel into dutchies, or win provinces *with a nimble galliard*.
The truth is, that the poet's matter failed him in the fifth act, and
he was glad to fill it up with whatever he could get; and not even
Shakespeare can write well without a proper subject. It is a vain
endeavour for the most skilful hand to cultivate barrenness, or to
paint upon vacuity.

ACT V. SCENE v. (V ii 305–402)

We have here but a mean dialogue for princes; the merriment
is very gross, and the sentiments are very worthless.

This play has many scenes of high dignity, and many of easy merriment. The character of the King is well supported, except in his courtship, where he has neither the vivacity of *Hal*, nor the grandeur of *Henry*. The humour of *Pistol* is very happily continued; his character has perhaps been the model of all the bullies that have yet appeared on the *English* stage.

The lines given to the chorus have many admirers; but the truth is, that in them a little may be praised, and much must be forgiven; nor can it be easily discovered why the intelligence given by the chorus is more necessary in this play than in many others where it is omitted. The great defect of this play is the emptiness and narrowness of the last act, which a very little diligence might have easily avoided.

(from *Works of Shakespeare*,
ed. Samuel Johnson, 1765)

MRS INCHBALD

THE death of Falstaff also, told in a humorous but most natural manner, will be as impressive, on some minds, as any of those scenes where the poet has frequently made state, pomp, or bitterest calamity, attendant on the dying man. – That pining obscurity in which the supercilious Sir John was compelled to live, when his royal comrade became ashamed of him, is a subject well worth the reflection of many a luckless parasite – and now, this stealing to his bed; stealing to his grave, without one tragic bustle, except that which his conscience makes, so well describes the usual decease of a neglected profligate, that every man who thinks, will own the resemblance, and take the warning conveyed.

(from *Henry V, With remarks by Mrs Inchbald*, 1807)

A. W. SCHLEGEL

KING Henry the Fifth is manifestly Shakespeare's favourite hero in English history: he paints him as endowed with every chivalrous and kingly virtue; open, sincere, affable, yet, as a sort of reminiscence of his youth, still disposed to innocent raillery, in

the intervals between his perilous but glorious achievements.
However, to represent on the stage his whole history subsequent
to his accession to the throne, was attended with great difficulty.
The conquests in France were the only distinguished event of his
reign; and war is an epic rather than a dramatic object. For
wherever men act in masses against each other, the appearance
of chance can never wholly be avoided; whereas it is the business
of the drama to exhibit to us those determinations which, with a
certain necessity, issue from the reciprocal relations of different
individuals, their characters and passions ... If we would have
dramatic interest, war must only be the means by which something else is accomplished, and not the last aim and substance
of the whole ... With great insight into the essence of his art,
[Shakespeare] never paints the fortune of war as a blind 'deity
who sometimes favours one and sometimes another; without
going into the details of the art of war (though sometimes he even
ventures on this), he allows us to anticipate the result from the
qualities of the general, and their influence on the minds of the
soldiers; sometimes, without claiming our belief for miracles, he
yet exhibits the issue in the light of a higher volition: the consciousness of a just cause and reliance on the protection of Heaven
give courage to the one party, while the presage of a curse hanging over their undertaking weighs down the other ...

However much Shakespeare celebrates the French conquest of
Henry, still he has not omitted to hint, after his way, the secret
springs of this undertaking. Henry was in want of foreign war to
secure himself on the throne; the clergy also wished to keep him
employed abroad, and made an offer of rich contributions to
prevent the passing of a law which would have deprived them of
the half of their revenues. His learned bishops consequently are
as ready to prove to him his indisputable right to the crown of
France, as he is to allow his conscience to be tranquillized by them
... After his renowned battles, Henry wished to secure his conquests by marriage with a French princess; all that has reference
to this is intended for irony in the play. The fruit of this union,
from which the two nations promised to themselves such happiness in future, was the weak and feeble Henry VI, under whom

every thing was so miserably lost. It must not, therefore, be imagined that it was without the knowledge and will of the poet that a heroic drama turns out a comedy in his hands, and ends in the manner of Comedy with a marriage of convenience.

(from *Lectures on Dramatic Art and Literature*, 1809–11)

WILLIAM HAZLITT

HENRY V is a very favourite monarch with the English nation, and he appears to have been also a favourite with Shakespear, who labours hard to apologise for the actions of the king, by shewing us the character of the man, as 'the king of good fellows'. He scarcely deserves this honour. He was fond of war and low company: – we know little else of him. He was careless, dissolute, and ambitious; – idle, or doing mischief. In private, he seemed to have no idea of the common decencies of life, which he subjected to a kind of regal licence; in public affairs, he seemed to have no idea of any rule of right or wrong, but brute force, glossed over with a little religious hypocrisy and archiepiscopal advice. His principles did not change with his situation and professions. His adventure on Gadshill was a prelude to the affair of Agincourt, only a bloodless one; Falstaff was a puny prompter of violence and outrage, compared with the pious and politic Archbishop of Canterbury, who gave the king *carte blanche*, in a genealogical tree of his family, to rob and murder in circles of latitude and longitude abroad – to save the possessions of the church at home. This appears in the speeches in Shakespear, where the hidden motives that actuate princes and their advisers in war and policy are better laid open than in speeches from the throne or woolsack. Henry, because he did not know how to govern his own kingdom, determined to make war upon his neighbours. Because his own title to the crown was doubtful, he laid claim to that of France. Because he did not know how to exercise the enormous power, which had just dropped into his hands, to any one good purpose, he immediately undertook (a cheap and obvious resource of sovereignty) to do all the mischief he could. Even if absolute monarchs had the wit to find out objects of laudable ambition, they could only 'plume up their wills' in adhering to the more sacred formula of the royal prerogative, 'the right divine of kings to govern wrong,' because will is only then triumphant when it is opposed to the will of others, because the pride of power is only then shewn, not when it consults the rights and interests of others, but when it insults and tramples on all justice and all humanity. Henry declares his resolution 'when France is his, to bend it to his awe, or break it all to pieces' – a resolution worthy of a conqueror, to destroy all that he cannot enslave; and what adds to the joke, he lays all the blame of the consequences of his ambition on those who will not submit tamely to his tyranny. . . .

Henry V it is true, was a hero, a King of England, and the conqueror of the king of France. Yet we feel little love or admiration for him. He was a hero, that is, he was ready to sacrifice his own life for the pleasure of destroying thousands of other lives: he was a king of England, but not a constitutional one, and we only like kings according to the law; lastly, he was a conqueror of the French king, and for this we dislike him less than if he had conquered the French people. How then do we like him? We like him in the play. There is he a very amiable monster, a very splendid pageant. As we like to gaze at a panther or a young lion in their cages in the Tower, and catch a pleasing horror from their glistening eyes, their velvet paws, and dreadless roar, so we take a very romantic, heroic, patriotic, and poetical delight in the boasts and feats of our younger Harry, as they appear on the stage and are confined to lines of ten syllables; where no blood follows the stroke that wounds our ears, where no harvest bends beneath horses' hoofs, no city flames, no little child is butchered, no dead men's bodies found piled on heaps and festering the next morning – in the orchestra! . . .

It is worth observing that in all these plays, which give an admirable picture of the spirit of the *good old times*, the moral inference does not at all depend upon the nature of the actions, but on the dignity or meanness of the persons committing them. 'The eagle England' has a right 'to be in prey', but 'the weazel Scot' has none 'to come sneaking to her nest', which she has left

to pounce upon others. Might was right, without equivocation
or disguise, in that heroic and chivalrous age. The substitution
of right for might, even in theory, is among the refinements and
abuses of modern philosophy. . . .

The behaviour of the king, in the difficult and doubtful circumstances in which he is placed, is as patient and modest as it
is spirited and lofty in his prosperous fortune.

(from *Characters of Shakespear's Plays*, 1817)

THOMAS CARLYLE

THAT battle of Agincourt strikes me as one of the most perfect
things, in its sort, we anywhere have of Shakspeare's. The description of the two hosts: the worn-out, jaded English; the dread
hour, big with destiny, when the battle shall begin; and then that
deathless valour: 'Ye good yeomen, whose limbs were made in
England!' There is a noble Patriotism in it, – far other than the
'indifference' you sometimes hear ascribed to Shakspeare. A true
English heart breathes, calm and strong, through the whole
business; not boisterous, protrusive; all the better for that. There
is a sound in it like the ring of steel. This man too had a right
stroke in him, had it come to that!

(from *On Heroes, Hero-Worship, and the Heroic in History*, 1841)

CHARLES KNIGHT

STANDING now upon the vantage-ground of four centuries of
experience, in which civilization has marched onwards at a pace
which could only be the result of great intellectual impulses, we
may, indeed, say that, if Henry V was justly fitted to be a leader
of chivalry, – fearless, enterprising, persevering, generous, pious,
– he was, at the same time, rash, obstinate, proud, superstitious,
seeking after vain renown and empty conquests, instead of making his people happy by wise laws and the cultivation of sound
knowledge. But Henry's character, like that of all other men, must
be estimated by the circumstances amidst which he moved. After
four centuries of illumination, if we find the world still suffering

under the dominion of unjust governors and ambitious conquerors, we may pardon one who acted according to his lights, believing that his cause justified his attempt to seize upon another crown, instead of wearing his own wisely and peacefully. At any rate, it was not for the poet to regard the most popular king of the feudal times with the cold and severe scrutiny of the philosophical historian. It was for him to embody in the person of Henry V the principle of national heroism; it was for him to call forth 'the spirit of patriotic reminiscence'. There are periods in the history of every people when their nationality, lifting them up almost into a frenzy of enthusiasm, is one of the sublimest exhibitions of the practical poetry of social life. In the times of Shakspere such an aspect of the English mind was not unfrequently presented. Neither in our own times have such manifestations of the mighty heart been wanting. But there have been, and there may again be, periods of real danger when the national spirit shows itself drooping and languishing. It is under such circumstances that the heart-stirring power of such a play as *Henry V* is to be tested. Frederick Schlegel says, 'The feeling by which Shakspere seems to have been most connected with ordinary men is that of nationality.' But how different is his nationality from that of ordinary men. It is reflective, tolerant, generous. It lives not in an atmosphere of falsehood and prejudice. Its theatre is war and conquest; but it does not hold up war and conquest as fitting objects for nationality to dedicate itself to, except under the pressure of the most urgent necessity. Neither does it attempt to conceal the fearful responsibilities of those who carry the principle of nationality to the last arbitrement of arms, nor the enormous amount of evil which always attends the rupture of that peace, in the cultivation of which nationality is best displayed. Shakspere, indeed, speaks proudly as a member of that English family

Whose blood is fet from fathers of war-proof;

but he never forgets that he belongs to the larger family of the human race. When Henry tells the people of Harfleur,

The gates of mercy shall be all shut up,

and draws that most fearful picture of the horrors of a sacked city, the poet tells us, though not in sententious precepts, that nationality, when it takes the road of violence, may be driven to put off all the gentle attributes of social life, and, assuming the 'action of the tiger', have the tiger's undiscriminating bloodthirstiness.

(from *Studies in Shakspere*, 1849)

G. G. GERVINUS

IN outward bearing, the piece resembles the second part of *Henry IV*. The choruses seem to announce that here the 'brightest heaven of invention' is to be ascended; yet this is reached rather in a patriotic and ethical sense than in an aesthetic one. The lack of all plot and the prose of the low scenes check the poetic flight; some of these scenes, such as that between Katherine and Alice, and that between Pistol and Le Fer, might even be well omitted. Here and there the poetry in this piece rises, it must be admitted, to the most lofty expression, and this especially in the choruses. This unequal form seems to reflect the deep nature of the subject displayed. Interpreters regarded these choruses as a means for investing the piece with an epic character, for which the simple battle material seemed to them more adapted. But these choruses are maintained in a bold, ardent, figurative diction, utterly opposed to the epic; Shakespeare rather employs this more elevated poetry to place the hero of his poem in the splendid heroic light in which from his unassuming nature he cannot place himself, and in which, when arrived at the height of his fame, he expressly wishes not to be seen by those around him. Garrick felt very justly that in representation these choruses ought not only not to be omitted, but that they ought to be placed most prominently forward: he spoke them himself . . .

Throughout the whole play, throughout the whole bearing of the king, sounds the key-note of a religious composure, of a severe conscientiousness, and of an humble modesty . . . Shakespeare has in no wise attributed to the king this pious humility and fear of God as an occasional quality, upon which he places

no more value than upon any other; we see from the repeated
reference to it, we see from the nature of the character and its
consequent bearing in various circumstances, we see from the
plan of the whole play, that this trait is intended to form the
central point of the whole. The poet works with the same idea in
which Aeschylus wrote his warlike pieces, *The Persians* and *The
Seven before Thebes*: namely, that terrible is the warrior who fears
God, and that on the other hand the blossom of pride ripens into
the fruit of evil and the harvest of tears. For entirely in this
sense has Shakespeare depicted the camp of the French and their
princes, in Xerxes-like arrogance and crime, in opposition to the
little troop of Britons and their intrepid pious hero.

(from *Shakespeare Commentaries*, trs. 1863)

THOMAS KENNY

THE drama of *King Henry V* is, in some respects, deserving of
the special notice of the students of Shakespeare's genius. The
poet had here a magnificent scene to delineate. The subject was
sure to be popular with his audience, and it is evident that he himself felt in it an unusual amount of interest. We do not know any
other work of his in which his national or personal predilections
have made themselves so distinctly visible: and yet it is impossible
to class this play among the great productions of his genius. . . .
The truth is, that the subject itself did not admit of perfect
dramatic treatment. It is a heroic history, and such a history, to be
dealt with effectively, should be dealt with epically or lyrically.
Henry V is here exhibited as a complete, harmonious, self-
possessed character; but such characters are not dramatic. In
the epic delineation of great personages and great exploits we
are dominated by them. In dramatic representation we are comparatively independent of the agents in the scene. We see them
caught in the struggle of passions which we know to be but distant and latent elements in our own nature. In epic narration it is
our admiration that is mainly or exclusively awakened; in the
dramatic exhibition of life it is our critical, discriminating,
illuminating sympathy that is called into action. The play of

King Henry V is the representation, not of great passions, but of great events, and it naturally fails to attain the highest dramatic vitality and movement. A large portion of its story has to be told, or merely indicated, by the choruses, in which the poet himself has to appear, and to confess the inability of his art to reproduce the march and shock of armies, and, above all, the great scene on the field of Agincourt. It is in some measure, perhaps, in obedience to his sympathy with the inevitable conditions of his work that he here appears for once in his own personality; and it may be that we have in this change another proof of the wonderful harmony of his imagination with every form of life which it seeks to revive. There is much in these scenes that is noble and imposing, and, in particular, it is impossible to witness without admiration the frank and gallant bearing of the king. But the work, on the whole, is forcible, eloquent, and declamatory, rather than vital, passionate, and dramatic. . . .

Among the comic sketches in this work we are specially struck by the scene (Act III, scene vii) in which the fantastic conceit of the Dauphin and the sarcastic temper of the Constable of France are so strangely delineated. The nature of the relations which must have prevailed between the two characters seems to have been utterly disregarded by the poet. It was impossible that a French subject should indulge in this contemptuous banter towards the heir to the French crown; and so far the form of the dialogue is wholly incongruous. But in its substance we are very much disposed to think that this is the most singular and the most distinctly Shakespearian scene in the whole drama. Amidst the light and even coarse indifference of its whole tone it displays throughout that firmness of touch, and that reckless truth to nature, which so often startle us in the manifestations of Shakespeare's genius.

(from *The Life and Genius of Shakespeare*, 1864)

EDWARD DOWDEN

THE historical plays lead up to *Henry V*, in the chronological succession of Shakspere's plays the last of the series. The tragedies lead up to *The Tempest*, which closes Shakspere's entire career as dramatist. Gervinus has spoken of King Henry V as if he were Shakspere's ideal of highest manhood, and other critics have assented to this opinion. It is an opion which, stated in an unqualified way, must be set aside as not warranted by the facts of Shakspere's dramas. But it is clear and unquestionable that King Henry V is Shakspere's ideal of the *practical* heroic character. He is the king who will not fail. He will not fail as the saintly Henry VI failed, nor as Richard II failed, a hectic, self-indulgent nature, a mockery king of pageantry, and sentiment, and rhetoric; nor will he only partially succeed by prudential devices, and stratagems, and crimes, like his father, 'great Bolingbroke'. The success of Henry V will be sound throughout, and it will be complete. With his glorious practical virtues, his courage, his integrity, his unfaltering justice, his hearty English warmth, his modesty, his love of plainness rather than of pageantry, his joyous temper, his business-like English piety, Henry is indeed the ideal of the king who must attain a success complete, and thoroughly real and sound.

But is this practical, positive, efficient character, with his soldier-like piety and his jolly fashion of wooing, is this the highest ideal of our supreme poet? Is this the highest ideal of Shakspere, who lived, and moved, and had his being not alone in the world of limitation, of tangible, positive fact, but also in a world of the soul, a world opening into two endless vistas, the vista of meditation and the vista of passion. Assuredly it is not so. We turn to the great tragedies, and what do we there discover? In these Shakspere is engaged in a series of studies not concerning success in the mastery of events and things, but concerning the higher success and the more awful failure which appear in the exaltation or the ruin of a soul. This with Shakspere is the true theme of tragedy. . . .

The central element in the character of Henry is his noble realisation of fact. To Richard II life was a graceful and shadowy ceremony, containing beautiful and pathetic situations. Henry IV saw in the world a substantial reality, and he resolved to obtain mastery over it by courage and by craft. But while Bolingbroke with his caution and his policy, his address and his ambition, penetrated only a little way among the facts of life, his son, with a true genius for the discovery of the noblest facts, and of all facts, came into relation with the central and vital forces of the universe, so that, instead of constructing a strong but careful life for himself, life breathed through him, and blossomed into a glorious enthusiasm of existence. And therefore from all that was unreal, and from all exaggerated egoism, Henry was absolutely delivered. A man who firmly holds, or rather is held by the beneficent forces of the world, whose feet are upon a rock, and whose goings are established, may with confidence abandon much of the prudence, and many of the artificial proprieties of the world. For every unreality Henry exhibits a sovereign disregard – for unreal manners, unreal glory, unreal heroism, unreal piety, unreal warfare, unreal love. The plain fact is so precious it needs no ornament.

From the coldness, the caution, the convention of his father's court (an atmosphere which suited well the temperament of John of Lancaster), Henry escapes to the teeming vitality of the London streets, and the tavern where Falstaff is monarch. There, among ostlers, and carriers, and drawers, and merchants, and pilgrims, and loud robustious women, he at least has freedom and frolic. 'If it be a sin to covet honour,' Henry declares, 'I am the most offending soul alive.' But the honour that Henry covets is not that which Hotspur is ambitious after:

> By heaven, methinks it were an easy leap
> To pluck bright honour from the pale-faced moon.

The honour that Henry covets is the achievement of great deeds, not the words of men which vibrate around such deeds. . . . Nor is his heroic greatness inconsistent with the admission of very humble incidents of humanity:

> *Prince.* Doth it not show vilely in me to desire small beer?
> *Poins.* Why, a prince should not be so loosely studied as to remember so weak a composition.
> *Prince.* Belike, then, my appetite was not princely got; for by my troth I do now remember the poor creature, small

beer. But indeed these humble considerations make me out of love with my greatness.

Henry with his lank frame, and vigorous muscle (the opposite of the Danish Prince who is 'fat and scant of breath'), is actually wearied to excess and thirsty, and he is by no means afraid to confess the fact; his appetite at least has not been pampered. 'Before God, Kate,' such is Henry's fashion of wooing, 'I cannot look greenly, nor gasp out my eloquence, nor I have no cunning in protestation; only downright oaths, which I never use till urged, nor never break for urging. . . . I speak to thee plain soldier; if thou canst love me for this, take me; if not, to say to thee that I shall die is true; but for thy love, by the Lord, no; yet I love thee too.'

And as in his love there is a certain substantial homeliness and heartiness, so is there also in his piety. He is not harassed like his son, the saintly Henry, with refinements of scrupulosity, the disease of an irritable conscience, which is delivered from its irritability by no active pursuit of noble ends. Henry has done what is right; he has tried to repair his father's faults; he has built 'two chantries, where the sad and solemn priests still sing for Richard's soul'. He has done his part by God and man, will not God in like-manner stand by him and perform what belongs to God? Henry's freedom from egoism, his modesty, his integrity, his joyous humour, his practical piety, his habit of judging things by natural and not artificial standards; all these are various developments of the central element of his character, his noble realisation of fact.

But his realisation of fact produces something more than this integrity, this homely honesty of nature. It breathes through him an enthusiasm which would be intense if it were not so massive. Through his union with the vital strength of the world, he becomes one of the world's most glorious and beneficent forces. From the plain and mirth-creating comrade of his fellow-soldiers he rises into the genius of impassioned battle. From the modest and quiet adviser with his counsellors and prelates, he is transformed, when the occasion requires it, into the terrible administrator of justice. . . .

Shortly before the English army sets sail for France the treason of Cambridge, Scroop, and Grey is disclosed to the King. He does not betray his acquaintance with their designs. Surrounded by traitors, he boldly enters his council chamber at Southampton (the wind is sitting fair, and but one deed remains to do before they go aboard). On the preceding day a man was arrested who had railed against the person of the King. Henry gives orders that he be set at liberty:

> We consider
> It was excess of wine that set him on;
> And on his more advice we pardon him.

But Scroop, and Grey, and Cambridge interpose. It would be true mercy, they insist, to punish such an offender. And then, when they have unawares brought themselves within the range of justice, Henry unfolds their guilt. The wrath of Henry has in it some of that awfulness and terror suggested by the apocalyptic reference to 'the wrath of the Lamb'. It is the more terrible because it transcends all egoistic feeling. What fills the king with indignation is not so much that his life should have been conspired against by men on whom his bounty has been bestowed without measure, as that they should have revolted against the loyalty of man, weakened the bonds of fellowship, and lowered the high tradition of humanity:

> O how hast thou with jealousy infected
> The sweetness of affiance! Show men dutiful?
> Why so didst thou: seem they grave and learned?
> Why so didst thou: come they of noble family?
> Why so didst thou: seem they religious?
> Why so didst thou: or are they spare in diet,
> Free from gross passion, or of mirth or anger,
> Constant in spirit, not swerving with the blood,
> Garnish'd and deck'd in modest complement,
> Not working with the eye without the ear,
> And but in purged judgement trusting neither?
> Such and so finely bolted didst thou seem:
> And thus thy fall hath left a kind of blot
> To mark the full-fraught man and best indued

> With some suspicion. I will weep for thee;
> For this revolt of thine, methinks, is like
> Another fall of man.

No wonder that the terrible moral insistance of these words can subdue consciences made of penetrable stuff; no wonder that such an awful discovery of high realities of life should call forth the loyalty that lurked within a traitor's heart. But though tears escape Henry he cannot relent:

> Touching our person seek we no revenge;
> But we our kingdom's safety must so tender,
> Whose ruin you have sought, that to her laws
> We do deliver you. Get you therefore hence,
> Poor miserable wretches, to your death,
> The taste whereof God of his mercy give
> You patience to endure, and true repentance
> Of all your dear offences!

And having vindicated the justice of God, and purged his country of treason, Henry sets his face to France with the light of splendid achievement in his eyes.

(from *Shakspere: A Critical Study of His Mind and Art*, 1875)

A. C. SWINBURNE

HARRY PERCY is as it were the true Sir Bedivere, the last of all Arthurian knights; Henry V is the first as certainly as he is the noblest of those equally daring and calculating statesmen-warriors whose two most terrible, most perfect, and most famous types are Louis XI and Caesar Borgia. Gain, 'commodity,' the principle of self-interest which never but in word and in jest could become the principle of action with Faulconbridge, – himself already far more 'a man of this world' than a Launcelot or a Hotspur, – is as evidently the mainspring of Henry's enterprise and life as of the contract between King Philip and King John. The supple and shameless egotism of the churchmen on whose political sophistries he relies for external support is needed rather to varnish his project than to reassure his conscience. Like

Frederic the Great before his first Silesian war, the future conqueror of Agincourt has practically made up his mind before
he seeks to find as good reason or as plausible excuse as were
likewise to suffice the future conqueror of Rosbach. In a word,
Henry is doubtless not the man, as old Auchindrane expresses it
in the noble and strangely neglected tragedy which bears solitary
but sufficient witness to the actual dramatic faculty of Sir Walter
Scott's genius, to do the devil's work without his wages; but
neither is he, on the like unprofitable terms, by any manner of
means the man to do God's. No completer incarnation could be
shown us of the militant Englishman – *Anglais pur sang*; but it is
not only, as some have seemed to think, with the highest, the
purest, the noblest quality of English character that his just and
far-seeing creator has endowed him. The godlike equity of
Shakespeare's judgment, his implacable and impeccable righteousness of instinct and of insight, was too deeply ingrained in the
very core of his genius to be perverted by any provincial or
pseudo-patriotic prepossessions; his patriotism was too national
to be provincial.

(from *A Study of Shakespeare*, 1880)

R. G. MOULTON

In *Henry V* Shakspere has embodied his conception of supreme
heroism; and in order that the conception may be individualized,
and not remain a mere poetic ideal, his choice of subject has given
it the practical tinge, which of all aspects of heroism is the one
most congenial to the English mind. Or rather, the hero of the
poem is the English nation itself, as typified in the popular king
who has caught the spirit of every class amongst his people, and
concentrates them all in himself; this effect being assisted by
constant contrast with the French nation, in which, as judged by
popular conception of it, the English nation finds its antithesis.
It would serve no purpose to analyze such character into its com-
ponent qualities, its best definition is to exhibit it in action. War
is chosen as representing action on the largest scale; and it is

interesting to note that here alone in all his works Shakspere betrays a consciousness of being straitened by dramatic form, and the prologues to the five acts, which paint so vividly successive stages of the war, are Shakspere's nearest approach to an epic poem. We have, moreover, in the play a thoroughly English conception of war: not a picture of a Napoleon, a glorious soldier at his work, but of a Wellington, supreme character displayed best by difficulty, and finding its highest climax in trouble. Looked at in this light the play illustrates one of the two species of Character-Development under consideration. There is no advance in the character of Henry itself. On the contrary, the point of the conversation between the bishops, with which the first act opens, is to bring out the sudden rise of a full-grown character in the king at the moment of his succession:

> The breath no sooner left his father's body,
> But that his wildness, mortified in him,
> Seem'd to die too; yea, at that very moment
> Consideration, like an angel, came
> And whipp'd the offending Adam out of him,
> Leaving his body as a paradise,
> To envelope and contain celestial spirits.

But this complete character is displayed before us in different phases, the succession of which is a progress to a goal. The whole picture is the heroism of achievement: as we have it we see first the formation of a great purpose; then in overcoming obstacles heroism is brought into contact with the treason which is its opposite; next we have heroism in the moment of action; the character then passes under the shadow of reverses, and reaches the crisis first of inward conflict, and then of outward action; finally, achievement being crowned by triumph, we have the reaction and unbending of the strain.

The first act paints formation of purpose so ideally that it is almost like a psychological process dramatized. The king will not hear the French ambassadors till he has been fully instructed in the rights of the matter, and we have a detailed exposition of the Salic law. Bishops and aged statesmen are rousing the young prince to war, while it is he himself who points out the difficulties to be provided against in the way of Scottish hostility. The whole discussion is based on highest considerations of State policy, and its climax is Canterbury's splendid application of the division of labour to political science, illustrated with his elaborate simile of the bees. Then, with suddenness like the fall of a hammer, calm deliberation passes into decisive resolution, and the ambassadors are called in. . . .

Achievement must of course be tested not only by difficulties in the action itself, but also by obstacles in the way of acting; and the conspiracy which threatens to delay Henry also gives opportunity for bringing the perfect man and national hero in contact with treachery, the supreme sin against both individual friendship and the nation. The progress of events is throughout the play painted by the emphatic points of successive stages; so here we have arraignment, denunciation, punishment, crowded into a single stroke – the sin and the perfect type sinned against are seen together in the blaze of light that accompanies a sudden discovery. There is no higher function for loftiness of soul than by its mere contact with what is base to shrivel it up into loathliness. So here: the physical suffering and other repulsive details of punishment do not appear, but the true punishment is Henry's outpouring of soul, which turns the light of heroism on to the sin of treason as he paints the trust and the treachery; the cunning fiend that inspired such a temptation hath got the voice in hell for excellence, the whole sweetness of affiance is infected with jealousy, it is like another fall of man! And the effect of such simple contact of natures is complete when Henry's eloquence is seen to have called forth the long-buried germs of goodness in the traitors themselves. They have grace enough to long for their death; and Henry, who has no weakness, not even the noble weakness of mercy, dismisses them to their fate.

We now reach the war itself, and the heroic spirit is displayed in the moment of action. Concentration of purpose is idealized in the speech before the walls of Harfleur:

> In peace, there's nothing so becomes a man
> As modest stillness and humility:
> But when the blast of war blows in our ears,

> Then imitate the action of the tiger;
> Stiffen the sinews, summon up the blood,
> Disguise fair nature with hard-favour'd rage.

Each fresh touch of description seems to string up the nerves another turn. . . .

The effect is continued in the summons to the town, and we must not allow our modern feelings, as to the horrors of sack and pillage, to hide from us that the concentration of heroic purpose in Henry is increased by the unhesitating way in which he fastens the full guilt of all that is to happen on the enemy that refuses to yield:

> Take pity of your town, and of your people,
> Whiles yet my soldiers are in my command;
> Whiles yet the cool and temperate wind of grace
> O'erblows the filthy and contagious clouds
> Of heady murder, spoil, and villainy.

. . . We now approach the crisis: and the critical point in external action is preceded by a still sharper crisis in the soul of Henry himself, marking the eve of the battle, which is brought before us in greater detail than any other point in the history. First, the leader's own personality has to be expended in stringing up the spirits of those around him to endurance and achievement. Henry's cheerfulness is unflagging, and he can extract some soul of goodness from every dull surrounding. As he moves about his camp in the darkness, and accosts every variety of his followers, he catches instantly the exact tone in which to address each, and calls forth from each a characteristic flash of enthusiasm. . . .

So far, he has been supported by the presence of others, and by having work to do: he must now experience the extremity of testing and self-review in a struggle with his own soul. Through his conversation with the soldiers has been present the thought of the loneliness of a king, and under his incognito as a private individual he has been craving for sympathy with the king as a man:

> I think the king is but a man as I am.

This has been rudely refused: they doubt whether the king's courage is more than a show to put spirit in others; they wish he were there by himself, as he could depend on ransom. Especially they touch the very point to doubt which at the moment of action is paralysis of soul – the justice of the cause; and they speak of the heavy reckoning the king will have to make, if the cause be not good, for the souls of those who have died,

some swearing, some crying for a surgeon, some upon their wives left poor behind them, some upon the debts they owe, some upon their children rawly left.

Indignantly the disguised king repudiates responsibility for the state of soul in which his subjects meet their death in doing their duty. But when he is alone the thought recurs and overwhelms him with a weight of responsibility, in the presence of which all the sense of kingly station, which raised him to moral greatness after the wildness of his youth, and which is still his support, seems to melt away into mere 'ceremony,' a tide of pomp breaking upon the high shore of this world, to no end but to rob him of the peaceful sleep and profitable labour of a peasant. On the threshold thus of morbid self-analysis the summons to action reaches him, and his self-searching intensifies into a single moment's agony of penitence and prayer:

> Not to-day, O Lord,
> O, not to-day, think not upon the fault
> My father made in compassing the crown!

So he passes into the battle on which his all is staked. As at the beginning we saw deliberation crystallize into decisive resolution, so all Henry's heart-searching and doubt has no effect but to draw every fibre of his soul on to the task before him. The fighting force of the army is the spirit of their king. Entering as Westmoreland is wishing for more numbers, Henry changes with a single speech the tone of all around him, and infuses into them his sin of coveting honour, by which he would grudge the sharing the danger of this glorious St Crispin's day with even one man more from England. He turns the same front of unswerving confidence to the scornful message of the enemy. Even where Henry is not present his spirit prevails none the less, and Suffolk and York have no thought in their bloody and heroic deaths but that with which the king has inspired them – the thought of dying as yoke-fellows in this glorious field. So through all incidents, glorious and pathetic, the full strain of resolution is maintained, until from the lips of the same herald, who had been the bearer of the insolent defiances, Henry first learns the full extent of his victory, the enormous slaughter of the enemy, and small English loss, which make the odds the greatest ever known. Then, indeed, his deep character perceives a point beyond triumph:

> O God, thy arm was here!

and he proclaims it death

> To boast of this, or take that praise from God
> Which is his only.

So tense a strain must in a healthy soul be followed by reaction: and the character-development which has displayed before us Henry's character in phase after phase with ever-increasing fulness, reaches completion by the glimpse the fifth act affords us of the hero unbending after achievement is finished. With free flow of humour he enters into the national vanity of Welsh Fluellen, and enjoys the practical jokes which have arisen out of his incognito. Above all, in his wooing of the Princess Katharine he gives full scope to the tenderness which is the reverse side of the warrior spirit, and which is thinly disguised under the rough exterior Henry affects to the mistress he is to win as the prize of arms.

(from 'On Character Development in Shakspere as illustrated
by Macbeth and Henry V', in Transactions of the New
Shakspere Society, 1880–86)

BARRETT WENDELL

GENERALLY, with purely dramatic purpose, Shakspere appears frankly to accept the conditions under which he must work. In

Henry V, he professes throughout that they bother him. So far as it goes, this very fact tends to show that his artistic purpose was not merely dramatic.

The general impression made by the play confirms this opinion. From beginning to end, Henry himself is always kept heroically in view; he is presented in the exasperating way which makes so ineffectual the efforts of moralizing scribblers, dear to Sunday-school librarians. . . . He is rather a moral hero than a dramatic. For all his humanity, you feel him rather an ideal than a man; and an ideal, in virtues and vices alike, rather British than human. He has sown conventional wild oats; he has reformed; he is bluff, simple-hearted, not keenly intellectual, courageous, above all a man more of action than of words. The Shakspere who propounds such an ideal, then, is limited more profoundly than by mere stage conditions; throughout his conception he reveals the peculiar limitation of sympathy which still marks a typical Englishman. In the honestly canting moods which we of America inherit with our British blood we gravely admire *Henry V* because we feel sure that we ought to. In more normally human moods, most of us would be forced to confess that, at least as a play, *Henry V* is tiresome.

(from *William Shakspere,*
a Study in Elizabethan Literature, 1894)

W. B. YEATS

I HAVE often had the fancy that there is some one Myth for every man, which, if we but knew it, would make us understand all he did and thought. Shakespeare's Myth, it may be, describes a wise man who was blind from very wisdom, and an empty man who thrust him from his place, and saw all that could be seen from very emptiness. It is in the story of Hamlet, who saw too great issues everywhere to play the trivial game of life, and of Fortinbras, who came from fighting battles about 'a little patch of ground' so poor that one of his captains would not give 'six ducats' to 'farm it,' and who was yet acclaimed by Hamlet and by all as the only befitting King. And it is in the story of Richard II, that unripened Hamlet, and of Henry V, that ripened Fortinbras. To poise character against character was an element in Shakespeare's art, and scarcely a play is lacking in characters that are the complement of one another, and so, having made the vessel of porcelain Richard II, he had to make the vessel of clay Henry V. He makes him the reverse of all that Richard was. He has the gross vices, the coarse nerves, of one who is to rule among violent people, and he is so little 'too friendly' to his friends that he bundles them out of doors when their time is over. He is as remorseless and undistinguished as some natural force, and the finest thing in his play is the way his old companions fall out of it broken-hearted or on their way to the gallows; and instead of that lyricism which rose out of Richard's mind like the jet of a fountain to fall again where it had risen, instead of that phantasy too enfolded in its own sincerity to make any thought the hour had need of, Shakespeare has given him a resounding rhetoric that moves men, as a leading article does to-day. His purposes are so intelligible to everybody that everybody talks of him as if he succeeded, although he fails in the end, as all men great and little fail in Shakespeare, and yet his conquests abroad are made nothing by a woman turned warrior, and that boy he and Katherine were to 'compound,' 'half French, half English,' 'that' was to 'go to Constantinople and take the Turk by the beard,' turns out a Saint and loses all his father had built up at home and his own life.

Shakespeare watched Henry V not indeed as he watched the greater souls in the visionary procession, but cheerfully, as one watches some handsome spirited horse, and he spoke his tale, as he spoke all tales, with tragic irony.

(from *Ideas of Good and Evil*, 1903)

GEORGE BERNARD SHAW

O N E can hardly forgive Shakespeare quite for the worldly phase in which he tried to thrust such a Jingo hero as his Harry V down our throats. The combination of conventional propriety and brute masterfulness in his public capacity with a low-lived blackguardism in his private tastes is not a pleasant one. No doubt he is true to nature as a picture of what is by no means uncommon in English society, an able young Philistine inheriting high position and authority, which he holds on to and goes through with by keeping a tight grip on his conventional and legal advantages, but who would have been quite in his place if he had been born a gamekeeper or a farmer. . . . His popularity, therefore, is like that of a prizefighter: nobody feels for him as for Romeo or Hamlet.

(from *Dramatic Opinions and Essays,* 1907)

SIDNEY LEE

SHAKESPEARE's *Henry V* is as far as possible removed from what is generally understood by drama. It is without intrigue or entanglement; it propounds no problems of psychology; its definite motive is neither comic nor tragic; women play in it the slenderest part; it lacks plot in any customary sense. In truth, the piece is epic narrative, or rather heroic biography, adapted to the purposes of the stage. The historical episodes – political debate, sieges, encampments, battles, diplomatic negotiations – with which the scenes deal, are knit together by no more complex bond than the chronological succession of events, the presence in each of the same *dramatis personae* and the predominance in each of the same character – the English King, in whose mouth the dramatist sets nearly a third of all the lines of the play. A few of the minor personages excite genuine interest, and there are some attractive scenes of comic relief, but these have no organic connection with the central thread of the play. Shakespeare's efforts were mainly concentrated on the portraiture of 'this star of England', King Henry, whom he deliberately chose out of the page of history as the fittest representative of the best distinctive type of English character.

When the play opens, the King is in his twenty-seventh year, in 'the very May morn of his youth'. Holinshed describes his person as of singular attraction; 'of stature and proportion tall and manly, rather lean than gross, somewhat long-necked, and black-haired, of countenance amiable; eloquent and grave was his speech and of great grace and power to persuade'.

Henry had already figured prominently in the two parts of Shakespeare's *Henry IV*, which immediately preceded the play of *Henry V*. There the Prince appears as a youth of untamable spirits, a lover of wild frolic and low company, addicted to riots, banquets, sports, and rough practical joking. But the close observer perceives even in the picture of his boisterous days the seeds of moral and mental strength and nobility. Even then he promises, when he is 'wanted', to cast off his profligacy – his 'coat of folly'. Even then he shows signs of remorse for idly profaning precious time. Even then he can fight gallantly, can display real kindness of heart, can appreciate the value of justice, can betray on occasion a determination of flint. The death of his father and his consequent call to the highest position in the state rouses to active and abiding life the sense of responsibility which, beneath all his giddy humours and vanities, only awaited fit occasion to assert sway over more superficial and less reputable characteristics. Under the stress of his change of fortune

> Consideration like an angel came
> And whipped the offending Adam out of him.

Simplicity and humility of mind lie at the root of his nature. Though fully sensible of the heavy burden of his new office, he sets no undue value on his rank. He knows that, as a king, 'he is a man as I am, the violet smells to him as it does to me; all his senses have but human conditions; his ceremonies laid by, in his nakedness he appears but a man'. In a simple, manly way he is strongly religious: he feels that whether suffering good or evil fortune he is under the protection of God. But his native geniality and homeliness of temperament give him at the same time the power of thoroughly enjoying life. The high spirits of his younger years are never completely tamed. He can still perpetrate on the impulse an innocent practical joke. In the dark hour preceding the dawn of the most momentous day in his career, on the very

eve of the engagement of Agincourt, he can, disguised in a soldier's cloak, set on foot a jest to embroil two comparatively
humble followers, and, as soon as the victory is won, he can turn
from more solemn pre-occupations to contrive the due fruition
of his merry plot. He lacks in the palace the polish usually identified with courts. His rough-and-ready wooing of the French
princess, though without offence, savours of uncouthness. But if
it lack refinement or delicate courtesy, it abounds in hearty
sincerity and the jollity of good-fellowship.

Yet one hardly pleasing trait must be alleged against Henry.
Like most typical Englishmen in positions of authority, who in
normal circumstances show a natural and easy-going heartiness,
he can on occasion develop an almost freezing austerity, he can
assume a frigid and terrifying sternness towards those who offend
not merely against law and order, but against his sense of dignity
or propriety. It is doubtful if he would make a truly sympathetic
friend. There may be good warrant for his remorseless condemnation to death of old acquaintances who play with treason, but his
harsh and intolerant treatment of the veteran sinner Falstaff, the
companion of his roaring youth, cannot easily win pardon.

It is as a soldier and an officer that Henry's character rises to its
full height. He is not merely brave in fight and prudent in strategy,
he is always cheery and frank in speech to friend and foe, and
possesses a rare gift 'to encourage' his men in seasons of danger
and difficulty by virtue of his power of eloquent and stirring
utterance. His nerve never fails him in the field, yet he is so 'free
from vainness and self-glorious pride', that he declines to allow
his bruised helmet and his bended sword to be paraded before
him on his triumphal entry into London after the victory. Similarly, he is fully conscious of the horrors of war and the duty of
rulers to aim at the preservation of the peace. The sword, which
must always spill guiltless blood, ought never to leave its sheath
except at the bidding of 'right and conscience'. Mindful of 'the
widows' tears, the orphans' cries', he conducts war with such
humanity as is practicable. He forbids looting, he forbids the use
of insulting language to the enemy. One of his own soldiers
who robs a church on the march is promptly hanged. 'When

lenity and cruelty play for a kingdom, the gentler gamester', he says, 'is the soonest winner.' Nevertheless the sternness that lurks in his nature can render him 'terrible in resolution'. There must be no luke-warmness, no weakness, no vacillation in the practical handling of a campaign. When the time comes for striking blows, they must be struck with all the force and fury of which the strikers are capable.

> In peace there's nothing so becomes a man
> As modest stillness and humility.
> But when the blast of war blows in our ears,
> Then imitate the action of the tiger.

With desperate severity he retaliates on the enemy as soon as they infringe the fair rules of war. He gives no quarter when his antagonist declines to face the fact of irretrievable defeat.

> What is it then to me if impious war,
> Array'd in flames like to the prince of fiends,
> Do, with his smirch'd complexion, all fell feats
> Enlink'd to waste and desolation?

Humanity demands, at every hazard, a prompt closing of a conflict when its issue is no longer in doubt.

Broadly speaking, Shakespeare has in no other play cast a man so entirely in the heroic mould as King Henry. Such failings as are indicated are kept in the background. On his virtues alone a full blaze of light is shed. . . . Alone in Shakespeare's gallery of English monarchs does Henry's portrait evoke at once a joyous sense of satisfaction in the high potentialities of human character and a sense of pride among Englishmen that a man of his mettle is of English race.

(from *Henry V*, ed. Sidney Lee, 1908)

A. C. BRADLEY

BOTH as prince and as king [Henry] is deservedly a favourite, and particularly so with English readers, being, as he is, perhaps the most distinctively English of all Shakespeare's men. In *Henry*

V he is treated as a national hero. In this play he has lost much
of the wit which in him seems to have depended on contact with
Falstaff, but he has also laid aside the most serious faults of his
youth. He inspires in a high degree fear, enthusiasm, and affection; thanks to his beautiful modesty he has the charm which is
lacking to another mighty warrior, Coriolanus; his youthful
escapades have given him an understanding of simple folk, and
sympathy with them; he is the author of the saying, 'There is
some soul of goodness in things evil'; and he is much more
obviously religious than most of Shakespeare's heroes. Having
these and other fine qualities, and being without certain dangerous tendencies which mark the tragic heroes, he is, perhaps, the
most *efficient* character drawn by Shakespeare, unless Ulysses, in
Troilus and Cressida, is his equal. And so he has been described
as Shakespeare's ideal man of action; nay, it has even been declared that here for once Shakespeare plainly disclosed his own
ethical creed, and showed us his ideal, not simply of a man of
action, but of a man.

But Henry is neither of these. The poet who drew Hamlet and
Othello can never have thought that even the ideal man of action
would lack that light upon the brow which at once transfigures
them and marks their doom. It is as easy to believe that, because
the lunatic, the lover, and the poet are not far apart, Shakespeare
would have chosen never to have loved and sung. Even poor
Timon, the most inefficient of the tragic heroes, has something
in him that Henry never shows. Nor is it merely that his nature
is limited: if we follow Shakespeare and look closely at Henry,
we shall discover with the many fine traits a few less pleasing.
Henry IV describes him as the noble image of his own youth;
and, for all his superiority to his father, he is still his father's son,
the son of the man whom Hotspur called a 'vile politician'.
Henry's religion, for example, is genuine, it is rooted in his
modesty; but it is also superstitious – an attempt to buy off
supernatural vengeance for Richard's blood; and it is also in part
political, like his father's projected crusade. Just as he went to
war chiefly because, as his father told him, it was the way to keep
factious nobles quiet and unite the nation, so when he adjures the

Archbishop to satisfy him as to his right to the French throne, he knows very well that the Archbishop *wants* the war because it will defer and perhaps prevent what he considers the spoliation of the Church. This same strain of policy is what Shakespeare marks in the first soliloquy in *Henry IV*, where the prince describes his riotous life as a mere scheme to win him glory later. It implies that readiness to use other people as means to his own ends which is a conspicuous feature in his father; and it reminds us of his father's plan of keeping himself out of the people's sight while Richard was making himself cheap by his incessant public appearances. And if I am not mistaken there is a further likeness. Henry is kindly and pleasant to every one as Prince, to every one deserving as King; and he is so not merely out of policy: but there is no sign in him of a strong affection for any one, such an affection as we recognise at a glance in Hamlet and Horatio, Brutus and Cassius, and many more. We do not find this in *Henry V*, not even in the noble address to Lord Scroop, and in *Henry IV* we find, I think, a liking for Falstaff and Poins, but no more: there is no more than a liking, for instance, in his soliloquy over the supposed corpse of his fat friend, and he never speaks of Falstaff to Poins with any affection. The truth is, that the members of the family of Henry IV have love for one another, but they cannot spare love for any one outside their family, which stands firmly united, defending its royal position against attack and instinctively isolating itself from outside influence.

(from 'The Rejection of Falstaff' in
Oxford Lectures on Poetry, 1909)

JOHN MASEFIELD

THIS play bears every mark of having been hastily written. Though it belongs to the great period of Shakespeare's creative life, it contains little either of clash of character, or of that much tamer thing, comparison of character. It is a chronicle or procession, eked out with soldiers' squabbles. It seems to have been written to fill a gap in the series of historical plays ... The lines of the epilogue show that Shakespeare meant the play to give an image of worldly success between images of failure in the other plays ...

It is about a popular hero who is as common as those who love him. But in its place it is tremendous. Henry V is the one commonplace man in the eight plays. He alone enjoys success and worldly happiness ... He has the knack of life that fits human beings for whatever is animal in human affairs.

(from *William Shakespeare*, 1911)

HARLEY GRANVILLE-BARKER (1925)

WELL, here he is, an acknowledged master of his craft and in the full flush of success, setting out to write a fine play, a spacious play, with England as its subject, no less a thing. He is now to crown the achievement of the earlier histories and, above all, of the last two, in which he had so 'found himself'. He is to bring that popular favourite Prince Hal to a worthy completion; and to this obligation – though against his formal promise to the public – he sacrifices Falstaff. It is easy to see why. Could Falstaff reform and be brought back into the company of the reformed Henry? No. Once before Shakespeare has hinted to us that the fat knight, if he grow great shall grow less, purge, leave sack, and live cleanly. But not a bit of it. *Henry IV*, *Part II*, when it came, found him more incorrigible than ever. On the other hand, had Falstaff made his unauthorized way to France, how could Henry's new dignity suffer the old ruffian's ironic comments on it? He had run away with his creator once: better not risk it. So to his now unimpeachable hero Shakespeare has to sacrifice his greatest, his liveliest creation so far. Does the hero reward him? No one could say that Henry is ill-drawn or uninteresting. But, when it comes to the point, there seems to be very little that is dramatically interesting for him to do. Here is a play of action, and here is the perfect man of action. Yet all the while Shakespeare is apologizing – and directly apologizing – for not being able to make the action effective. Will the audience, for heaven's sake, help him out? One need not attach too much importance to the formal modesty of the prologue.

> O pardon! Since a crooked figure may
> Attest in little place a million,
> And let us, ciphers to this great accompt,
> On your imaginary forces work.

This might be merely the plea of privilege that every play-wright, ancient or modern, must tacitly make. But when we find the apology repeated and repeated again, and before Act V most emphatically of all; when we find there the prayer to his audience

> . . . to admit the excuse
> Of time, of numbers, and due course of things
> Which cannot in their huge and proper life
> Be here presented –

does it not sound a more than formal confession, and as if Shake-speare had distressfully realized that he had asked his theatre – mistakenly; because it must be mistakenly – for what it could not accomplish?

Turn now to Henry himself. When do we come closest to him? Not surely in the typical moments of the man of action, in

> Once more unto the breach, dear friends, once more . . .

and upon like occasions. But in the night before Agincourt, when, on the edge of likely disaster, he goes out solitary into the dark and searches his own soul. This is, of course, no new turn to the character. Prince Hal at his wildest has never been a figure of mere fun and bombast. Remember the scenes with his father and with Hostpur. Still, soul-searching is – if one may use such a phrase of Majesty – not his long suit; and the passage, fine as it is, has the sound of a set piece. It is rhetoric rather than revelation.

In the later speech to Westmoreland:

> We few, we happy few, we band of brothers . . .

Henry, set among his fellows, is more himself. But Shakespeare makes practically no further attempt to show us the inner mind of the man. The Henry of the rest of Act IV is the Henry of the play's beginning. While, since for Act V some new aspect of the hero really must be found, we are landed with a jerk (nothing in the character has prepared us for it) into a rollicking love scene. And this well-carpentered piece of work is finished. I daresay it

was a success, and the Shakespeare who lived to please and had
to please to live, may have been content with it. But the other, the
daring, the creative Shakespeare, who had now known what it
was to have Shylock, Mercutio, Hotspur, and Falstaff come to
life, and abound in unruly life, under his hands – was he satisfied?
No doubt he could have put up as good a defence as many of his
editors have obliged him with both for hero and play, for its epic
quality and patriotic purpose. Though he had read in the preface
to the admirable Arden edition that –

Conscientious, brave, just, capable and tenacious, Henry
stands before us the embodiment of worldly success, and as such
he is entitled to our unreserved admiration . . .

I think he would have smiled wryly. For he was not the poet to
find patriotism an excuse for the making of fine phrases. And he
knew well enough that neither in the theatre nor in real life is it
these 'embodiments of worldly success' that we carry closest to
our hearts, or even care to spend an evening with.

No, he had set himself this task, and he carried it through
conscientiously and with the credit which is sound workman-
ship's due. But I detect disappointment with his hero, and – not
quite fancifully, I believe – a deeper disillusion with his art. The
'daemonic' Shakespeare, then, was only a lesson to the good. But
it was a valuable lesson. He had learnt that for presenting the
external pageantry of great events his theatre was no better than
a puppet-show; and that though the art of drama might be the art
of presenting men in action, your successful man of action did not
necessarily make the most interesting of heroes. For behind the
action, be the play farce or tragedy, there must be some spiritually
significant idea, or it will hang lifeless. And this is what is lacking
in *Henry V*.

> (from *From 'Henry V' to 'Hamlet'*, 1925; rev. ed. 1933)

H. B. CHARLTON

IN popular estimation Shakespeare's Henry V is probably a more
perfect king than Henry IV. Admittedly he is a far more likeable

fellow – once he has ceased to explain his wild oats. And what
enterprises of kingship he undertakes he performs no less successfully than did his father. But Shakespeare can only allow him
to purchase our personal affection by considerably reducing his
duties as a king. His father had to exercise the whole art of
government, maintaining peace at home and securing glory
abroad. It was in the more exacting office of governing at home
that his subtlest craft was needed. But Hal is largely relieved of
these routine trials, and for the most part his kingship is circum-
scribed to military leadership. At the head of his army, in embarkation, in siege, and in battle, he treads the surest of traditional
ways to popular acclamation. He is a great commander whose
greatness as a king is tacitly and sentimentally assumed. In a field-
command he can keep so much of the humanity he would per-
force have to leave outside the door of civil office. Soldiers are
much more obviously human than clerks of the Treasury.

But on the rare occasions when Hal is called upon for a
definitely political decision, are the factors determining political
wisdom different from what they were in his father's case? Hal's
mode of leading his army to victory is his most obvious national
asset. But it was, so to speak, a secondary achievement, and the
good it did was entirely dependent on the prior decision to make
war on France. The first scene of *Henry V* – a scene which critics
curiously pass by – unmistakably deprives Hal of all personal
credit for that decision. He is trapped into declaration of war by
the machinations of a group of men whose sole and quite explicit
motive is to preserve their own revenues; and the political implication is more flagrant in that these men are an ecclesiastical
synod. Hal, in fact, owes his political achievement, not as did his
father, to his own insight, but rather to something so near to
intellectual dullness that it permits of his being jockeyed into his
opportunities. He can be saved from such imputation only by the
assumption that he saw through the bishops' subtlety and quietly
used them as an excuse to embark on a foreign war with the idea
of securing domestic peace, even as his father in his dying words
had advised him to do. But such Machiavellian astuteness does
not fit in with the indubitable traits of Hal's nature. On one

occasion, and on one occasion only, there is a faint suspicion of
political sophistication. In the preceding play, Hotspur contri-
buted to his own political ruin by a noble gesture of bravado.
Too eager to await reinforcements, he joined immediate battle
with the vaunt that the reduction of his forces

> lends a lustre and more great opinion,
> A larger dare to our great enterprise.

As a moral attitude its effect is magnificent; as a political decision
it is disastrous. But on a similar occasion, Henry V displays a like
temper. When, on the night before Agincourt, Westmoreland
wishes that they had but one ten thousand more recruits from
England, Henry will have none of it.

> The fewer men, the greater share of honour,
> ... Wish not a man from England.
> God's peace, I would not lose so great an honour
> As one man more methinks would share from me.

He exceeds Hotspur in moral generosity and in thirst for glory:
he would even reduce the army he has:

> Rather proclaim it, Westmoreland, through my host,
> That he which hath no stomach to this fight,
> Let him depart: his passport shall be made
> And crowns for convoy put into his purse –

and all because

> we would not die in that man's company
> That fears his fellowship to die with us.

But his gesture does not lead to defeat. It is not in fact a procla-
mation and a firm offer to the army. It is merely a remark to one
of his chiefs of staff. Nor would there have been much opportunity for wholesale demobilization on the very eve of battle. The
offer, which was no offer, was either a piece of strategy or the
natural outcome of Henry's military enthusiasm. Either his
guardian spirit once more urges Henry to make what, in spite of
first appearances, proves in the end to be the politic move, or
Henry is sounder in the theory of military numbers than he

appears in this speech to be. There is more of the general's acumen in another of his battle-prayers:

> O God of battles, steel my soldiers' hearts,
> Possess them not with fear; take from them now
> The sense of reckoning, if the opposed numbers
> Pluck their hearts from them.

Altogether, then, the play of *Henry V* does not really imply substantial modifications in Shakespeare's apprehension of the political life. There remains in it the sense that what is good in the world of politics is entirely unrelated to and generally the opposite of what makes for goodness in the moral life. It is the distinction between Machiavelli's *virtu* and the moralist's virtue, or, as Mr G. B. Shaw puts it, between virtue and goodness. . . . Henry IV achieves political greatness and proves his political worth by the deliberate exercise of his political acumen: whence our coldness to him as a man. To a large extent, Henry V is thrust into political greatness by sheer instinct. His genius leads him to take steps his moral nature would have prohibited his taking; and his ingratiating commonplaceness of mind hides from him their immoral implications or even glosses them with conventional moral sanctions. He is secured in our affections, because he is dispensed by Shakespeare from requiring such intellectual greatness as his father had. He stands before us always as the great plain man, and there is a sort of gratification felt by Shakespeare, as by most of us, in installing the plain man in high political office. Illogical, it probably is; a mere gamble with fate. We trust that a blind instinct will prompt the plain man to do those things the competent politician would clearly see to be necessary; and we are willing to take our chance, though at such very long odds against us, because, as human beings and unpolitical animals, we prefer to sacrifice the probability of good government to secure ourselves against the fear of exploitation by the expert. A pledge to do nothing at all is not without advantages as an electioneering cry. Henry V wins our hearts as the greatest of plain men. His common text is that the king is but a man; that all his senses have but human conditions, and that, his ceremonies laid by, in his nakedness he appears but a man. Note, however, how his guardian angel saw to it that he should preserve his incognito whilst preaching this sermon. Henry has all the admirable propensities of the average Englishman, his conventions, his manners, and his opportune lack of them, his prejudices, and even his faith. He would have welcomed Robinson Crusoe as a brother in God. In all except generalship, he is that most attractive and delightful being, the magnificent commonplace, and we needs must love the glorified image of ourselves.

Thus did Shakespeare sweeten the savour of the political life, without giving the lie to what he had apprehended of its sordid necessities. Though it may be largely hidden, the truth as Shakespeare grasped it, remains even in *Henry V*: the sense that not only is politics a nasty business, but that a repugnant unscrupulousness is an invaluable asset in the art of government. That is the burden of the English History Plays, jubilant as they are in pride of country and of race.

(from Shakespeare, Politics and Politicians,
English Association Pamphlet, no. 72, April 1929)

WILLIAM EMPSON

THERE is a variety of the 'conflict' theory of poetry which says that a poet must always be concerned with some difference of opinion or habit between different parts of his community; different social classes, ways of life, or modes of thought; that he must be several sorts of men at once, and reconcile his tribe in his own person. . . .

In the following full-blown ornamental comparison men and bees are the two social types, with each of which the poet must be in sympathy.

> for so work the honey-bees . . .
> They have a king, and officers of sorts . . .
> Others, like soldiers, armed in their stings,
> Make boot upon the summer's velvet buds;
> Which pillage they with merry march bring home,

> To the tent-royal of their emperor;
> Who, busied in his majesty, surveys
> The singing masons building roofs of gold;
> The civil citizens kneading up the honey;   (1 ii 320)

and so forth. The commentators have no grounds for deciding from this passage, of course, whether Shakespeare knew much or little about bees: we can only see what effects he was producing by a distorted account of their habits. It is a vision of civil order conceived as natural, made at once charming and convincing by its expression in terms of creatures so petty and apparently so irrelevant. The parallel passage in Vergil uses the same methods; it pokes fun at bees and their pretensions to humanity, and so, with a sad and tender generosity, elevates both parties in the mind of the reader by making a comparison between them. For matters are so arranged that the only things the reader thinks of as in common between men and bees are the more tolerable things about either of them, and since, by the compactness of the act of comparison, a wide variety of things in which bees and men are alike have appeared in his mind, he has a vague idea that both creatures have been adequately described. Both, therefore, are given something of the charm, the suppression of unpleasing detail, and the cosiness (how snug they all are down there!) of a bird's-eye view.

I shall only consider the line about *masons*.* Bees are not forced by law or immediate hunger to act as *masons*; 'it all comes naturally to them'; as in the Golden Age they *sing* with plenty and the apparent freedom of their social structure. On the other hand, *bees* only *sing* (indeed, can only sing) through the noise produced by their working; though happy they are not idle; and the human opposition between the pain of work and the waste of play has been resolved by the hive into a higher unity, as in Heaven. Milton's 'the busy hum of men' makes work seem agreeable by the same comparison in a less overt form.

* G. K. Chesterton had praised this line, I think in one of his detective stories. He had great powers as a verbal critic, shown mainly by incidental remarks, and I ought to have acknowledged how much I was using them.

Roofs are what they are *building*; the culmination of successful work, the most airy and striking parts of it; also the Gothic tradition gave a peculiar exaltation to *roofs*, for instance, those magnificent hammer-beam affairs which had angels with *bee*-like wings on the hammers, as if they were helping in the *singing* from a heavenly choir; and to have *masons*, building a stone *roof*, with mortar instead of nails, is at once particularly like the methods of *bees* and the most solid and wealthy form of construction. But *bees build* downwards from the *roof*, so that they are always still *building* the *roof*, in a sense; the phrase is thus particularly applicable to them, and the comparison with men makes this a reckless or impossible feat, arguing an ideal security. In the same way, both parties are given wealth and delicacy because the yellow of wax is no surface gilding, not even such as in the temple of Solomon (built without sound of hammer, in the best *bee* tradition, though it was) shone thickly coated upon ivory, but all throughout, as the very substance of their labours, is its own pale ethereal and delicious *gold*.

(from *Seven Types of Ambiguity*, 1930; rev. ed. 1953)

E. M. W. TILLYARD

IN one historical matter *Henry V* is unique in Shakespeare: its partiality to things Welsh refers obliquely to that side of the Tudor myth ... which Spenser and Warner, among the poets, developed.

> *Fluellen.* All the water in Wye cannot wash your majesty's
> Welsh plood out of your pody, I can tell you that.
> God pless it and preserve it, as long as it pleases his
> grace, and his majesty too!
> *Henry.* Thanks, good my countryman.

I fancy too that Shakespeare spares the French king the ridicule he heaps on the Dauphin, because he was father of Katharine, who, widowed of Henry V, married Owen Tudor and became the ancestress of Henry VII. The French king always speaks with dignity.

Henry V [is] constructed without intensity. It is worth mentioning one or two points in which this is true. After the Archbishops' fable of the bees there is little of the cosmic lore that marks the other History-Plays. When Shakespeare's mind was working intensely it was aware of the whole range of the universe: events were not isolated but took place concurrently with other events on all the planes of existence. But the settings of the different scenes in this play are simple and confined. Even the battle of Agincourt evokes no correspondences in the heavens or elsewhere. A second sign of slack construction is the unevenness of the verse. There are passages of flatness among the rhetoric. The rhetoric has been better remembered than the flatness. But take the opening of II iv (the first scene showing the French court) up to the arrival of Exeter: it is written in the flattest verse, a relapse into the style of the more primitive parts of *1 Henry VI*; and, though Exeter proceeds to liven things a little, the verse remains lethargic. Nor is there much energy in the verse portions of the play's last scene. A third sign of weak construction is the casualness of the comic scenes. Whereas in *Henry IV* these were linked in all sorts of ways with the serious action, in *Henry V* they are mainly detached scenes introduced for mere variety. The farewell scene of Pistol and the Hostess in London is good enough in itself, but it is quite episodic. It would be unfair, however, not to mention the redeeming brilliance of Fluellen. For sheer original invention Shakespeare never made a better character. Had the rest of the play backed him up, he would (as his creator probably meant him to do) have filled the place of Falstaff not unworthily.

I fancy, too, that Fluellen helps us to understand Shakespeare's state of mind when he wrote *Henry V*. Fluellen is an entire innovation, like nobody else in Shakespeare before (though many years after he may have begotten the Baron of Bradwardine); and he suggests that Shakespeare was now wanting to do something fresh. Whenever Fluellen, the new character, is on the stage, Shakespeare's spirits seem to rise and he ceases to flog himself into wit or rhetoric. There are other things in the play that suggest Shakespeare's longing for a change. The coarseness of Henry's

courtship of Katharine is curiously exaggerated; one can almost
say hectic: as if Shakespeare took a perverse delight in writing
up something he had begun to hate. Henry's reproof of Scroop,
... alien in tone to the norm of the play, has a quality as new as
the character of Fluellen; for it is tragic and looks forward to
Shakespeare's future bent of mind –

> May it be possible that foreign hire
> Could out of thee extract one spark of evil
> That might annoy my finger? 'tis so strange
> That, though the truth of it stands off as gross
> As black and white, my eye will scarcely see it.

That is one of the tragic themes: the unbelievable contradiction
of appearance and reality; felt by Troilus about Cressida, by
Hamlet about his mother, and by Othello about Desdemona. It
has nothing to do with ... politics, with patterns of history, with
ancestral curses, with England's destiny and all the order of her
society. It is a personal and not a public theme.

(from Shakespeare's History Plays, 1944)

J. I. M. STEWART

FALSTAFF's corner of *Henry V* is extremely wonderful; the rest
is a slack-water play, stirred here and there by simple patriotic
feeling. For comedy now Shakespeare had so little list that he
fell back upon comic Scots, Irish and Welshmen – the resource,
I think I may say, of a professional entertainer hard pressed
indeed. Moreover, that the poet of *Romeo and Juliet* should have
executed the wooing of Katherine – that *ne plus ultra* of all
obtuseness – must fill us with dismay until we persuade ourselves
(with a school of critics romantic, no doubt) that there here glints
at us from behind the mask the master's most inscrutable smile.

(from Character and Motive in Shakespeare, 1949)

ARTHUR SEWELL

ROYALTY has its unmistakable style and reveals itself as certainly
as greatness of soul in a work of art. It is the style in which a

particular address to the world, a royal address, is transformed
into poetry, and I dare say, unmistakable as it is, and absolutely
unmistakable in Henry V, it defies analysis. Young Arthur has it,
when he`pleads with Hubert. Royalty does not exempt a man
from stupidity or even from wickedness; it alone does not qualify
a man to rule his kingdom. But for Shakespeare political order
was something more than temporal, and was not to be explained
in the handbook. There was in it a mystical element, which not
prose but only poetry could represent, and a part of this element
is royalty.

The histories are concerned with rebellion, usurpation, conspiracy, and war. These events are hatched in the minds of men
and are exercised by the purposes of men. Certainly the idea of
Fate is present in the histories, and we are continually reminded
of historic expiation and retribution. But these are represented as
involved with the moral nature of man, and this moral nature is
apprehended in terms of its political manifestations. So it is that
character is created. . . . Political order and political disorder, and
those workings of man's moral nature which generate them, are
all apprehended together, implying and involved with each other.
Henry V is not the reconstruction of a political theorist; he is a
poet's representation of a king. . . .

The histories raise the problem of character-presentation in a
special form. The persons in these plays, whether taken from
Plutarch or Holinshed, had already, before Shakespeare dealt
with them, their particular life in men's imaginations. They were
known as treacherous or ambitious; their policies had brought
them victory or had come to nothing; for kings and counsellors
they were famous predecessors and known examples. The
audience had already formed some attitude to these characters,
and, of course, this attitude was largely determined by the contemporary idea of political order. . . . Shakespeare, without playing tricks, can take very good advantage of such a character: as
of Hal, in his treatment of Falstaff or in the situation of Henry
V's wooing, or, more movingly, in the talk with the common
soldiers on the eve of Agincourt. We should remember, however, that even in these more private moments a public, a political

character is being represented. ... Every moment is, in its own way, an image of man in political society and in these moments the character is conceived. Into the political world the study of character, however humane and individual, is extraverted.

How then is character active in the historical plays? Over all, as the presiding vision, there is a poet's idea of political order about which Shakespeare leaves us in no doubt. In *Richard II* the gardener develops the analogy between the state and the garden:

> We at time of year
> Do wound the bark, the skin of our fruit-trees,
> Lest, being over-proud in sap and blood,
> With too much riches it confound itself:
> Had he done so to great and growing men,
> They might have lived to bear and he to taste
> Their fruits of duty; superfluous branches
> We lop away, that bearing boughs may live:
> Had he done so, himself had borne the crown,
> Which waste of idle hours hath quite thrown down.

In *Henry V*, in another comparison, Shakespeare sees political society in the honey-bees, who teach 'the act of order to a peopled kingdom'. The significance of the vision expressed in these analogies in its relation to character is unmistakable. This vision, as it were, gets to know itself more concretely and more variously in such characters as Bolingbroke, Hotspur, Henry V, and Falstaff. The primary activity of character is apprehended as shaping or mis-shaping political order. And we should note that political disapproval does not imply an absolute disapproval. The bark of the tree must be wounded

> Lest, being over-proud in sap and blood,
> With too much richness it confound itself.

There is no simple opposition of sheep and goats in the internecine tensions of political society. But the political judgement, sometimes sadly enough, must override all others. ...

It is a consequence of all this that, in general, the characters of the historical plays have no truly private emotions. What inner feeling they may be thought to have is *public emotion*. When

Henry IV complains of his sleeplessness the emotion is, as it were, a show. When Richard II takes a handful of English earth in his hands and weeps over it, the action and the feeling belong not to his private but to his public life. Even when Henry V walks round the English camp in the darkness and speaks to the common soldiers, what he says as man enlarges what he is as king.

The imagery in the historical plays has an important part in determining in what world – and in what manner – these emotions are felt. It is imagery which finds the equivalents for emotion in the world of public and political behaviour, and so this emotion takes a relevant part in our imaginative apprehension of political order.

> Why, rather, sleep, liest thou in smoky cribs,
> Upon uneasy pallets stretching thee,
> And hush'd with buzzing night-flies to thy slumber,
> Than in the perfumed chambers of the great,
> Under the canopies of costly state,
> And lulled with sounds of sweetest melody?

In such a way – this is a simple example – is the treatment of character subordinate to the comprehensive vision of the play, and in the presentation of character we are at all times reminded by the imagery of the political society to which character belongs.

(from *Character and Society in Shakespeare*, 1951)

G. WILSON KNIGHT

HENRY V's 'Crispin' speech may serve as a starting-point for an inquiry into Shakespeare's use of proper names. It contains examples of two main literary uses: (i) a good list of place-names to make a poetic cluster, though these are, it is true, personal titles; and (ii) a single personal name 'Crispin', acting as a verbal talisman, in which more 'is meant', as Milton says of the old myths in *Il Penseroso*, 'than meets the ear'. . . .

It is comparatively easy to strike fire from 'Christendom', 'Agincourt', and 'Harfleur', but what is so remarkable is Shakespeare's ability to use English or Welsh names, with all their lack,

at least to us, of exotic colour and appeal, in such a way as still
to entrance us: an excellence found pre-eminently in the first part
of *Henry IV*. Scottish place-names attain a high dramatic intensity in *Macbeth*. In such instances the personal, or spiritual, even
moral, powers seem to be present within the places themselves;
each separate place is, as it were, no less richly charged than the
one word 'Rome'. The simple words 'England' and 'English'
are obvious powers. Examples abound. We may point simply to
Henry V's

> And you, good yeomen,
> Whose limbs were made in England ... (iii i 25)

The poet relies, simply, on emotions, or powers, which are
assumed; and somehow he always succeeds. It is the same with
that remarkable cluster in his 'Crispin' speech:

> Then shall our names,
> Familiar in his mouth as household words,
> Harry the King, Bedford and Exeter,
> Warwick and Talbot, Salisbury and Gloucester,
> Be in their flowing cups freshly remember'd.
>   (iv iii 51)

Apart from the name 'Harry', the power here seems to radiate
less from thought of the persons concerned than from that of the
places. Why are they so effective? It is as though the places have
become themselves, as places, personal. We could say that, in time
of war, if this simple grouping of names, as Shakespeare handles
it, does not raise a flutter of patriotic feeling, nothing will.

Throughout the Histories English place-names are exquisitely
handled, either in themselves – as in the immortality given by
Falstaff to 'Shrewsbury clock' (*1 Henry IV*, v iv 151) – or as
titles, where the places are one with the people. When Richard,
Duke of Gloucester, refers to 'the faultless blood of pretty Rutland' (*Richard III*, i iii 178), words typical of Shakespeare's
feeling for the pathos of slaughtered youth, 'Rutland' gathers to
itself all the warmth of a Christian name. But there is a personal
dignity, or sovereignty, in the title too; as when Buckingham in
Henry VIII bitterly comments on his loss of the ringing title

'Duke of Buckingham' and his return to simple 'Edward Bohun' (II i 103). The material is too rich and obvious for detailed comment. . . .

We now turn to the second type of name found in our 'Crispin' speech; that is, names following the type of 'Crispin' itself; personal names which, without being exactly 'labels', yet carry undertones of significance, and often of a certain personal dignity, or royalty, which repay study. The play on 'Crispin' working up to the climax of 'Crispin Crispian' most excellently suggests, without forcing, the word 'Christian', and this is why it can function so well as the pivot-mechanism of Shakespeare's key-speech in delineation of Christian warriorship; the very fact that it suggests, without asserting, the word 'Christian', subtly underlining a recognition of the complexities and difficulties involved: 'Christ' or 'Christian' would not, in such a context, have done so well.

The other personal name of importance here is 'Harry': 'Harry the King, Bedford, and Exeter' (IV iii 53). This is to Shakespeare a talismanic name, as in that strange phrase 'a little touch of Harry in the night' (IV Chorus 47). But its force is felt most vividly in an earlier speech addressed by the King to his brothers and also, in effect, to the Lord Chief Justice, who had had cause to correct him before he became king, and is, on his accession, terrified of what may now be in store for him. The new king disabuses them all, not by argument, and with no fine sentiments, but in these simple words:

> Brothers, you mix your sadness with some fear:
> This is the English, not the Turkish, court;
> Not Amurath an Amurath succeeds,
> But Harry Harry.　　　　　　　(*2 Henry IV*, v ii 46)

There, in two lines made of two names, we have the whole story of what England, throughout the centuries, stands for, or what at least we should like to think that England stands for: what, anyway, Shakespeare's England stands for. Henry is its personification: 'We are no tyrant, but a Christian king' (I ii 241).

(from *The Sovereign Flower*, 1958)

ANN RIGHTER

THE Chorus speeches of *Henry V*, with their insistence upon the gap between reality and the pretensions of illusion, the poverty of resource of the stage, give perhaps the first warning of an attitude towards the theatre which was to emerge far more fully in succeeding plays. A kind of mock humility, a studied obeisance to the all-powerful audience, certainly plays its part in those references to the 'flat unraised spirits', the 'unworthy scaffold', the 'huge and proper life' of things beyond the scope of any 'wooden O', even as it does in the epilogue's description of Shakespeare's 'rough and all-unable pen'. Yet there is a restlessness in these formal apologies and invocations to the imagination of the audience to 'force a play' which strikes a new and not altogether cheerful note. In a sense, these Chorus passages seem to point beyond the noble actors of *Hamlet* or *Julius Caesar* to the 'strutting player' of *Troilus and Cressida* and *Macbeth*, to a period when Shakespeare, his faith in the power of illusion seemingly gone, would turn to the exploration of resemblances between the world and the stage which were negative and curiously grim.

(from *Shakespeare and the Idea of the Play*, 1962)

PART TWO
Longer Studies

Gerald Gould

IRONY AND SATIRE IN
HENRY V (1919)

NONE of Shakespeare's plays is so persistently and thoroughly misunderstood as *Henry V*, and one is tempted to think that there is no play which it is more important to understand. Irony is an awkward weapon. No doubt the irony of *Henry V* was meant to 'take in' the groundlings when it was first produced: had it failed to take them in, it would have invited bitter and immediate unpopularity. But Shakespeare can scarcely have intended that force of preconception should, hundreds of years after his death, still be preventing the careful, the learned, and the sympathetic from seeing what he so definitely put down. *The play is ironic:* that is, I venture to think, a fact susceptible of detailed proof. Yet we still find, for instance, Mr J. A. R. Marriott taking it at its face value as an example of 'patriotism'; while the critics who counter this error by a reminder of the more hideous 'Prussianisms' with which Shakespeare has endowed his Henry fail to press the argument home, and are content with a sort of compromise reading.

That Shakespeare was a patriot there is neither reason nor excuse for denying. What must be denied is that *Henry V* is patriotic. Precisely because Shakespeare *was* patriotic, he must have felt revolted by Henry's brutal and degrading 'militarism'. The question of how far Shakespeare's reading of Henry is historically accurate does not arise: Shakespeare chose Henry, as he chose Antony, to illustrate and enforce a certain reading of life. And he never allowed himself to be limited by his materials.

The misunderstandings of *Henry V* have varied. Hazlitt was bitterly opposed to the conventional interpretation. He detested Henry, and said so: but he made the mistake of supposing that

that detestable character was a 'favourite' character of Shakespeare's. Dr A. C. Bradley, as is his habit, has come nearest to the
detection and exposition of the essential: and to differ from Dr
Bradley on any point of Shakespearean criticism is an act of pre-
sumption which no one will venture lightly. Yet even he declares
to be inconceivable that reading of *Henry V* which is demon-
strably the right one: and it is impossible, if one is wrong about
Henry V, to be altogether right about the rest of Shakespeare.
Henry V is central and conclusive, and that in spite of the fact
that it is certainly not one of the best plays. It is central actually
in time: and this in itself makes us mildly wonder why it is *not*
one of the best plays. It happens to be one of the few whose
date can be determined with certainty and precision. It belongs
to 1599: that is to say, it comes between Shakespeare's greatest
comic period, the period which saw the creation of Falstaff, and
his greatest tragic period, the period which began with *Julius
Caesar* and *Hamlet*. Is it not odd that work so circumstanced
should be so largely lacking in indications of Shakespeare's
tragic or comic greatness? Touches of greatness, certainly, there
are: the death of Falstaff is in the high sense 'Shakespearean'.
But for the most part the serious scenes are full of a loud clanging
rhetoric, which lacks almost wholly the intensity and profundity
of tragic poetry, and the humours are mainly crude and verbal.
The play, both in its 'serious' parts and in its comedy, is specially
popular with schoolboys. Some of the more miserable jocosities
are, it is true, borrowed from an old play: but that is neither
excuse nor (to anyone who has studied Shakespeare's ways of
using his materials) explanation. On the other hand, this particular argument must not be pushed too far. It is certain that the
middle period of Shakespeare saw, at any rate, some other work
of inferior character, and consequently we cannot pretend that
the inferiority òf *Henry V* was necessarily intentional and
'tendencious'.

Again, if the examination of the play shows us – as it does –
various discrepancies and contradictions, we must hesitate as to
how far we press the argument from these. The contradictions
in Shakespeare vary in kind. In the early plays they seem often

to be nothing but the results of technical carelessness and incompetence. The contradictions of time in *Othello*, on the other hand, seem to be carefully inserted in order to secure the dramatic effect of 'double time', while, as against that, when we go on to *Lear*, we find confusions and discrepancies for which no critical scheme can account. The contradictions in *Henry V*, then, must be judged on their own merits, and brought to one simple test: the test of whether they do or do not appear to follow a definite line, illustrate a definite tendency, and fix a definite character. If they do so appear, it will scarcely be fair to dismiss them as technical errors. Rather, we shall have to consider them as the means of Shakespeare's irony. *Henry V* is a satire on monarchical government, on imperialism, on the baser kinds of 'patriotism', and on war. This can be proved by quotation from the play itself, even if we consider the play itself in isolation. But we ought not to consider it in isolation. It is definitely the concluding portion of a trilogy. The character of Henry V is perfectly consistent throughout: both in the two parts of *Henry IV* and in *Henry V* he puts forward consistent and convincing explanations of his apparent 'wildness' and the change from that to his assumption of public dignity. His explanations differ only when they have different objects to subserve. He is the perfect hypocrite. Even in soliloquy he sometimes keeps up the pretences which he uses elsewhere to deceive his acquaintances or the public: the fact being that his pretences have penetrated to the subconscious deeps of his character. (It is instructive to compare the soliloquies of Iago, in which that supreme villain searches about in his consciousness, of course unsuccessfully, for motives which are not there at all – motives which ought rather to be sought in the subconscious 'urge' of an unrealised moral jealousy.) Never once, throughout the three plays in which he figures, the trilogy of which he is the unifying centre, does Henry perform an act of spontaneous generosity or kindliness. When he displays magnanimity, as towards the Lord Chief Justice, it is always in order to repay some return in political advantage. His 'magnanimity' to the Lord Chief Justice is in sharp, immediate, and intentional contrast to his rejection of Falstaff. There was nothing to be 'got' by being magnanimous, or even fair, to Falstaff: quite the contrary. Octavius in *Antony and Cleopatra* displays a magnanimity similar to Henry's both in manner and in motive. Shakespeare, in short, was constantly preoccupied with the contrast between cold successfulness and the generous infirmities of human nature. He recurred again and again to this theme. In such 'militarism' as Henry's he saw an outstanding example of what cold successfulness means in the political and international sphere, and this impression was fortified by his reading of the characters of Henry's father and brother. In devoting the play of *Henry V*, which is both a complete play in itself and the conclusion of a trilogy, to a satire on 'militarism', he was providing a central and conclusive example of a constant theme. The case is threefold. If we read *Henry V* as part of a trilogy through which runs what may be called the Bolingbroke motif, the view that it is a satire is immeasurably strengthened. If we read it in the light of Shakespeare's work as a whole, that view is strengthened still more. Yet that view, I repeat, is unmistakable in the play itself, even apart from the just and necessary illumination provided by its context. I advance a general theory, which may be acceptable or unacceptable, of Shakespearean interpretation. If the general theory is rejected, still the particular reading of *Henry V* remains.

Shakespeare's main moral line of demarcation, then, was (like Christ's) between successful self-righteousness (which he hated) and erring loving humanity (which, however 'gross and miserable' its error, he loved). This point has been suggested in so masterly a fashion by Dr Bradley that I will not presume to labour it here: even Dr Bradley, however, has missed some of its implications. Shakespeare loved Antony and hated Octavius. He sympathised with Shylock and hated Antonio. . . . Shakespeare sympathised (in *Measure for Measure*) with Claudio, and hated Isabella. . . . Above all, Shakespeare loved Falstaff and hated Prince Hal (Henry V). He hated not only Prince Hal, but also his father and his brother; the hereditary psychology of the family fascinated him. Prince John of Lancaster, fresh from the most dastardly treachery (*Henry IV, Part II*, iv ii), meets Falstaff (iii), and is summed up by him as 'this same young sober-

blooded boy', in the same speech in which Prince Hal's own
natural cold blood is insisted upon – 'the cold blood he did naturally inherit of his father'. It is true the whole speech, characteris-
tically Falstaffian and absurd, is to prove that one Prince is
valiant because he drinks 'fertile sherris', the other not, because
he does not: that, of course, is only Falstaff's way of proclaiming
his affection for the one Prince and his distaste for the other. Here
is pathos, too, for within a very little that greater warmth in
Prince Hal (on which, for all his wilfully farcical explanation of
it, Falstaff has seriously counted) is to be found lacking. The
famous 'rejection scene', if judged on its merits, bears but one
interpretation. Falstaff takes with dignity his double rebuff, cruel,
ungrateful, and cowardly as it is: our hearts go out to him, and
turn away sickened from the prig Henry. . . .

To come to *Henry V* itself. It is about war. The King makes
war – war which, whether it is justifiable or not, is admittedly
not thrust upon him. In war lies the whole glory of the play and
its hero, such as that glory is. We can scarecely, therefore, shut
our eyes to the irony with which Shakespeare makes Henry
declare (IV i):

> The slave, a member of the country's peace,
> Enjoys it; but in gross brain little wots
> What watch the King keeps to maintain the peace,
> Whose hours the peasant best advantages.

It may well be said here that the 'peace' referred to is not international peace, but legal and domestic. Even so, the contrast is
sufficiently striking, and none the less so if we accept the view
that Henry's war-making can somehow be justified. But can it?

The actual words used in *Henry V* about the French war are
foreshadowed at the end of *Henry IV* in the speech of Prince
John of Lancaster (and as to Shakespeare's view of *his* cynicism
there can be no doubt):

> I will lay odds that, ere this year expire,
> We bear our civil swords and native fire
> As far as France: I heard a bird so sing,
> Whose music, to my thinking, pleased the King.

'Pleased the King' – that is the point. That forestalls all the arguments by which, in the early part of *Henry V*, the justification of
a war against France is urged. But even earlier there has been an
indication of the militarist motive. In *Henry IV*, *Part II*, IV v,
the dying Henry IV says to his son, who is to succeed him:

> Therefore, my Harry,
> Be it thy course to busy giddy minds
> With foreign quarrels; that action, hence borne out,
> May waste the memory of the former days.

The pleas of justification for the war, with which we are bound
to begin any detailed examination of *Henry V* are open to two
main criticisms. Even if they were convincing on their merits,
they would prove only that the war was justified as a *dynastic* war.
And are dynastic wars ever justified? – seeing that they cost the
blood of the common people who have nothing to do with
dynasties. To say this is not to import 'modern' ideas into
Shakespeare: the point was fully appreciated, long before Shakespeare, by Sir Thomas More. So much, however, is conjecture:
the sound and unanswerable criticism is that, even *as* a dynastic
claim, Henry's claim to the French crown could be justified, as he
indeed seeks to justify it, by his descent from Edward III and by
that only: and *since he was not descended in the eldest line, the claim
had no shadow of justification.* He held the English throne by vote
of Parliament; but even he could scarcely think that the English
Parliament could vote him the French crown. Nor can it be said
that we are here going outside Shakespeare to mere historical
fact: Henry himself admits his position as a usurper's son (IV i):

> Not to-day, O Lord,
> O, not to-day, think not upon the fault
> My father made in compassing the crown!

All the Archbishop's talk about the 'Salic law' (I ii) is utterly
beside the point. Granted the refutation of the 'Salic law',
granted Edward III's claim, still the heir was not Henry but
Mortimer. It is true that Shakespeare was not clear about the
Mortimers. In *Henry IV*, *Part I*, he appears to confuse two differ-

ent ones, but there he does at least admit the position of the
Mortimer line (1 iii), though not on dynastic grounds. The only
conceivable case against the hereditary claim of that Mortimer
who was Earl of March would have been a denial of the power to
inherit through a woman – a denial which is expressly repudiated
(in fact, the repudiation is made the basis of the claim) in Henry's
own claim to the throne of France!

It is Act i, sc. i which at once gives the game away. Two prelates are discussing how they may avert a threatened law for the
disendowment of the Church:

> If it pass against us,
> We lose the better half of our possession,

says the Archbishop of Canterbury, and proposes to buy off the
King by offering him an unprecedentedly large sum towards the
expenses of a war with France – and *to explain to him*

> The severals and unhidden passages
> Of his true titles to some certain dukedoms,
> And generally to the crown and seat of France.

The cynicism of this, in the forefront of the play, needs no
elaboration – it is only amazing that it should ever have been
missed. Bear in mind that there is artistically, in dramatic construction, no reason or excuse whatever for this scene: unless its
intention is the obvious cynical one, there is no intention at all.
A later speech of Henry's own, again (1 ii) admits of only one
reading. He is explaining the wild courses of his youth, and
advances an argument so obviously outrageous for a seriously
patriotic play that one wonders even the 'rabble' could swallow
it:

> We never valued this poor seat of England;
> And therefore, living hence, did give ourself
> To barbarous licence; as 'tis ever common
> That men are merriest when they are from home.
> But tell the Dauphin I will keep my state,
> Be like a king and show my sail of greatness
> When I do rouse me in my throne of France.

If this is not a plain statement that the war with France was intended from long before, it is (to say nothing of the quaint 'patriotism' of the first line!) utterly meaningless. Then what are we to say of the hypocrisy which seeks to put the decision upon the Archbishop of Canterbury? Henry cannot have it both ways within three hundred lines. The Archbishop is adjured:

> And God forbid, my dear and faithful lord,
> That you should fashion, wrest, or bow your reading,
> Or nicely charge your understanding soul
> With opening titles miscreate, whose right
> Suits not in native colours with the truth;
> For God doth know how many now in health
> Shall drop their blood in approbation
> Of what your reverence shall incite us to.
> Therefore take heed how you impawn our person,
> How you awake our sleeping sword of war:
> We charge you, in the name of God, take heed. . . .

Then follows the Archbishop's exposition of the Salic law – an exposition which is, in any case, as we have seen, wholly irrelevant and certainly known to be insincere. Later, different suggestions of motives are allowed to peep out – not, we must suppose, without deliberate intention of contrast. Thus Ely urges:

> . . . my thrice puissant liege
> Is in the very May-morn of his youth,
> Ripe for exploits and mighty enterprises.

And Exeter:

> Your brother kings and monarchs of the earth
> Do all expect that you should rouse yourself,
> As did the former lions of your blood.

Henry's tendency, indulged already at great length, to deplore the waste of innocent blood in war, does not here move him to rebuke these 'militarist' incitements! Is there, again no hint of, irony in the Prologue to Act II?

> Now thrive the armourers, and honour's thought
> Reigns solely in the breast of every man.

Perhaps not. But can a king who has so recently been unsure of
his own claim be credited with sincerity when he tries to put on
those who resist it the whole blame of the war? Yet Henry's
emissary, Exeter, speaking to the French king (II iv), thus defines
his master's attitude:

> ... he ...
> ... bids you, in the bowels of the Lord,
> Deliver up the crown, and to take mercy
> On the poor souls for whom this hungry war
> Opens his vasty jaws; and on your head
> Turning the widows' tears, the orphans' cries,
> The dead men's blood, the pining maidens' groans,
> For husbands, fathers, and betrothed lovers,
> That shall be swallow'd in this controversy.

It is important to notice the extraordinary accumulation and
contradiction of motives with which the whole question of the
war's origin is confused. In the negotiation scene (II iv) the Dauphin's earlier and provocative message is admitted by implication
to be a mere side-issue. Now this message of the Dauphin's was
in answer to a demand of Henry's, not indeed for the crown of
France, but for 'some certain dukedoms': and *those* were claimed
'in the right of your great predecessor, King Edward the Third'.
That claim was made, then, long before the King had received
the Archbishop of Canterbury's decision about the Salic law and
the right of succession – and yet the Archbishop makes no distinction between the two claims when (II i) he speaks of Henry's

> ... true titles to some certain dukedoms,
> And generally to the crown and seat of France,
> Derived from Edward, his great-grandfather.

Besides, before the war irretrievably begins, the French King
relents from the Dauphin's attitude, and fruitlessly offers Henry
his daughter's hand and what the Prologue to Act III describes as

> Some petty and unprofitable dukedoms.

Confusion on confusion! Leaving aside the fact that Henry had
no claim to the French crown at all, and judging only the English

case as presented by the English in the play, what do we find? The claim to certain dukedoms is identical with the claim to the whole Erench Kingdom: both depend on the inheritance from Edward: yet the former claim is put forward irrespective of the latter, and is refused by the Dauphin. The Dauphin's refusal is made the occasion of violent threats against the French people – threats which are later in a slightly different form repeated to the French King as the penalty of refusing the *second* claim, not the first. Indeed, as has been said, the French King is willing to depart from the Dauphin's attitude and to compromise: but it is too late. Why, since the Dauphin's insult is admitted to be irrelevant? Because the Archbishop has decided that Henry has a claim, not merely to the dukedoms which he *had* claimed, but to the Kingdom of France. But Henry had previously intended to conquer the Kingdom of France anyway: the whole course of his youth is explained by that single intention. Yet the responsibility of his enterprise is to rest, firstly, on the Archbishop, who gives Henry the advice which he has already acted on before receiving it, and secondly on the King of France, who refuses a claim about which Henry himself has been extremely doubtful. War is a glorious thing, irrespective of its cause or object – a 'mighty enterprise' in which a King is expected to engage; yet it is so inglorious that the responsibility of embarking on it has at all costs of veracity and common sense, to be 'shelved'. It diverts men's minds from difficulties at home, and requires and receives the blessings of the Church! One can of, course, if one chooses, attribute all this wildness of contradiction and nonsense to carelessness or incompetence on Shakespeare's part. But to do so is an extreme step, in face of the satisfying completeness with which every contradiction, every absurdity, fits in with the further insincerities of Henry's character to make of that character a comprehensive and comprehensible whole.

The second main indictment against Henry is his unscrupulous brutality. This is so clear, so insistent, that it can be neither missed nor explained away. Commentators have sometimes taken the discreet course of ignoring it. It should, alone, be sufficient to silence the suggestion that we are meant to admire Henry. But it does not stand alone. It is inextricably mingled with the old hypocrisy, the continual confusion of motive. In Act IV sc vi every soldier is ordered to kill his prisoners, merely as a precautionary measure ('Give the word through'); yet in the next scene we find, first, that this measure *has* been adopted for quite a different reason, and, secondly, that the threat of such a measure (had the word not been 'given through'?) is to be used in negotiation, and that as a preface to it Henry says:

> I was not angry since I came to France
> Until this instant.

Unfortunately, the anger of such cold-blooded worldlings can be produced to order, like their magnanimity, when 'profits will accrue'. One wonders how, if not by anger, Henry can have excused his previous ravings, almost incredible in their mingled brutality and hypocrisy, before Harfleur:

>   . . . as I am a soldier,
> A name that in my thoughts becomes me best,
> If I begin the battery once again,
> I will not leave the half-achieved Harfleur
> Till in her ashes she lie buried.
> The gates of mercy shall be all shut up,
> And the flesh'd soldier, rough and hard of heart,
> In liberty of bloody hand shall range
> With conscience wide as hell, mowing like grass
> Your fresh-fair virgins and your flowering infants.
> What is it then to me, if impious war,
> Array'd in flames like to the prince of fiends,
> Do, with his smirch'd complexion, all fell feats
> Enlink'd to waste and desolation?
> What is 't to me, when you yourselves are cause,
> If your pure maidens fall into the hand
> Of hot and forcing violation?
>
>   Therefore, you men of Harfleur,
> Take pity of your town and of your people
> Whiles yet my soldiers are in my command.
>
> If not, why, in a moment look to see
> The blind and bloody soldier with foul hand

Defile the locks of your shrill-shrieking daughters;
Your fathers taken by the silver beards,
And their most reverend heads dash'd to the walls,
Your naked infants spitted upon pikes. ...

Is it seriously maintained that Shakespeare means us to admire
Henry *here?*

The scene in which the King, disguised, talks with the soldiers
is very much to my purpose: it is too famous to bear much quotation, but I may point out how completely and deliberately Henry
confuses the issue. Bates and Williams argue that there is heavy
responsibility on the King '*if the cause be not good*', and that they,
having no choice but to obey, do not know whether the cause is
good or not. Williams says:

I am afeard there are few die well that die in a battle; for how
can they charitably dispose of anything, when blood is their
argument?

to which Henry replies with an irrelevant and hypocritical discourse on the sins that may have been committed *before* the war.
What do those who take Henry seriously as a patriot argue here?
Do they suggest Shakespeare was so obtuse as not to know when
he was making one of his characters argue dishonestly? Follows
the famous speech on Kingship, closely parallel to a similar outbreak, in a previous play, of the arch-humbug, Henry IV, who
there deplored the crown which he had won by such ill means.
The ground on which, in the present scene, Henry defends war
reveals the very grotesqueness of insincerity, especially when
contrasted with his own previous expatiation on its horrors.
Consider this:

Therefore should every soldier in the wars do as every sick
man in his bed, wash every mote out of his conscience; and dying
so, death is to him advantage; or not dying, the time was blessedly
lost wherein such preparation was gained.

The inglorious and 'profiteering' side of war is hit off in two
lines delivered by Pistol in Act II, sc. i:

... for I shall sutler be
Unto the camp, and profits will accrue.

So later, on the death of Falstaff, Pistol says:

> Yoke fellows in arms,
> Let us to France; like horse-leeches, my boys,
> To suck, to suck, the very blood to suck!

Nor, when in Act IV, sc. iv, we find Bardolph and Nym hanged for stealing, can we forbear the reflection that they have only done on a small scale what Henry has done on a large.

The part played by Fluellen as ironic commentator is highly significant. He is unimpressed by Henry's characteristic comment after victory (IV_viii):

> O God, thy arm was here;
> And not to us, but to thy arm alone,
> Ascribe we all!

– with which we may profitably compare Prince John's epilogue to his own successful but contemptible treachery in *Henry IV, Part II*, IV ii:

> God, and not we, hath safely fought to-day.

When Fluellen asks:

Is it not lawful, an't please your majesty, to tell how many is killed?

the King replies:

> Yes, captain, but with this acknowledgment,
> That God fought for us.

Is there anyone who will contend that Fluellen's rejoinder – 'Yes, my conscience, he did us great good' – is not ironic? Nor is the same note hard to discern in his reference to Falstaff:

As Alexander killed his friend Cleitus, being in his ales and his cups; so also Harry Monmouth, being in his right wits and his good judgments, turned away the fat knight with the great-belly doublet.

About Fluellen, however, opinions may easily vary. They cannot easily vary about the treatment of Falstaff. Our reading of the rejection-scene is more than confirmed by *Henry V*. The two scenes, Act II, sc. ii and iii, are in this connection decisive. They comprise the unmasking of the treachery of Cambridge, Scroop, and Grey, *with enormous stress laid on the sin of ingratitude towards a former comrade* – and the death of Falstaff, the victim of *the King's ingratitude towards a former comrade.* The irony of the contrast is unmistakable – it is indeed 'laid on almost too thick'. The whole character of Henry 'pivots', as it were, on his relation to Falstaff. It is the familiar antithesis – cold success and sinful humanity – which runs through the whole trilogy and through the whole of Shakespeare. It runs through the play of *Henry V* like a rhythm. 'Nay,' says Exeter, speaking, not of the King's treachery towards Falstaff, but of a conspirator towards the King:

> Nay, but the man that was his bedfellow,
> Whom he hath dull'd and cloy'd with gracious favours. . . .

The King thanks God for having graciously intervened on his behalf – and it is then that we go on to the famous and touching scene in which Falstaff's death is described. Those whom the fat knight has wronged stay by him: only the King has proved a false friend. It is Shakespeare's final moral judgment.

SOURCE: 'A New Reading of *Henry V*', in *The English Review* (1919).

E. E. Stoll

SHAKESPEARE'S PRESENTATION
OF A CONTEMPORARY HERO (1930)

SHAKESPEARE's *Henry V* is the last of his English 'histories',
which cover the line of kings from Richard II to Richard III.
Though itself not one of his greatest plays, it was written, in
1599, when Shakespeare had entered into the plenitude of his
powers, had almost finished his series of comedies, and was about
to touch the pinnacle of his art in *Hamlet, Othello, King Lear*, and
Macbeth. That – from 1602 to about 1607 – was the period of
tragedy; this, of history and comedy; that, the period of gloom
and terror; this, of love and joy and 'high, heroic things'. Not
that the prevailing mood of either period is necessarily to be
taken for the mood of Shakespeare the man. A man who writes
tragedy may himself be not uncheerful. just as one has been
known to write jokes for the newspapers at a time when his heart
was breaking. But so far as the plays themselves are concerned,
the period which ends with *Henry V* and *Twelfth Night* reflects
a joy in life and an exuberance of spirits, which then, for some
reason, suddenly pass away. This is true not only of the substance
but of the style. The expression now is highly colored, lavish of
poetry and the beauty of phrase and figure. In the great tragedies
ornament seems to be disdained, and the sweetness of the master's
style is sometimes almost lost in its Titanic strength.

To this more human and genial period *Henry V* wholly
belongs. In it are mingled the serious and the comic, as in *Henry
IV*, and the shadow of Fate nowhere appears. Shakespeare is
here following the older tradition of the English 'history',
though much improving upon it. Marlowe, in his *Edward II* (*c.*
1592), had eliminated the comic element; and Shakespeare, in
Richard III and *Richard II*, had followed suit. These 'histories'
are really tragedies; and both have the pomp and (the earlier, at

least) the horror of the older Elizabethan tragic manner. There is the supernatural machinery of the plot, inherited from the tragic poet Seneca – Fate lowering in the background, ghosts shrieking in the foreground, and omens and premonitions, prophecies and curses, fulfilled to the last jot and tittle. And there are atrocious crimes and deeds of violence, and fierce men and comparatively fiercer women, with long high-flown speeches in their mouths, passionate, declamatory, full of introspection and self-consciousness, and often not very closely fitted to the business in hand.

In *Henry IV* and *Henry V*, then, Shakespeare turned back somewhat from the Marlowesque history to the earlier popular tragi-comedy, but he pretty much abandoned the Senecan tragic machinery to be found in both. There were no doubt several reasons for this. In the first place, he must have felt that this tragic manner was too stiff and heavy for some of the material in English history which he wished to present. Henry IV was too businesslike, Hotspur too high-souled and eccentric, to lend himself to such a style. In the second place, he inclined to hearken to the popular cry. Before Marlowe English audiences had delighted in tragedy (or history) blended with comedy, just as they had done in the Middle Ages; such had always been the popular dramatic taste; and Shakespeare instinctively knew that only by satisfying this deep-seated craving could the artistic miracle be wrought – when, as with an electric shock, artist and public come vitally in contact. How then could he meet the popular demand without stooping to it? One of the readiest ways was to drop the portentous and atrocious old tragic manner and adopt one that more nearly accommodated itself to the sobriety and simplicity of life as we know it. Titans and ogres and men heroically mounted on stilts do not mingle readily with jolly good fellows and clowns: you cannot always be sure which set you are meant to laugh at. In *Henry IV* the serious part blends with the comic much more readily than in *Titus Andronicus* or *King John*, if for no other reason, simply because it is more within human reach and compass. And, in the third place, he now wished to treat a subject which demanded this blending of the comic and the serious, of low life and high life, by its very nature. Henry V combined the two elements in his single self. The hero of Agincourt had in life, as in Shakespeare's previous play, been a madcap and boon companion. To the popular heart this was the most interesting thing about his character – on the popular stage it was the one thing that could not be omitted or ignored. In these plays, then, in which he appears, *Henry IV* and *Henry V*, comedy was essential; and to harmonize with the comedy, as well as to fit the historical subject, the serious part must step down a bit to a more human level.

The greatest success in 'history' that Shakespeare attained was in the *First Part of Henry IV*. Here is to be found his liveliest and most richly-colored picture of tavern and country; here is to be found Falstaff, and Falstaff at his best; and here, in Hotspur, and in young Harry roused to emulation, are to be found a pair of Shakespeare's most radiant figures of English youth and chivalry. But the main thing is that the two elements, serious and comic, hold together better here than in *Henry V*. The Prince of Wales still belongs to both worlds; and both worlds, that is, the court and the Boar's Head in Eastcheap, are made to reflect or echo one another. At court for instance, Henry IV complains of his son's debauchery and takes him to task; at the Boar's Head, the actual scene between them is enacted by the Prince and Falstaff in burlesque; and then the alarm of war breaks in upon that haunt of jollity, and brings it and the court together, driving the droll and motley crew to Shrewsbury, not in quest of honor, to be sure, though young Harry – roused from his indifference – is in quest of nothing else.

I

In *Henry V* the hero has already forsaken Eastcheap for ever; Falstaff and his companions he has banished from his sight; and though after Falstaff's death his scurvy cronies follow the army into France, they do not enter the King's presence or indeed have much to do with his story. They are in the play, not so much because they belong there, as because, having been in the play preceding, they might be expected to be in this – the audience craving, like the clientèle of the present-day newspaper, the comic characters it already knows; and because the introduction of new comic characters, more closely connected with the King, had been made difficult by his reformation.

Plot, indeed, is not the strong point of this 'history'. *Henry V* is, as has been said, rather a series of tableaux. The choruses, which not only effect the transitions but also introduce glowing descriptions, elsewhere out of place, indicate as much. Pictures of life, interspersed with poetry and eloquence – these make up the story. A drama, of course, requires a struggle; and the King, by his reform, is past that. His career is simply a triumphal progress from Harfleur to Agincourt, and from Agincourt on to the French crown and the French princess' hand. There is even no external struggle, because there must be, in this patriotic drama, no enemy able to withstand him.

Wherein, then, lies the value of the drama? In the quality of the pictures of life and character, on the one hand; and in the quality of the eloquence and poetry – the patriotic passion which runs through the play – on the other. It is the latter, the patriotic fervor, along with the dominant figure of the King, that gives the play unity of effect. Nowhere else in Shakespeare is there so much of it as here. John of Gaunt's great speech in *Richard II*, – and that is no more than a speech – is the only thing to compare with it. Shakespeare in general was not so patriotic, or at least not so imperialistic, as his contemporaries Sidney, Raleigh, Spenser, Daniel, and Drayton; he was not interested in America, or 'Virginia', as they were, or in the greatness of England there, or in Europe, or on the sea. He had nothing to say, as they had, of the Queen, and the glory of her arms, the vast empire that then was making. He was not highly patriotic, just as he was not a partisan, whether in matters of state or of church. He loved men, loved Englishmen, more than England. But, as he always did, he rose to the occasion: he was enough in love with everything to do that. The choruses and the King's speeches to his soldiers stir and quicken your blood, and ring in your memory, after the book has been laid down:

Once more unto the breach, dear friends, once more,
Or close the wall up with our English dead.
... And you, good yeomen,
Whose limbs were made in England, show us here
The mettle of your pasture.

The words thrill us, who in these years have but sat at home,
now more than ever, for we know that they were read and uttered
of late by thousands of Englishmen on French soil, facing this
time, happily, a different foe. Like the words of the Prayer-book
and of the devotional parts of the Bible, they have been made
sacred by the lips, now silent, which repeated them. Like those,
they have become part of the litany of the nation, and of her
daughter nations too.

II

Apart from this, the play interests us most as a picture of life and
character. The patriotism, though ardent, is not highly enlightened. The war is for no good cause; Henry's claim to the throne
is, for all that he believes in it, unfounded. And the ideal of the
English is, so far as it is expressed, honor and glory, not love of
country, or liberty, or devotion to one's faith. It is a feudal,
chivalric war, waged, not for a cause like a crusade, but like a
tournament for a victor's crown. Henry, before the action,
rejoices that Englishmen are not there in greater numbers, partly
indeed, because 'if we are mark'd to die we are enow to do our
country loss'; but much more because 'the fewer men, the greater
share of honour'. Henry has the mind of a king but the soul of a
paladin. He speaks for the moment the language of knight-
errantry, – the language of Sidney, Raleigh, and Drake, to be
sure, and all very noble and glorious, but in these days, when
bloodshed is of itself more abhorrent, exceedingly remote. For
the ethics of statecraft and warfare were, in Shakespeare's time,
not so clearly and soundly established as today. English rulers
then were a little like some continental ones of late, and apart
from the motive of honor, they were for war from motives of
calculating expediency. Henry IV is made by Shakespeare twice

to express the opinion of the poet's friend, the Earl of Essex, that peace and unity at home were to be secured by waging foreign wars. In *Henry V* even the Archbishop advises waging one in order to save the endowments of the Church. Like some of the political leaders and writers of late, war they thought the great domestic curative and tonic. And like these, Englishmen then, as well as other Europeans, believed in waging a war of terror. The historical Henry V was no lamb, though he was not quite the lion that Shakespeare makes of him, roaring before the gates of Harfleur:

> If I begin the battery once again,
> I will not leave the half-achieved Harfleur
> Till in her ashes she lies burièd.
> The gates of mercy shall be all shut up,
> And the flesh'd soldier, rough and hard of heart,
> In liberty of bloody hand shall range
> With conscience wide as hell, mowing like grass
> Your fresh fair virgins and your flow'ring infants.
>
> (III iii 7–14)

His bark is worse than his bite, we trust; but even so his words are not out of keeping with the gentle poet Edmund Spenser's views on the subjugation of Ireland; or with the Spanish ways in Holland – and the Catholic ways in France – of stamping out heresy and dissent; or with the policy of the strong arm and violence as taught by the teacher and mentor of our contemporary Professor Treitschke and General Bernhardi – Niccolò Machiavelli – less than a century before Shakespeare's day.

But Shakespeare was not a political or moral theorist. He was not a theorist at all, not even, in any abstract or analytic sense of the word, a thinker. He was an artist, which is something widely different. His morals and his politics, his science and his history, were those of his time or one still earlier; but his art was for the ages. He was not a philosopher, a seer, an oracle, as some worshippers have taken him to be; he was not, of course, a prophet living in spirit in the nineteenth century while working in the sixteenth; but he was a man and dramatist as others were – Sophocles, Molière, Lope de Vega – and as such he was not very different from a great painter, sculptor, or musician. Like theirs, his work was to reveal not truth but beauty, to imitate and ennoble life, not analyze or expound it. Plot and situation, dialogue and character, style and meter, – these are the elements of his art in which he wrought as he strove to produce the illusion of life upon the stage. These are the things that we should attend to as we, in turn, strive to discover how far he succeeded in producing the illusion of life upon the stage. And in this particular play, as we have seen, plot and situation count for little, dialogue and characters for nearly all.

III

Chief of the characters is, of course, the King. He is, on the whole, done according to historical and popular tradition; he is the Hal of *Henry IV*, reclaimed and sobered. He has the manliness, the physical strength and ability, the personal courage, the generalship, the ruthlessness (as well as the mercifulness toward the poor and the weak), the piety (though not the bigotry and intolerance), and the exalted patriotic temper, which the chronicler Holinshed had attributed to the great popular hero of the land. But the mere transcription of traits will not go far towards making a character; and Shakespeare gave him many other features, and put in his nostrils the breath of life besides.

The most remarkable thing about him is the way that Shakespeare reforms him and yet contrives to keep him human and recognizable. Reformations are ticklish things to handle on the stage; edifying, but alienating, they ordinarily lead beyond the province of art and poetry into the dry and sterile air of morals or the dank atmosphere of sentimentality. This on the whole the royal reformation does not do. Henry is a knight and a hero, a king and a wise ruler, and a general who has put almost all petty personal considerations under his feet; but he is still a friendly good fellow, has his joke before battle and in the midst of battle, and woos the French princess in no silken terms of gallantry, but more like a captain of cavalry than a king, though more like a

king than a suitor, with fire in his heart though with a twinkle
in his eye. Wine, at times, is still a bit too good for him; like his
princely younger self, he has now and then a longing for the
poor creature, small beer. Bardolph, Pistol, and Falstaff himself,
risen from the dead, would have known him, though to recall
him and what he had been to them, both in purse and in person,
would now have cost them a pang. There is in the hero of Agincourt that mixture of the serious and the humorous, of the digni-
fied and the simple and naïve, which was impossible in French
tragedy until it came, in the nineteenth century, under Shakespeare's own influence, but which, in some form, is to be found
in many of his best characters and is one of the most authentic
signs of their reality. They are not mere rôles – not wraiths which
the moon shines through.

Some readers may object a little to Henry's obtrusive morality
and his familiarity with the Most High. They may be reminded
of later czars and kaisers, likewise engaged in wars of aggression,
and be inclined to call it all hypocrisy or official cant. Shakespeare
surely did not mean it so; the Elizabethans would not have taken
it so; and such monarchs, again, like their parties, are specimens
of times and manners, now long out of date, but not out of date
in the age of Elizabeth. In any case, Shakespeare has deliberately
brushed away much of the piety clinging to him in Holinshed.
He has added, to be sure, the prayer the night before the battle,
in which he speaks of King Richard's death. But that really is a
relief; Henry is not so pious as penitent, and would make amends
for his father's wrong, by which he profits. And a striking positive change is made when the action is about to begin. The
speech he now utters (IV iii 18–67), part of which has been quoted
above, is all of honor; but the corresponding passage in Holinshed has something of the twang and snuffle of a Puritan preacher's
cant:

But if we should fight in trust of multitude of men, and so get
the victorie (our minds being prone to pride), we should there-
upon peradventure ascribe the victorie not so much to the gift
of God, as to our owne puissance, and thereby provoke his high
indignation and displeasure against us.

That, for a man of action, at such a moment, is not in Shakespeare's vein. Piety and humility for the night-time; but 'amid the clang of arms', as Mr Stone says, he would have his hero 'speak in a rapture of martial ardor which sweeps every other thought from his mind'. Now he must think only of battle and drink delight of battle. Instead of preaching in such an hour or praying, Shakespeare would have him assert himself, let himself go a bit, like, say, George Washington, another hero who sometimes seemed something of a prig and (in popular legend at least) was always the pink of propriety, but who in battle went so far as to break out spontaneously into oaths. 'God's will!' cries King Henry, 'I pray thee, wish not one man more ... God's peace! I would not lose so great an honour.' Like Nelson at Copenhagen, he 'would not be elsewhere for thousands'. Like Roland of old, he would not have wound his horn. 'The game's afoot,' as he cried to his men before Harfleur; his blood is up; and the name of God rises to his lips only in oaths or in the war-cry, 'God for Harry, England, and St George.' Like every man of action, when the time of action arrives he thinks of nothing – feels the need of nothing – save to get into it. And in that hour he has no religion but that of the old English adage, 'God helps him who helps himself.'

Was Henry, then, as some have thought, Shakespeare's ideal? Gervinus and other German critics have declared he was, being the antithesis of Richard II and Hamlet. Some of them have even gone so far as to say that Henry is Shakespeare himself, with his practical genius and well-balanced nature, his taste for the low as well as the lofty, and his sense of humor in the midst of duty – his liking for play when at work. Mr W. B. Yeats holds just the contrary. Poet of the Celtic twilight, of them that went forth to battle but always fell, he thinks that Shakespeare infinitely preferred Richard; and that Henry is given the 'gross vices and coarse nerves', and 'resounding rhetoric, as of a leading article', which befit a man who succeeds, though his success was really failure. 'Shakespeare watched Henry V, not indeed as he watched the greater souls in the visionary procession, but cheerfully, as one watches some handsome spirited horse, and he spoke his tale,

as he spoke all tales, with tragic irony.' But when Shakespeare –
when any popular dramatist – is ironical, we the people must
needs know it; or else his popular art has failed him and missed the
mark. Here is no evidence of either. Instead of being sly, or
insinuating, or pregnant of innuendo, he is more exuberant and
enthusiastic than usual; the choruses, which are the authentic
voice of the poet himself, put that beyond the peradventure of a
doubt. And the likelihood is that Professor Dowden is nearer
the truth; Henry V, at least in some measure, approaches
Shakespeare's ideal of the practical man, which is not his highest
ideal. Shakespeare, no doubt, admired success, though without
worshipping it; he himself succeeded, not inconsiderably in
his brief two score and ten; but the men he admired most, I
daresay, were the finer spirits such as Hamlet, Brutus, or Pros-
pero, whether they succeeded or failed. It was their devotion
and gallantry that he admired, not (pessimistically or sentimentally) their devotion and gallantry foiled or thrown away.

It is more to the point to say that Henry is the ideal of England,
not Shakespeare's but his country's notion of their hero-king.
He is the king that audiences at the Globe would have him be.
This is particularly true as regards what we nowadays consider
his bragging, his priggishness and cant. The obtrusive morality
and piety were expected; for that matter they are like the sort of
thing you find in a Speech from the Throne or our American
Presidential Thanksgiving proclamations at the present day.
Officially, piety has been ever in favor; even in ungodly America
ceremonies so diverse as the laying of a cornerstone and the conferring of the German degree of Ph.D. are performed in the name
of the Father, the Son, and the Holy Ghost; and in the new
Assembly of Southern Ireland, I notice, the order is given by the
Speaker to 'call the roll in the name of God'.

And on the Elizabethan stage piety and morality are as inseparable from the ideal king as the crown on his head, the royal 'we'
in his mouth, or the 'strut' (lingering down to the eighteenth
century to be admired by Sir Roger de Coverley) with which his
royal legs must tread the stage. There is in all Elizabethan dramatic art something naïve – something self-descriptive – in the lines,

which in the three centuries of evolution towards the more purely and strictly dramatic has nearly disappeared. The wicked, like Richard III in his first soliloquy, know that they are wicked; the good, that they are good; heroes like Julius Caesar boast and vaunt their prowess; and a king, like a god on the stage, must every minute remember, and make us remember too, that he is nothing less. Henry's preaching, swaggering, and swinging of the scepter may repel us a bit today; but that is because as we read we democratically take him for no more than a man, as people at the Globe did not nor were expected to do. Even we, at the theater, are perhaps not so different and enlightened as we think. King Edward VII, not emulating the ceremoniousness of his ancestors, walked and talked like other people; but on the stage, not more than a score of years ago, Richard Mansfield, as Henry V, found it expedient to strut and swagger a bit again, in the fashion that pleased Sir Roger.

Or if Henry's blatant piety still offend us, surely we should find relief from it in his bragging and swearing. For these efface any impression of sanctimoniousness – these are royal, too, in the genuine antique style. Fancy William the Conqueror, Richard the Lion-hearted, or a king of Henry of Lancaster's kidney, shorn of all these high privileges and immunities of utterance, particularly on the stage. A medieval king can hardly be expected to talk like a gentleman in top hat and gaiters. The lion must not speak small – leviathan must not speak soft words unto thee – but have his roar. Despite our enlightenment, most of us, I suppose, have a sneaking notion of a king as one who talks and does, with a superlatively grand air, pretty much as he pleases. At the theater – at the Elizabethan theater far more than at ours – many, for the time being, have hardly any other notion of him at all. 'We are the makers of manners,' says Henry himself. And something of this loftiness and liberty of utterance must be granted him even in his morality and piety.

For through it all the man appears. Like Shakespeare's other characters Henry has an individual tone, his own voice, not just anybody's, and one unmistakably human. It swells and subsides, pulses and undulates, alive as a limb in a Rubens or a Raphael.

Here are both man and king, both individual and Englishman,
in Henry's mingled downrightness and moderation, as he flings
his cards upon the table, though ready enough for all that to play
on:

> There's for thy labour, Montjoy.
> Go bid thy master well advise himself,
> If we may pass, we will; if we be hind'red,
> We shall your tawny ground with your red blood
> Discolour; and so, Montjoy, fare you well.
> The sum of all our answer is but this:
> We would not seek a battle, as we are;
> Nor as we are, we say we will not shun it.
> So tell your master.

That's the voice of a king, a man, an Englishman, and yet not
quite that of any other that I know....

IV

In *Henry V* the supreme comic figure does not appear; that was
a risk not to be taken. The reformed young king could not
decorously permit of him in his presence; and, in his presence or
out of it, he would have upset the balance, and broken the unity,
of the play. So, like Cervantes with Don Quixote, and Addison
with Sir Roger de Coverley, he kills him off to keep him from
falling into weaker hands. His death is reported, not presented;
and that too is well ordered, for the death of a comic character
should not touch us too nearly. Here it does not: as it is told by
Mrs Quickly, the pathetic and the comic were never better
blended by mortal pen. And the whole little scene is the best
thing in the play – whether it be for Falstaff's cronies as they
comment and engage in reminiscences, or for the fat knight himself as his shade is thus summoned up before our eyes again.

It is a scene that might easily have become sentimental or
maudlin. But sullen and dogged Bardolph is still himself, even
in this the one exalted moment of his life: 'Would I were with
him, wheresome'er he is, either in heaven or in hell!' And

motherly, consolatory Quickly, who had always looked on the bright side, and called shady things by fair names, is still herself as she smoothes Sir John's pillow and bids him ' 'a should not think of God, – I hoped there was no need to trouble himself with any such thoughts yet.' The 'fine *end*', she thinks, is all that matters, hell or heaven. And now that he has got to one or the other, she will not have it that he is in hell, but in Arthur's bosom, if ever man went to Arthur's bosom. That British bosom for Abraham's, and not troubling oneself with God till the very pinch of death is at one's throat, are typical of her simple heathen soul. Her own legendary king is more to her than your alien patriarch; superstition is deeper rooted in her heart than the Christian faith; and the blossoming there is the kindliness of naked and benighted human nature, not of piety. She knows and notes the immemorially ominous signs and seasons – the hour just between twelve and one – even at the turning of the tide – and his fumbling with the sheets, playing with flowers, and smiling upon his fingers' ends. All that she noticed; and still, woman and heathen that she was, she comforted him by bidding him not yet think of God. But the fine end he made justified her – 'an it had been any christom child', she said of it – for not having put him to that sore 'trouble'. For he, a heathen too, who had avoided trouble and endeavoured to be 'o' good cheer' all his life long, took her comfort readily and thought of God no more. Even the fat knight, though now his nose be sharp as a pen, seems still himself. 'Peace, good Doll!' he had said in his latter heyday, 'do not speak like a death's-head; do not bid me remember mine end' . . .

SOURCE: *Poets and Playwrights* (1930).

Charles Williams

THE HONOUR OF KING HENRY V
(1936)

WITH *Henry V* Shakespeare reached the climax of exterior life; it is at once a conclusion and a beginning. It is not primarily a patriotic play, for the First Chorus knows nothing of patriotism nor of England, but only of a *Muse of fire which would ascend the brightest heaven of invention* by discovering a challenge between mighty monarchies. Patriotism certainly keeps breaking in, but rather like the army itself: the mass behind Henry is dramatically an English mass, and as the play proceeds he becomes more and more an English king. So much must be allowed to the patriots; it is, however, for them to allow that he becomes something else and more as well, and it is in that something more that his peculiar strength lies.

Before defining that, however, and his own words define it, it may be well to remark a few of the differences between *Henry V* and its precedent *Henry IV*. The newer manner of the blank verse itself is accentuated; it gains in speed. Less even than in *Henry IV* are there any involutions or adornments; its movements, like the action of the persons, admit of no delay. It has lost superfluity, though it has not yet gained analysis. No word blurs, but each word does not yet illuminate, as each was to illuminate in that later play of action and vision, *Antony and Cleopatra*. Here it is equivalent to the King's desire and the King's deed, and equals the one with the other. But there is, at first, no variation between the King and other characters, as there is variation between the Prince and Hotspur and Falstaff in *Henry IV*: what the King is, he is, and the others are apart from him. In fact, the next differences between the two plays are (i) the omission of Hotspur, and (ii) the omission of Falstaff. It will be said that Hotspur is dead before *Henry IV* ends and Falstaff dies soon after *Henry V* begins. But whatever historical necessity or moral convenience compelled those two deaths, the result is to leave the stage free not only for King Henry himself, but for something else – for the development of the idea of honour. In *Henry IV* honour had been peculiarly the property of Hotspur, and it had seemed like being his property in a narrower sense. He had regarded it almost as if it were something he owned as he owned his armour, something that he could capture and possess.

> By heaven methinks it were an easy leap
> To pluck bright honour from the pale-fac'd moon,
> Or dive into the bottom of the deep,
> Where fathom-line could never touch the ground,
> And pluck up drowned honour by the locks;
> So he that doth redeem her thence might wear
> Without corrival all her dignities:

Against this splendid and egotistical figure is the figure of Falstaff. Up to the last act of *2 Henry IV* the distinction of Falstaff had been that, though he may want a lot for his comfort, he does not need it for his complacency. Hotspur, without a sense of his own honour, feels himself deficient; it is why he rebels. Falstaff, without the same sense, feels himself free; it is why he runs away or fights as circumstances and his own common sense dictate. Henry V might have been made like either of them; in fact, he was made like neither. Neither Hotspur nor Falstaff could suit the Muse of fire or the brightest heaven. Honour must for Henry in his own play be something consonant with that brightness, and that invention discovered a phrase which made honour more than reputation – whether for possession or repudiation.

> And those that leave their valiant bones in France,
> Dying like men, though buried in your dunghills,
> They shall be fam'd; for there the sun shall greet them,
> And draw their honours reeking up to heaven,
> Leaving their earthly parts to choke your clime.

Their bodies are dead; their honours live, but not as fame upon earth. The heaven of invention is to suggest this other heaven;

the honour of poetry is to show the honour of the spirit in challenge. It is a little reminiscent of *Lycidas*; where also Fame is
transmuted into something pleasing to 'all-judging Jove'. The
honours which so live are the spirits and souls of the righteous –
anyhow; of the righteous at Agincourt. It is to Henry that the
identification is given; it is for him that honour is now a name
for man's immortal part. If that venture of war which is the result
of the challenge between two great worldly powers, two mighty
monarchies, is defeated, this end at least is left to those who carry
themselves well in that venture.

As far as the war itself is concerned, the play did not attempt
any illusion. It put war 'in the round'. The causes of it are there;
dynastic claims are the equivalent of the modern prestige of
governments. The force of the verse carries the sincerity of the
intention, and the tennis-balls are part of the cause of the war; that
is, the other monarchy is also involved. Any insincerity is part of
the way of things, but insufficient to cloud the glory of the change.
In this sense Shakespeare threw over the diplomatic advice of
the King in *Henry IV* as well as the martial egotism of Hotspur.

Besides the causes of war there is, in the first Harfleur scene,
what a soldier-poet called 'Joy of Battle'; so, with a horrid faithfulness, in the second Harfleur scene, is the usual result of Joy
of Battle. So, finally, in the field before Agincourt, is a kind of
summing-up. War is not so very much more dangerous than
peace; one is almost as likely to be killed one way as the other.
'Every soldier's duty is the King's, but every subject's soul is his
own', which if he keep clean, it does not very much matter
whether he lives or dies. Death is not all that important – to
Henry (who in the play was going to fight), to the lords, to the
army, and, as a consequence, to the citizens of Harfleur. The
Duke of Burgundy's oration in the last Act describes all the general
advantages of peace, but it does not do more. Peace, as a general
thing, is preferable to war, but life is pretty dangerous any way –
pretty bloody, in every sense of the word – and a healthy male
adult should be prepared for death at any moment. So what does
it matter? It is not the modern view, but we are not Elizabethans,
and our police are efficient.

Honour then – the capacity to challenge the world and to endure the result of challenge – is the state to be coveted.

> But if it be a sin to covet honour,
> I am the most offending soul alive.

Those lines come from the most famous of Henry's speeches. But there is another and much shorter and less famous speech which throws a stronger light on Henry. There had been a minor crisis – the conspiracy in the Second Act – before the great crisis of Agincourt. But as no one has the least interest in the Lord Scroop of Masham, and as no one can feel the King himself has had time to love him behind the scenes either in *Henry IV* or *Henry V*, the conspiracy fails to excite. We are left to listen to the King being merely vocal. When, however, the central crisis approached, Shakespeare had another way of being equivalent to it. This comes in the English camp by night before the battle, very soon after the greatest thing in the play, the sublime Fourth Chorus. In that Chorus a change had been presented as coming over the whole war. The venture had gone wrong, the challenge delivered to the world of the French had been accepted and that French world had trapped the English army and was on the point of destroying it. At the point of that pause the Fourth Chorus delivers its speech, describing the night, the gloom, and the danger. But its speech, if the words are literally followed, has two futures. The first is Agincourt; the second is the tragedies. There is not only a change in *Henry V*; there is a still darker change away from *Henry V*. The Muse of fire has been ascending her heaven - that is the poetry's own description of what it has been trying to do. But now it directly suggests that it is doing something quite different.

> Now entertain conjecture of a time
> When creeping murmur and the poring dark
> Fills the wide vessel of the universe.

The word 'universe' means, certainly, earth and heaven in that darkness before the battle. But there seems no reason why it should not also mean 'universe' in the accepted sense, the whole

world and the whole heaven, including the brightest heaven of
poetry with which we began. It is all this which is beginning to
be filled with creeping murmur and the poring dark. Poetry and
(so to speak) life are being occupied by this universal noise and
night. It is not yet so fixed; it is but a guess and a wonder. 'Now
entertain conjecture – ' It is the prelude to all the plays that were
to come.

From poetry thus conceiving of its own probable business,
both locally at Agincourt and universally, and its future, two
other enlargements follow. One concerns the English army; the
other, the King.

The *Muse of Fire* is compelled to behold the army as 'so many
horrid ghosts', and the description of the soldiers is that of men
who are in the state she has described. It is an army but it is also
humanity. To 'sit patiently and inly ruminate the morning's
danger' is a situation familiar enough to us in peace as to them in
war, if 'danger' also may be given a wider meaning than that of
battle. Illness, unemployment, loneliness, these are the things
that make sacrifices of 'the poor condemned English', that make
them 'pining and pale'. It is among such a host of spectral images
of mankind that the King moves, and the Chorus imagines him
as their contrast and support: 'the royal captain of this ruined
band'. It remains true, however, that the Chorus has to do this
without having had, up to that point, much support from the
play itself. Henry had been cheerful and efficient and warlike and
friendly, but he has not suggested to us his capacity for being an
almost supernatural 'little touch of Harry in the night'. The wider
and the darker the night, the more that gleam shines. But why?

The cause follows. When the King appears he is speaking,
more or less lightly, of the advantages which evil chances bring
with them. It is not a particularly original remark, not a moment
of 'great insight', and we need not perhaps suppose it is meant to
be solemn or serious. It is in the next speech that the sudden
difference between Henry and all the rest appears.

> 'Tis good for men to love their present pains
> Upon example; so the spirit is eas'd:
> And when the mind is quicken'd, out of doubt,

> The organs, though defunct and dead before,
> Break up their drowsy grave, and newly move
> With casted slough and fresh legerity.

This is the centre of Henry's capacity. He 'loves' his present pains, and his spirit is therefore eased. He has rather more than accepted darkness, danger, defeat, and death, and loves them. It is this which gives him a new quickening of the mind, new motions of the organs; it destroys sloth and the drowsy grave of usual life. It is this love and the resulting legerity of spirit which enable him to be what the Chorus describe, and what the rest of the Act accentuates.

> Upon his royal face there is no note
> How dread an army hath enrounded him;

how can there be when he loves being enrounded?

> But freshly looks and overbears attaint
> With cheerful semblance and sweet majesty.

It is precisely a description of what he has done within himself. Therefore every wretch 'plucks comfort from his looks', receiving the 'largess universal' from his liberal eye – from the eased spirit, the quickened mind, the moving organs, which are the effect of his love for present pains.

Perhaps this also was something of the explanation of the dead Falstaff; perhaps Henry was more like his old acquaintance than he altogether knew. Only the word 'love' can hardly be used of Falstaff in any sense; it was by no accident or haste that Shakespeare could not show him in more 'love' than the odd possibility of lechery excites. He enjoyed his dilemmas in the sense that he enjoyed being equal to them, but Henry enjoys them because he is careless of them.

There is a distinction, and it lies in the fact that the King's spirit is 'honour' whereas Falstaff's is the rejection of 'honour'. It also lies in the fact that Falstaff does die when he cannot conquer 'the King's unkindness'. If ever Falstaff's spirit was drawn reeking up to heaven, he would only enter it on his own terms, but Henry will enter it on Heaven's terms. It is Falstaff's greatness that we are delighted to feel heaven give way to him; Henry's that we are eased by his giving way to heaven. But the artistic difference is that there is no more to be done in the method of Falstaff - he is complete and final. He can be continually varied and repeated, but he cannot be developed. Henry is complete, but not final. For he, in whose honour there is no self-contradiction, could love his pains simply because there was nothing else to do except run away, and that the same honour forbade. The genius of Shakespeare proceeded, however, immediately to imagine an honour in which self-contradiction did passionately exist; it emerged as Brutus, and was set in front of a power which was more 'monstrous' than that of the French army; he called that monstrosity Caesar, and made another play out of those other conditions, in which the crisis is a more deeply interior thing, and the heaven of honour begins itself to be at odds.

Henry then has made of his crisis an exaltation of his experience; he has become gay. This gaiety - a 'modest' gaiety, to take another adjective from the Chorus - lasts all through the Act. It lightens and saves the speech on ceremony; more especially, it illuminates the speech to Westmoreland. In view of the King's capacity the stress there may well be on the adjective rather than the substantive: 'We few, we *happy* few.' His rejection of all those who have no stomach for the fight, his offer of crowns for convoy, is part of the same delight: so far as possible he will have no one there who does not love to be there. He makes jokes at the expense of the old men's 'tall stories' of the battle, and at the French demand for ransom. We are clean away from the solemn hero-king, and therefore much more aware of the Harry of the Chorus, and of the thing he is - the 'touch of Harry in the night'. The very last line of that scene - 'how thou pleasest, God, dispose the day' - is not a prayer of resignation but a cry of complete carelessness. What does it matter what *happens?*

It is a legerity of spirit, the last legerity before the tragedies. Hamlet was to have a touch of it, but there is little else, in the greater figures, until, as from beyond a much greater distance, it is renewed by a phrase Kent uses of the Fool in *Lear*. Who, says a Gentleman on the moor, is with the King?

> None but the Fool, who labours to outjest
> His heart-struck injuries.

Henry's injuries are not heart-struck; he is no tragic figure. But he deserves more greatly than has perhaps always been allowed. The Muse, *entertaining conjecture* of a new and dreadful world, conjectured also a touch in the night, the thawing of fear, a royal captain of a ruined band, and conjectured the nature of the power of love and consequent lightness that thrills through the already poring dusk.

SOURCE: *Shakespeare Criticism: 1919–1935*, ed. Anne Bradby (1936).

Mark Van Doren

THE FRAGMENTATION OF THE
HEROIC IDEA IN *HENRY V* (1939)

SHAKESPEARE in *Henry IV* had still been able to pour all of his thought and feeling into the heroic drama without demolishing its form. His respect for English history as a subject, his tendency to conceive kings in tragic terms, his interest in exalted dialogue as a medium through which important actions could be advanced – these, corrected by comedy which flooded the whole with the wisdom of a warm and proper light, may have reached their natural limit, but that limit was not transgressed. *Henry IV*, in other words, both was and is a successful play; it answers the questions it raises, it satisfies every instinct of the spectator, it is remembered as fabulously rich and at the same time simply ordered. *Henry V* is no such play. It has its splendors and its secondary attractions, but the forces in it are not unified. The reason probably is that for Shakespeare they had ceased to be genuine forces. He marshals for his task a host of substitute powers, but the effect is often hollow. The style strains itself to bursting, the hero is stretched until he struts on tiptoe and is still strutting at the last insignificant exit, and war is emptied of its tragic content. The form of the historical drama had been the tragic form; its dress is borrowed here, but only borrowed. The heroic idea splinters into a thousand starry fragments, fine as fragments but lighted from no single source.

Everywhere efforts are made to be striking, and they succeed. But the success is local. *Henry V* does not succeed as a whole because its author lacks adequate dramatic matter; or because, veering so suddenly away from tragedy, he is unable to free himself from the accidents of its form; or because, with *Julius Caesar* and *Hamlet* on his horizon, he finds himself less interested than before in heroes who are men of action and yet is not at the moment provided with a dramatic language for saying so. Whatever the cause, we discover that we are being entertained from the top of his mind. There is much there to glitter and please us, but what pleases us has less body than what once did so and soon will do so with still greater abundance again.

The prologues are the first sign of Shakespeare's imperfect dramatic faith. Their verse is wonderful but it has to be, for it is doing the work which the play ought to be doing, it is a substitute for scene and action. 'O for a Muse of fire', the poet's apology begins. The prologues are everywhere apologetic; they are saying that no stage, this one or any other, is big enough or wealthy enough to present the 'huge and proper life' of Henry's wars; this cockpit cannot hold the vasty fields of France, there will be no veritable horses in any scene, the ship-boys on the masts and the camp-fires at Agincourt will simply have to be imagined. Which it is the business of the play to make them be, as Shakespeare has known and will know again. The author of *Romeo and Juliet* had not been sorry because his stage was a piece of London rather than the whole of Verona, and the storm in *King Lear* will begin without benefit of description. The description here is always very fine, as for example at the opening of the fourth act:

> Now entertain conjecture of a time
> When creeping murmur and the poring dark
> Fills the wide vessel of the universe.
> From camp to camp through the foul womb of night
> The hum of either army stilly sounds,
> That the fix'd sentinels almost receive
> The secret whispers of each other's watch;
> Fire answers fire, and through their paly flames
> Each battle sees the other's umber'd face;
> Steed threatens steed, in high and boastful neighs
> Piercing the night's dull ear; and from the tents
> The armourers, accomplishing the knights,
> With busy hammers closing rivets up,
> Give dreadful note of preparation.

But it is still description, and it is being asked to do what description can never do – turn spectacle into plot, tableau into tragedy.

The second sign of genius at loose ends is a radical and indeed
an astounding inflation in the style. Passages of boasting and
exhortation are in place, but even the best of them, whether from
the French or from the English side, have a forced, shrill, windy
sound, as if their author were pumping his muse for dear life in
the hope that mere speed and plangency might take the place of
matter. For a few lines like

> Familiar in his mouth as household words (IV iii 52)
>
> The singing masons building roofs of gold (I ii 198)
>
> I see you stand like greyhounds in the slips,
> Straining upon the start   (III i 31–2)

there are hundreds like

> The native mightiness and fate of him   (II iv 64)
>
> With ample and brim fullness of his force (I ii 150)
>
> That caves and womby vaultages of France
> Shall chide your trespass and return your mock.
>   (II iv 124–5)

Mightiness and fate, ample and brim, caves and vaultages, tres-
pass and mock – such couplings attest the poet's desperation, the
rhetorician's extremity. They spring up everywhere, like birds
from undergrowth: sweet and honey'd, open haunts and popularity, thrive and ripen, crown and seat, right and title, right and
conscience, kings and monarchs, means and might, aim and butt,
large and ample, taken and impounded, frank and uncurbed,
success and conquest, desert and merit, weight and worthiness,
duty and zeal, savage and inhuman, botch and bungle, garnish'd
and deck'd, assembled and collected, sinister and awkward, culled
and choice-drawn, o'er-hang and jutty, waste and desolation,
cool and temperate, flexure and low bending, signal and ostent,
vainness and self-glorious pride. Shakespeare has perpetrated
them before, as when in *Henry VI* he coupled ominous and fearful, trouble and disturb, substance and authority, and absurd and
reasonless. But never has he perpetrated them with such thought-
less frequency. Nor has he at this point developed the compound
epithet into that interesting mannerism – the only mannerism he

ever submitted to – which is to be so noticeable in his next half-dozen plays, including *Hamlet*. The device he is to use will involve more than the pairing of adjectives or nouns; one part of speech will assume the duties of another, and a certain very sudden concentration of meaning will result. There is, to be sure, one approximation to the device in *Henry V* – 'the quick forge and working-house of thought' (Prologue, v 23). But our attention is nowhere else held and filled by such lines as these in *Hamlet*:

> In the dead waste and middle of the night
>
> The perfume and suppliance of a minute
>
> Unto the voice and yielding of that body
>
> And in the morn and liquid dew of youth
>
> The slings and arrows of outrageous fortune
>
> Which is not tomb enough and continent;

or these in *Troilus and Cressida*:

> The sinew and the forehand of our host
>
> For the great swing and rudeness of his poise
>
> The unity and married calm of states
>
> Than in the pride and salt scorn of her eyes;

or these in *Measure for Measure*:

> Whether it be the fault and glimpse of newness
>
> Now puts the drowsy and neglected act
>
> There is a prone and speechless dialect.

In such lines there is not merely the freshness and the emphasis which an expert distortion of conventional meanings can give; there is a muscled cadence, an abrupt forward stride or plunge of sound. All this is lacking for the most part in the style of *Henry V*, which is fatty rather than full, relaxed instead of restrung.

The third sign is a direct and puerile appeal to the patriotism of the audience, a dependence upon sentiments outside the play

that can be counted on, once they are tapped, to pour in and
repair the deficiencies of the action. Unable to achieve a dramatic
unity out of the materials before him, Shakespeare must grow
lyrical about the unity of England; politics must substitute for
poetry. He cannot take England for granted as the scene of conflicts whose greatness will imply its greatness. It must be great
itself, and the play says so – unconvincingly. There are no conflicts. The traitors Scroop, Cambridge, and Grey are happy to
lose their heads for England (II ii), and the battles in France,
even though the enemy's host is huge and starvation takes its
toll, are bound to be won by such fine English fellows as we have
here. If the French have boasted beforehand, the irony of their
doing so was obvious from the start. But it was patriotism,
shared as a secret between the author and his audience, that made
it obvious. It was not drama.

And a fourth sign is the note of gaiety that takes the place here
of high passion. The treasure sent to Henry by the Dauphin is
discovered at the end of the first act to be tennis-balls: an insult
which the young king returns in a speech about matching rackets
and playing sets – his idiom for bloody war. When the treachery
of Scroop, Cambridge, and Grey is detected on the eve of his
departure for France he stages their discomfiture somewhat as
games are undertaken, and with a certain sporting relish watches
their faces as they read their dooms. The conversation of the
French leaders as they wait for the sun to rise on Agincourt is
nervous as thoroughbreds are nervous, or champion athletes
impatient for a tournament to commence; their camp is a locker
room, littered with attitudes no less than uniforms (III vii). The
deaths of York and Suffolk the next day are images of how young
knights should die. They kiss each other's gashes, wearing their
red blood like roses in the field, and spending their last breath
in terms so fine that Exeter, reporting to the King, is overcome
by 'the pretty and sweet manner of it' (IV vi 28). And of course
there are the scenes where Katharine makes fritters of English,
waiting to be wooed (III iv) and wooed at last (V ii) by Henry
Plantagenet, 'king of good fellows'. 'The truth is', said Dr
Johnson, 'that the poet's matter failed him in the fifth act, and he

was glad to fill it up with whatever he could get; and not even Shakespeare can write well without a proper subject. It is a vain endeavour for the most skilful hand to cultivate barrenness, or to paint upon vacuity.' That is harsh, but its essence cannot be ignored. The high spirits in which the scenes are written have their attraction, but they are no substitute for intensity.

Nor do they give us the king we thought we had. 'I speak to thee plain soldier,' boasts Henry in homespun vein. 'I am glad thou canst speak no better English; for, if thou couldst, thou wouldst find me such a plain king that thou wouldst think I had sold my farm to buy my crown. I know no ways to mince it in love, but directly to say, "I love you." ... These fellows of infinite tongue, that can rhyme themselves into ladies' favours, they do always reason themselves out again. ... By mine honour, in true English, I love thee, Kate' (v ii). 'I know not', breaks in Dr Johnson's voice once more, 'why Shakespeare now gives the king nearly such a character as he made him formerly ridicule in Percy. This military grossness and unskillfulness in all the softer arts does not suit very well with the gaieties of his youth, with the general knowledge ascribed to him at his accession, or with the contemptuous message sent him by the Dauphin, who represents him as fitter for the ball room than the field, and tells him that he is not "to revel into dutchies", or win provinces "with a nimble galliard".' Shakespeare has forgotten the glittering young god whom Vernon described in *Henry IV* – plumed like an estridge or like an eagle lately bathed, shining like an image in his golden coat, as full of spirit as the month of May, wanton as a youthful goat, a feathered Mercury, an angel dropped down from the clouds. The figure whom he has groomed to be the ideal English king, all plumes and smiles and decorated courage, collapses here into a mere good fellow, a hearty undergraduate with enormous initials on his chest. The reason must be that Shakespeare has little interest in the ideal English king. He has done what rhetoric could do to give us a young heart whole in honor, but his imagination has already sped forward to Brutus and Hamlet: to a kind of hero who is no less honorable than Henry but who will tread on thorns as he takes the path of duty –

itself unclear, and crossed by other paths of no man's making.
Henry is Shakespeare's last attempt at the great man who is also
simple. Henceforth he will show greatness as either perplexing
or perplexed; and Hamlet will be both.

Meanwhile his imagination undermines the very eminence on
which Henry struts. For the King and his nobles the war may be
a handsome game, but an undercurrent of realism reminds us
of the 'poor souls' for whom it is no such thing. We hear of
widows' tears and orphans' cries, of dead men's blood and pining
maidens' groans (II iv 104–7). Such horrors had been touched
on in earlier Histories; now they are given a scene to themselves
(IV i). While the French leaders chaff one another through the
night before Agincourt the English common soldiers have their
hour. Men with names as plain as John Bates and Michael Williams
walk up and down the dark field thinking of legs and arms and
heads chopped off in battle, of faint cries for surgeons, of men in
misery because of their children who will be rawly left. Henry,
moving among them in the disguise of clothes like theirs, asks
them to remember that the King's cause is just and his quarrel
honorable. 'That's more than we know', comes back the disturbing cool voice of Michael Williams. Henry answers with much
fair prose, and the episode ends with a wager – sportsmanship
again – which in turn leads to an amusing recognition scene
(IV viii). But the honest voice of Williams still has the edge on
Henry's patronizing tone:

> *Williams.* Your Majesty came not like yourself. You appear'd
> to me but as a common man; witness the night, your
> garments, your lowliness; and what your Highness
> suffer'd under that shape, I beseech you take it for your
> own fault and not mine. . . .
> *King Henry.* Here, uncle Exeter, fill this glove with crowns,
> And give it to this fellow. Keep it, fellow;
> And wear it for an honour in thy cap
> Till I do challenge it.   (IV viii 53–64)

Henry has not learned that Williams knows. He is still the plumed
king, prancing on oratory and waving wagers as he goes. That he
finally has no place to go is the result of Shakespeare's failure

to establish any relation between a hero and his experience. Henry
has not absorbed the vision either of Williams or of Shakespeare.
This shrinks him in his armor, and it leaves the vision hanging.

The humor of the play, rich as it sometimes is, suffers likewise
from a lack of vital function. The celebrated scene (ii iii) in which
the Hostess describes Falstaff's death shuts the door forever on
Henry IV and its gigantic comedy. Pistol and Bardolph continue
in their respective styles, and continue cleverly; the first scene of
the second act, which finds them still in London, may be indeed
the best one ever written for them – and for Nym in his pompous
brevity.

I cannot tell. Things must be as they may. Men may sleep,
and they may have their throats about them at that time; and
some say knives have edges. It must be as it may.

Pistol was never excited to funnier effect.

> O hound of Crete, thinks't thou my spouse to get?
> No! to the spital go,
> And from the powdering-tub of infamy
> Fetch forth the lazar kit of Cressid's kind,
> Doll Tearsheet she by name, and her espouse.
> I have, and I will hold, the quondam Quickly
> For the only she; and – *pauca*, there's enough.
> Go to.

Yet this leads on to little in France beyond a series of rather
mechanically arranged encounters in which the high talk of
heroes is echoed by the rough cries of rascals. 'To the breach,
to the breach!' yells Bardolph after Henry, and that is parody.
But Henry has already parodied himself; the device is not needed,
any more than the rascals are. Shakespeare seems to admit as much
when he permits lectures to be delivered against their moral
characters, first by the boy who serves them (iii ii 28–57) and
next by the sober Gower (iii vi 70–85), and when he arranges
bad ends for them as thieves, cutpurses, and bawds.

There is a clearer function for Fluellen, the fussy Welsh pedant
who is for fighting wars out of books. Always fretting and out
of breath, he mourns 'the disciplines of the wars', the pristine

wars of the Romans, now in these latter days lost with all other learning. There was not this tiddle taddle and pibble pabble in Pompey's camp. The law of arms was once well known, and men – strong, silent men such as he fancies himself to be – observed it without prawls and prabbles. He has no shrewdness; he mistakes Pistol for a brave man because he talks bravely, and there is his classic comparison of Henry with Alexander because one lived in Monmouth and the other in Macedon and each city had a river and there were salmons in both. He has only his schoolmaster's eloquence; it breaks out on him like a rash, and is the one style here that surpasses the King's in fullness.

> *Fluellen.* It is not well done, mark you now, to take the tales out of my mouth, ere it is made and finished. I speak but in the figures and comparisons of it. As Alexander kill'd his friend Cleitus, being in his ales and his cups; so also Harry Monmouth, being in his right wits and his good judgements, turn'd away the fat knight with the great belly doublet. He was full of jests, and gipes, and knaveries, and mocks; I have forgot his name.
> *Gower.* Sir John Falstaff.
> *Fluellen.* That is he. (IV vii 43–55)

Fluellen reminds us of Falstaff. That is a function, but he has another. It is to let the war theme finally down. Agincourt is won not only by a tennis-player but by a school-teacher. Saint Crispin's day is to be remembered as much in the pibble pabble of a pedant as in the golden throatings of a hollow god. Fluellen is one of Shakespeare's most humorous men, and one of his best used.

SOURCE: *Shakespeare* (1939).

Una Ellis-Fermor

SHAKESPEARE'S PORTRAIT OF
THE STATESMAN-KING (1945)

THE solution of the problems of the two parts of *Henry IV* and
Henry V is the peculiar contribution of Shakespeare's Elizabethan
phase to the summation of his idea of a king, of the man who
should fit at every point the demands laid upon him by public
office. Henry IV has all the qualities necessary to a king and
avoids all the weaknesses of temperament in the portrayal of
which the positive qualities have, so far, been implied. He has
shrewdness, tenacity and self-command that already approaches
self-concealment; he has the true Tudor sense of the value of
discreet popularity. He is as astute as a badger and has very much
the same tough courage. He is not self-indulgent, he is not vain,
he is not self-absorbed. He is not even a saint or a poet. He is an
exceedingly able, hard-working statesman whose career reveals
gradually but clearly the main qualification for kingship, the
king's sense of responsibility to his people, that sense of service
which, while making him no more than the state's greatest ser-
vant, makes all his privileges and exemptions, even a measure of
autocracy itself, no more than necessary means for that service.
Domineering he is, at times, like Shakespeare's prototype of
Tudor monarchy, but he has, in the main, decent intentions, and
he possesses, through thick and thin, an unfailing, humorous sense
of proportion.

Having, then, such potentialities, why is he not the final figure
in the group? The answer is obvious after the study of *Richard II*.
The flaw in Henry's title, the fatal act of usurpation with which
Richard had made such fine play, does indeed cripple his power
and, through that, his mental stature, eating into his confidence
and bringing down all loftiness of gesture or intention to the
necessity of cunning and circumspection. Character no less than

tenure suffers thus under the nemesis for an outrage done to the sacredness of inheritance. Henry IV is in nearly all things a potential Henry V and, trembling upon the verge of achievement, he looks into the promised land, and, as so often happens, speaks more explicitly of it than those who have dwelt in it familiarly. That is why it is, I think, impossible to understand Henry V as Shakespeare saw him, the Henry V who never speaks out, unless we can see his position and his intentions through the eyes of Bolingbroke's frustration:

> Heaven knows, my son,
> By what by-paths, and indirect, crook'd ways
> I met this crown: and I myself know well
> How troublesome it sat upon my head.
> To thee, it shall descend with better quiet,
> Better opinion, better confirmation:
> For all the soil of the achievement goes
> With me, into the earth.

It is left to Henry V to gather up in himself all that is fitting and necessary to a king and to remain as the epitome of the Elizabethan idea of the 'polliticke vertues'. Shakespeare has at last resolved his demands upon such a figure into certain clearly defined qualifications and summed them all in Henry V, with his unflawed, hereditary title and his assured possession of all kingly attributes. With his broad-based popularity, his genuine love of public service for its own sake, his strong sense of responsibility, and his equally clear sense of its relation to privilege, his shrewd statesman's brain, successfully masked as that of a simple soldier, he stands where, perhaps, no king in drama has stood before or after him. Church and state, commoners and noblemen, soldiers and civilians, he knows them all, with a knowledge rooted in the taverns of Eastcheap, and holds them in his hand, too practised, popular, and secure to make a show of mastery. He was a statesman fulfilling Burke's demand – he knew how the whole world lived. He was a monarch, modelled upon the greatest of the Tudors, Elizabeth herself. It probably happens to every man to believe, at one time or another, for a time at least, that the greatest of the arts is conduct. And it is some such experience as this, in

Shakespeare's career, that lies, I think, at the base of the great historical studies culminating in the figure of Henry V.

But if this were all, the composite figure would be shorn of half its subtlety and magnitude. We are aware already in this play that Shakespeare has gone beyond the experience he is primarily describing; that, implicit in this carefully balanced study, this culmination of so long and careful an exploration, is the germ of some later revulsion of thought which refutes it, as the great destructive speeches of Timon refute Ulysses' speech on the beauty of degree, of the ordered hierarchical state. For a while, it may be, between the writing of *Henry IV* and *Henry V*, Shakespeare believed the highest achievement of man to be the ordered state he afterwards described in *Troilus and Cressida*, the image of the ordered universe, of the cosmos with its regulated spheres.

> The Heavens themselves, the planets, and this centre,
> Observe degree, priority, and place,
> Insisture, course, proportion, season, form,
> Office, and custom, in all line of order . . .
>   But when the planets
> In evil mixture to disorder wander,
> What plagues, and what portents, what mutiny?
> What raging of the sea? Shaking of earth?
> Commotion in the winds, frights, changes, horrors,
> Divert and crack, rend and deracinate
> The unity and married calm of states
> Quite from their fixture? O, when degree is shak'd,
> (Which is the ladder to all high designs)
> The enterprise is sick. How could communities,
> Degrees in schools, and brotherhoods in cities,
> Peaceful commerce from dividable shores,
> The primogenitive and due of birth,
> Prerogative of age, crowns, sceptres, laurels,
> (But by degree) stand in authentic place?
> Take but degree away, untune that string,
> And hark what discord follows.

The keystone of this order was the figure of the perfect public man, of Henry V. All the implications of the foregoing plays point to this ultimate emergence of the complete figure. In all the

anticipations that lead up to him, and particularly in the later
scenes of the second part of *Henry IV*, Shakespeare has, he would
seem to imply, 'in this rough work, shaped out a man'; the great
art of conduct, and of public conduct at that, is at last truly
understood.

But has he? Or has he, as it were unawares, and led already on
to some perception beyond his immediate purpose, shaped out
instead something that is at once more and less than a man. Henry
V has indeed transformed himself into a public figure; the most
forbidding thing about him is the completeness with which this
has been done. He is solid and flawless. There is no attribute in
him that is not part of this figure, no desire, no interest, no habit
even that is not harmonized with it. He is never off the platform;
even when, alone in a moment of weariness and of intense
anxiety, he sees with absolute clearness the futility of privilege
and the burden of responsibility, he still argues his case in general
terms, a king's life weighed against a peasant's, peasant against
king. No expression of personal desire escapes him; though he
makes almost the same comparison as Henry VI, he is detached
alike from king and shepherd, commenting upon them, but
wasting no more strength on imagining what cannot be than on
deluding himself, like Richard, with the empty glories of his
state. He has inured himself so steadfastly to the life of a king,
lived so long in councils and committees, weighing, sifting, deciding, commanding, that his brain automatically delivers a public
speech where another man utters a cry of despair, of weariness
or of prayer. It is in vain that we look for the personality of Henry
behind the king; there is nothing else there. We know how his
brain works upon any one of half a dozen problems; the treachery
of Cambridge, Grey, and Scroop, the fomenting of wars abroad
to preserve peace at home, the disaffection in the army, the difficulties of a formidable campaign, and the equally great dangers
of a crushing victory. We see the diplomacy, the soldiership, the
vigilant, astute eye upon the moods of people and barons, the
excellent acting of a part in court and camp and council-room,
and only when we try to look into the heart of the man do we find
that it is hardly acting, after all, that the character has been con-

verted whole to the uses of this function, the individual utterly eliminated, sublimated, if you will. There is no Henry, only a king.

I think Shakespeare was profoundly interested in this particular study. Not, indeed, by the character, for there is no character, but by the singular circumstances of its disappearance. Neither we the readers nor Henry himself nor his God ever meets the individual that had once underlain the outer crust that covers a Tudor monarch, for there is nothing beneath the crust; all has been converted into it; all desires, all impulses, all selfhood, all spirit. He is never alone, even with his God – least of all when he prays, for then he is more than ever in the council chamber driving an astute bargain, a piece of shrewd diplomacy, between one kind and another.

> O God of battles, steel my soldiers' hearts,
> Possess them not with fear. Take from them now
> The sense of reckoning, if th' opposed numbers
> Pluck their hearts from them. Not to-day, O Lord,
> O, not to-day, think not upon the fault
> My father made, in compassing the crown.
> I Richard's body have interred new,
> And on it have bestowed more contrite tears,
> Than from it issued forced drops of blood.
> Five hundred poor I have in yearly pay,
> Who twice a day their wither'd hands hold up
> Toward Heaven, to pardon blood. And I have built
> Two chantries, where the sad and solemn priests
> Sing still for Richard's soul. More will I do,
> Though all that I can do is nothing worth;
> Since that my penitence comes after all,
> Imploring pardon.

This king, as Shakespeare portrays him, is indeed 'a wondrous necessary man', the keystone upon which the sixteenth-century state depends, and individuality has at last been subjugated wholly to the demands of office. But it is not for nothing that generations of Shakespeare's readers have found little to love in this play.

Unless we read it in the light of a certain bitter, underlying commentary, implicit in the orientation of the chief character, there is little there but that most grievous product of unremitting office, a dead man walking.

For the truth is that Shakespeare himself, now that he has built the figure with such care, out of the cumulative experience of eight plays, begins to recoil from it. It has been an experiment, an exploration, like, but for its larger scale, his brief but effective exploration of the system of Machiavelli, and, as he did with that system, so he does with this vast body of assembled evidence on public life: he rejects its findings as invalid before the deeper demands of the less explicit but immutable laws of man's spirit.

So much, then, for the Elizabethan phase of Shakespeare's portrait of the statesman-king, for the record of the period when he for a time believed that the wide canvas of public life was greater than the illimitable experience of the spirit. The contrast between the private and public virtues has been made clear, the qualifications of the great statesman have been slowly selected, tested, and built up into a single figure. Such characteristics as did not contribute to his public self have been eliminated (and they are seen, somewhat surprisingly, to be nearly co-terminous with character). More than this, certain of the loyalties, decencies, and ideals most prized in an individual are found to be incompatible with the public virtues. Henry, who rejected Falstaff in circumstances which cannot be forgiven, will also, in the moment of crisis, bargain with his God like a pedlar. His religion and his love for his people alike carry with them a tinge of expediency, a hint of the glib platform speaker.

It would seem, then, that in the very act of completing the figure, Shakespeare became aware of a certain insufficiency, and that dissatisfaction was already implicit in his treatment of Henry V, the culminating study of the series. What was there implicit is revealed by degrees in his treatment in the later plays of similar characters, or characters similarly placed.

SOURCE: 'Shakespeare's Political Plays', in *The Frontiers of Drama* (1945; 2nd ed. 1964).

J. H. Walter

SHAKESPEARE'S CHRISTIAN
EPIC HERO

THE reign of Henry V was fit matter for an epic. Daniel omits
apologetically Henry's reign from his *Civil Wars*, but pauses to
comment,

> O what eternal matter here is found
> Whence new immortal *Iliads* might proceed;

and there is little doubt that this was also the opinion of his
contemporaries, for not only was its theme of proper magnitude,
but it also agreed with Aristotle's pronouncement that the epic
fable should be matter of history. Shakespeare, therefore, in
giving dramatic form to material of an epic nature was faced with
difficulties. Not the least was noted by Jonson, following Aristotle, 'As to a *Tragedy* or a Comedy, the Action may be convenient, and perfect, that would not fit an *Epicke Poeme* in
Magnitude' (*Discoveries*, ed. 1933, p. 102). Again, while Shakespeare took liberties with the unity of action in his plays, insistence on unity of action was also a principle of epic construction
(*Discoveries*, p. 105) and could not lightly be ignored. Finally,
the purpose of epic poetry was the moral one of arousing admiration and encouraging imitation. Sidney writes,

> as the image of each action styrreth and instructeth the mind, so
> the loftie image of such Worthies most inflameth the mind with
> desire to be worthy, and informes with counsel how to be worthy.
> (*Apologie for Poetry*, 1924 ed., p. 33)

Shakespeare's task was not merely to extract material for a play
from an epic story, but within the physical limits of the stage and
within the admittedly inadequate dramatic convention to give the
illusion of an epic whole. In consequence *Henry V* is daringly

novel, nothing quite like it had been seen on the stage before. No wonder Shakespeare, after the magnificent epic invocation of the Prologue, becomes apologetic; no wonder he appeals most urgently to his audiences to use their imagination, for in daring to simulate the 'best and most accomplished kinde of Poetry' (*Apologie*, p. 33) on the common stage he laid himself open to the scorn and censure of the learned and judicious.

Dover Wilson points out that Shakespeare accepted the challenge of the epic form by writing a series of historic tableaux and emphasizing the epical tone 'by a Chorus, who speaks five prologues and an epilogue'. Undoubtedly the speeches of the Chorus are epical in tone, but they have another epical function, for in the careful way they recount the omitted details of the well-known story, they secure unity of action. Shakespeare, in fact, accepts Sidney's advice to follow the ancient writers of tragedy and 'by some *Nuncius* to recount thinges done in former time or other place' (*Apologie*, p. 53). Indeed, it is possible that the insistent emphasis on action in unity in I ii 180–213, with illustrations drawn from music, bees, archery, sundials, the confluence of roads and streams, is, apart from its immediate context, a reflection of Shakespeare's concern with unity of action in the structure of the play.

The moral values of the epic will to a large extent depend on the character and action of the epic hero, who in renaissance theory must be perfect above the common run of men and of royal blood, in effect, the ideal king. Now the ideal king was a very real conception. From Isocrates onwards attempts had been made to compile the virtues essential to such a ruler. Christian writers had made free use of classical works until the idea reached its most influential form in the *Institutio Principis*, 1516, of Erasmus. Elyot and other sixteenth-century writers borrowed from Erasmus; indeed, there is so much repetition and rearranging of the same material that it is impossible to be certain of the dependence of one writer upon another. Shakespeare knew Elyot's *Governor*, yet he seems closer in his general views to the *Institutio* and to Chelidonius' treatise translated from Latin into French by Bouvaisteau and from French into English by James

Chillester as *Of the Institution and firste beginning of Christian Princes,* 1571. How much Shakespeare had assimilated these ideas will be obvious from the following collection of parallels from Erasmus,[1] Chelidonius and *Henry V*.

It is assumed that the king is a Christian (I ii 241, 2 Chorus 6; Chel. p. 82; Eras. *Prefatory Letter,* p. 177 etc.) and one who supports the Christian Church (I i 23, 73; Chel. p. 82; Eras. passim). He should be learned (I i 32, 38–47; Chel. p. 57, c. VI.; Eras. *Prefatory Letter*) and well versed in theology (I i 38–40; Eras. p. 153). Justice should be established in his kingdom (II ii; *2 Henry IV,* v ii 43–145; Chel. p. 42, c. X; Eras. pp. 221–37) and he himself should show clemency (II ii 39–60; III iii 54; III vi 111–18; Chel. pp. 128–37; Eras. p. 209) not take personal revenge (II ii 174; Chel. p. 137; Eras. pp. 231–3) and exercise self-control (I i 241–3; Chel. p. 41; Eras. pp. 156–7). He should allow himself to be counselled by wise men (I ii; II iv 33; Chel. c. VI; Eras. p. 156), and should be familiar with humble people (IV i 85–235; Chel. pp. 129, 131; Eras. p. 245) though as Erasmus points out he should not allow himself to be corrupted by them (p. 150). The king seeks the defence and preservation of his state (I ii 136–54; II ii 175–7; Chel. p. 148; Eras. pp. 160, 161, etc.), his mind is burdened with affairs of state (IV i 236–90; Eras. p. 160) which keep him awake at night (IV ii 264, 273–4, 289; Eras. pp. 162, 184, 244). The kingdom of a good king is like the human body whose parts work harmoniously and in common defence (I i 178–83; Chel. p. 166; Eras. pp. 175–6) and again like the orderly bee society (I i 183–204; Chel. pp. 18–21; Eras. pp. 147, 165) with its obedient subjects (I i 186–7; Chel. p. 21; cf Eras. p. 236). He should cause idlers, parasites and flatterers to be banished or executed (the fate of Bardolph, Nym, Doll, etc.; Chel. Prologue; Eras. p. 194 etc.). The ceremony and insignia of a king are valueless unless the king has the right spirit (IV i 244–74; Eras. pp. 150–2); some titles are mere flattery (IV i 269; Eras. p. 197); at all costs flattery is to be avoided (IV i 256–73; Chel. Prologue; Eras. pp. 193–204). Although it is customary to compare kings with great men of the past, the kings must remember that as Christians they are far better than such men as Alexander (IV vii

13–53; Eras. pp. 153, 203; cf Chel. denunciation of Alexander
for murdering Cleitus, p. 129). The king should consider his
responsibility in war for causing the deaths of so many innocent
people (IV i 135–49; Eras. pp. 253–4). The evils of war are described (II iv 105–9; III iii 10–41; v ii 34–62; Chel. pp. 169–71;
Eras. pp. 253–4). It is a good thing for a king to enter into the
honourable estate of matrimony (v ii; Chel. p. 179).[2] Eramus
regards marriage for the sake of an alliance as liable to create
further strife (pp. 241–3).

There are, too, some small points of resemblance. Chelidonius
gives a full account of the society of bees (pp. 18–21) taken
mainly from Pliny, *Naturalis Historiae*, XI, and St Ambrose,
Hexaemeron, and his opening phrasing is similar to Shakespeare's
'they have their King, and seeme to keepe a certaine forme of a
kingdome', and he too stresses obedience as a civic virtue. The
episode of the man who railed against Henry has a close parallel.
Chelidonius, p. 137, refers to a story of Pyrrhus, king of Epirus,
who pardoned some soldiers who spoke 'uncomly and indecēt
wordes of him' because they were drunk with wine. (Shakespeare,
however, may have remembered the incident in Plutarch.)

The Conversion of Prince Henry

It is just this portrait of Henry, the ideal king, that most commentators have found difficult to reconcile with Prince Hal, and
to describe Henry as Hal 'grown wise' is to avoid the issue. If
Henry V is the end that crowns *1* and *2 Henry IV*, then King
Henry V must come to terms with Prince Hal. The heart of the
matter is the nature of the change that came over Henry at his
coronation, and this must be examined in detail.

Shakespeare gives only one observer's account of what happened, that by the Archbishop of Canterbury I i 25–34:

> The breath no sooner left his father's body,
> But that his wildness, mortified in him,
> Seem'd to die too; yea, at that very moment,
> Consideration like an angel came,

And whipp'd the offending Adam out of him,
Leaving his body as a paradise,
T'envelop and contain celestial spirits,
Never was such a sudden scholar made;
Never came reformation in a flood,
With such a heady currance, scouring faults.

This deftly intricate passage is based mainly on the Baptismal Service from the Book of Common Prayer. Compare,

he being dead unto sin ... and being buried with Christ in his death, maye crucifye the olde man, and utterlye abolyshe the whole bodye of sinne,

and,

graunt that the olde Adam in this child may be so buryed, that the new man may be raised up in him,

and,

that all carnall affections maye dye in him, and that all thynges belonginge to the Spirite may lyve and growe in him.

(Boke of Common Prayer, 1560)

Again the baptismal 'washing away of sins' is almost certainly responsible for the flood imagery in lines 32-4. Not only is Baptism the 'only true repentance' in Jeremy Taylor's phrase, but it is also a means of 'spiritual regeneration'.

This, however, is not all. Lines 28-30, besides containing an obvious allusion to the casting forth of Adam and Eve from the Garden of Eden (Gen. III 23-4), have a deeper significance. The word 'consideration' is usually glossed as 'reflection' or 'contemplation', but this is surely an unsatisfactory gloss here. Its usage in this period points to another connotation. In the Authorized Version the verb 'consider' is frequently used where it is almost equivalent to an exhortation to repent from evil doing or at least in association with evil doing (Deut. xxxii 29; Ps. l. 22; Hag. i 5; Isa. i 3; Jer. xxiii 20; xxx 24, etc.). In Donne's sermons 'consideration' appears again with similar associations (*Sermons* XLV, LIV. § 2, LXIII, etc.), as it does in Hooker (*Works* (1850) II 242). Jeremy Taylor, *Holy Living* and *Holy Dying* uses

'consideration' in numerous section headings with the meaning
of spiritual contemplation, and again in the general context of
turning away from sin to the good life or the good death. It is
evident that the word was associated with intense spiritual contemplation, and self-examination, and not with merely thought
or reflection.

Centuries earlier, Bernard of Clairvaux, called upon to write
an exhortation that would encourage corrupt members of the
Church to repent and reform their lives, wrote *De Consideratione*.
'Consideration' for St Bernard is one of the 'creatures of Heaven'[3]
dominated on earth by the senses. He notes that St Paul's
ecstasies (2 Cor. xii 4) were departures from the senses and therefore forms of consideration or divine contemplation in which
men were 'caught up to Paradise'. Consideration, when the help
of heavenly beings is given – and such angelic help is given to
those who are the 'heirs of salvation' (Heb. i 14) – becomes perfection in the contemplation of God. There is no evidence that
Shakespeare knew Bernard's work, although it was regarded as
one of his most important writings and was very highly esteemed
in the Middle Ages. But the linking of significant words 'consideration', 'angel', 'paradise', 'celestial spirits', indicates that
Shakespeare was undoubtedly thinking of repentance and conversion in the religious sense.

In a later comment on the Prince's reformation, Canterbury
says,

> for miracles are ceas'd;
> And therefore we must needs admit the means
> How things are perfected.

Had it been doctrinally admissible Canterbury would have
acknowledged a miracle; as it is, he has to admit that to the Prince
by the revelation of divine grace is 'made known the supernatural
way of salvation and law for them to live in that shall be saved'
(Hooker, *Laws of Ecclesiastical Polity*, 1 xi 5).

Was there any suggestion of a religious conversion in the
historical sources? Hall and Holinshed both state briefly that the
Prince 'put on the new man', a phrase that had become proverbial

even in the sixteenth century and may therefore have lost its original scriptural significance. With two exceptions the earlier chroniclers are not very informative on this point; the exceptions are T. Elmham's *Liber Metricus de Henrico Quinto* (ed. C. A. Cole, in *Memorials of Henry V*, Rolls Series, 1958, p. 100), which gives a mere hint in the line 'rex hominem veterem sic renovare', and the *Vita et Gesta Henrici Quinti* (Pseudo-Elmham, ed. T. Hearne, 1727), written some thirty years after Henry's death. In this latter work, Henry, upon his father's death, spent the day in profound grief and repentance, he shed bitter tears and admitted his errors. At night he went secretly to a man of perfect life at Westminster and received absolution. He departed completely changed, 'felici miraculo convertitur' (pp. 14-15). The writer of the *Vita et Gesta* has no doubt that there was a miraculous conversion.

It is not certain that Shakespeare was acquainted with the *Vita et Gesta*, but it is highly probable, at least as probable as that he knew the *Gesta*.

It may be objected that this does not solve the problem, but only introduces almost literally a *deus ex machina*. Yet if we had read *1* and *2 Henry IV* with imagination, this turn of events would not appear arbitrary and inconsistent. Let us reconsider some of Hal's speeches and actions in these two plays. In *1 Henry IV*, 1 ii 217-39, Hal's declaration that he would throw off his unyoked idle humour when the time was ripe and thereby gain wide approbation has earned him accusations of cold-hearted, selfish scheming. Admittedly the speech is a clumsy dramatic device which Shakespeare also used in *Richard III* to let Gloucester announce that he was 'determined to prove a villain'. But it is not cold-blooded scheming, it is a piece of self-extenuation, a failure to reform which Hal justifies as unconvincingly as Hamlet does his failure to run Claudius through while he was at prayer. It is no more and no less than St Augustine's youthful prayer of repentance, 'O God, send me purity and continence – but not yet.' Henry's interview with his father brings about a partial change of his attitude, but he does not see beyond physical and material ends; his atonement is to match himself in battle

with Hotspur, in which he succeeds brilliantly. These taken with
Vernon's praise of him, *1 Henry IV*, v ii 51–68, suggest perhaps
not altogether fancifully, that Henry had reached physical perfection, the first of Aristotle's three ways of perfection.

In *2 Henry IV*, ii ii 51–61, we are given a clear warning not to
think that Henry is a hypocrite, and in iv iv 67–78 Warwick's
defence of the Prince's essential integrity. At the same time the
Prince and Falstaff are moving farther apart, Hal has nothing to
do with Falstaff's night of venery, nor with his capture of Cole-
ville. The soliloquy on the cares of kingship shows the Prince
beginning to realize his responsibilities; his profound grief
(mentioned twice it should be noted), his reconciliation with his
father, his committal of the powers of the law into the hands of
the Lord Chief Justice, suggest again that he is attaining the
second Aristotelian perfection, intellectual perfection, or as
Hooker phrased it, 'perfection civil and moral' (*Eccles. Polity*,
I xi 4).

Finally, Canterbury's account in *Henry V* shows Henry's
perfection, physical, intellectual and spiritual completed, he is
now the 'mirror of Christendom'.

It could not be otherwise. Medieval and Tudor historians
saw in the events they described the unfolding of God's plan,
history for them was still a handmaid to theology, queen of
sciences. Henry V, the epic hero and the agent of God's plan,
must therefore be divinely inspired and dedicated; he is every bit
as dedicated as is 'pius Aeneas' to follow the divine plan of a
transcendent God.

Within this all-embracing Christian Providence there was an
acceptance of classical beliefs of the innate tendency of states to
decay, and of the limitations and repetitions of human thoughts
and emotions throughout the ages consequent on the sameness
of the elements from which human bodies were formed. It was
hoped that men would return to the brilliance of pagan achievement in classical times, that highest peak of human endeavour,
since the conception of progress had not yet come to birth. In the
meantime classical writers were models for imitation and touch-
stones of taste, classical figures were exemplars of human actions

and passions, and the language of Cicero and Virgil, still current, foreshortened the centuries between. The modern was naturally compared with the ancient, Henry with Alexander. Calvary apart there could be no greater praise.

Only a leader of supreme genius bountifully assisted by Fortune and by the unity of his people could arrest this civic entropy and raise a state to prosperity. We do less than justice to Henry if we do not realize that in Elizabethan eyes he was just such a leader whose exploits were greater than those of other English kings, in Ralegh's words 'None of them went to worke like a Conquerour: saue onely King *Henrie* the fift.'

Shakespeare's Henry V

This is the man, and this his background. Let us now look more closely at Shakespeare's presentation of him in the major incidents of the play.

The conversation of Canterbury and Ely in the opening scene establishes economically the religious conversion of Henry on the highest authority in the country, Henry's support of the Church as a true Christian monarch, and his desire for guidance from learned churchmen, a procedure warmly recommended to kings by Erasmus, Chelidonius and Hooker. Later Canterbury demolishes the French objections to Henry's claim to the throne of France, and by his authority encourages Henry to undertake a righteous war. The characters of the two prelates have been heavily assailed, but Dover Wilson is surely right in his vindication of their integrity. Hall's bitter attack on the churchmen who sought to divert Henry's attention from the Bill by advocating war with France was followed more moderately by Holinshed.[4] Shakespeare, however, alters the order of events. Canterbury on behalf of Convocation offers Henry a subsidy to help him in the war with France which is already under consideration. His speech on the Salic Law is made at Henry's request to discover the truth behind the French objections to claims already presented, and not as in Hall and Holinshed thrust forward to divert his attention from the Lollard Bill by initiating a war with France. In 1585

in very similar circumstances the Earl of Leicester asked Archbishop Whitgift whether he should advise Queen Elizabeth to
fight on the side of the Low Countries against Spain. There was
talk, too, of seizing Church revenues to pay for the war, but
nevertheless the Church encouraged the war and offered a substantial subsidy.[5] Moreover, to portray Henry as the dupe of two
scheming prelates, or as a crafty politician skilfully concealing
his aims with the aid of an unscrupulous archbishop, is not consistent with claiming at the same time that he is the ideal king;
indeed it is destructive of the moral epic purpose of the play.

Yet Henry has been so calumniated. His invasion of France
has been stigmatized as pure aggression – though the word· is
somewhat worn – and Henry himself charged with hypocrisy.
Now Henry does not, as Bradley alleges, adjure 'the Archbishop
to satisfy him as to his right to the French throne', he urges that
the Archbishop should

> justly and religiously unfold
> Why the law Salic that they have in France
> Or should, or should not, bar us in our claim

and the remaining thirty-two lines of his speech are a most
solemn warning to the Archbishop not to

> wrest, or bow your reading,
> Or nicely charge your understanding soul
> With opening titles miscreate, whose right
> Suits not in native colours with the truth.

This does not sound like hypocrisy or cynicism. The Archbishop
discharges his duty faithfully, as it stands his reasoning is impeccable apart from any warrant given by the precedent of
Edward III's claims. Henry is not initiating aggression, in fact
Shakespeare omits from Exeter's speech in Hall the one argument
that has a predatory savour, namely, that the fertility of France
makes it a desirable addition to the English crown. And if Shakespeare did consider Henry's claims justified, he was thinking in
agreement with Gentili, the greatest jurist of the sixteenth
century, who quite uninvited expressed his opinion that the

claim of the English kings to the French throne was legal and valid:

... as the kings of England wished to retain their rights in the kingdom of France ... calling themselves their kings ... and thus they preserve a kind of civil possession. ... And that title is not an empty one ... (*De Iure Belli*).

Henry accepts the advice of his counsellors, but he it is who displays his foresight by asking the right questions. Shakespeare again adapts his sources to make Henry the first to raise the possibility of a Scottish invasion – not merely the incursion of marauding bands – during his absence in France, and then to assure himself of the essential unity of the country and its capacity to deal with such a threat.

In the presentation of the tennis balls by the French ambassadors Shakespeare has made a significant change from both Hall and Holinshed. Holinshed places the incident before Archbishop Chichele's speech in the Parliament of 1414, before there has been any suggestion of invading France; Hall places it after the speeches of Chichele, Westmoreland and Exeter, adding that, though he cannot be certain, this 'vnwise presente' among other things may have moved Henry to be 'determined fully to make warre in Fraunce'. In the play it is placed *after* Henry has determined to make war in France, it makes no difference to the issue. Shakespeare uses it to show Henry's christian self-control. To the French ambassadors, uneasy lest their message may cost them their lives, he declares:

> We are no tyrant, but a Christian king;
> Unto whose grace our passion is as subject
> As is our wretches fetter'd in our prisons.

The message itself he receives with unruffled urbanity:

> We are glad the Dauphin is so pleasant with us;
> His present and your pains we thank you for ...

and wittily turns the jest on the sender. Henry, the ideal king, is not to be incited to war by a personal insult; he reveals remarkable self-restraint, at the same time warning the Dauphin that his refusal to treat the English claims seriously will bring about bloodshed and sorrow.

While with some insensitiveness to irony we in this modern age may excuse Henry's invasion of France as arising from his limited medieval horizons, many are less inclined to pardon his rejection of Falstaff. Although Shakespeare's original intention was to portray Falstaff larding the fields of France, no doubt discreetly distant from Henry, he must accept responsibility for the play as it is. If he were prohibited from introducing Falstaff in person into *Henry V*, why was it necessary to mention Falstaff at all? In some slight way it might be regarded as fulfilling the promise in the epilogue of *2 Henry IV* that Falstaff might 'die of a sweat', or as containing a topical reference to the Oldcastle affairs, or as the best conclusion that could be made to cover the results of official interference; any or all of these might be offered as explanation. Surely the truth lies deeper. The 'finer end' that Falstaff made changes the tone of the play, it deepens the emotion; indeed, it probably deepened the tone of the new matter in Act IV. The play gains in epic strength and dignity from Falstaff's death, even as the *Aeneid* gains from Dido's death, not only because both accounts are written from the heart with a beauty and power that have moved men's hearts in after time, but because Dido and Falstaff are sacrifices to a larger morality they both ignore. Some similarities too between Aeneas and Henry may be noted; both neglect their duties for pleasant dalliance; both are recalled to their duty by divine interposition; thenceforth both submit to the Divine Will – it is significant that in *Aeneid*, IV 393, immediately after Dido's denunciation of him, Aeneas is 'pius' for the first time in that book – both display a stoic self-control for which they have been charged with coldness and callousness.

Falstaff has given us medicines to make us love him, he has bewitched us with his company just as Dido bewitched the imagination of the Middle Ages. We have considered him at once too lightly and too seriously: too seriously in that we hold him in the balance against Henry and England, and too lightly in that as a corrupt flatterer he stands for the overthrow of the divinely ordained political order. Erasmus expresses the opinion of the age when he reserves his severest censures for those flatterers who corrupt a prince, the most precious possession a country has (p. 194), and whom he would punish with death. Falstaff is such a one. If Henry's conversion and acceptance of God's will mean anything at all, they must be viewed in the light of the period to see Henry's full stature, even as a reconsideration of Virgil's religion enlarges and dignifies the character of Aeneas. The medieval habit of mind did not disappear with the Renaissance and Copernicus, on the contrary it is no longer a paradox that the Renaissance was the most medieval thing the Middle Ages produced. For both Middle Ages and Renaissance religion was planned, logical and integrated with everyday life, not as it is for many of their descendants a sentimental impulse to an occasional charity. So while a place may have been found for Falstaff with his crew of disreputable followers with Henry's army, there could be no room for him in Henry's tent on the eve of Agincourt.

It has been suggested that Henry deals with the conspirators with cat-like cruelty. Now Shakespeare has deliberately added to his immediate sources the pardoning of the drunkard who reviled Henry and the merciless attitude of the conspirators towards this man. While the latter may owe something to Le Fèvre, there is nothing of the kind in Hall or Holinshed. The reason is clear enough. Henry is to be shown as the ideal prince magnanimous enough to pardon offences against his person like Pyrrhus, king of Epirus, and the conspirators are to blacken themselves by their contrasting lack of mercy. Even when to high treason Scroop adds the personal disloyalty of a beloved and trusted friend, a treachery that disgusted Henry's nobles, Henry, consistent with his mercy to the drunkard, seeks no personal revenge:

> Touching our person seek we no revenge;
> But we our kingdom's safety must so tender,
> Whose ruin you have sought, that to her laws
> We do deliver you.

Henry's threats to Harfleur sound horrible enough, but he was precisely and unswervingly following the rules of warfare as laid down by Vegetius, Aegidius Romanus, and others. Harfleur he regards as his rightful inheritance, and those who withhold it from him are 'guilty in defence', because they wage an 'impious war'. He allows the besieged time to discover whether a relieving force is on its way, then warns them to surrender before he begins his main assault, which could not then be halted and which would have inevitable evil consequences. All this was in strict accord with military law:

This also is the reason for the law of God which provides that cities which do not surrender before they are besieged shall not be spared (Gentili, *De Iure Belli*, p. 217).

Henry again exercises his royal clemency by requiring Exeter to 'use mercy to them all'.

It is in Act IV that we see the full picture of Henry as the heroic leader. The devotion and enthusiasm he inspires indeed begin earlier, before he set foot in France. His personality has united England as never before (1 i 127), and already 'the youth of England are on fire' eager to follow the 'mirror of all Christian kings'. Something of the expectation in the air of 1598, when Essex was preparing his forces for Ireland has infected the spirit of these lines. A contemporary describes such a gathering:

They were young gentlemen, yeomen, and yeomen's sons and artificers of the most brave sort, such as did disdain to pilfer and steal, but went as voluntary to serve of a gaiety and joyalty of mind, all which kind of people are the force and flower of a kingdom.[6]

The heavy losses before Harfleur by battle and dysentery, the 'rainy marching in the painful field', the frightening size of the French army which might well have disheartened Henry's men, only united them closer still. Henry shares their dangers and is accepted into their fellowship which his exhilaration and leadership had made so strong. He shares too in the grim jesting of men bound in spirit in the eye of danger, who hobnob sociably with the Almighty, of Lord Astley at Edgehill and of the English soldier at Fontenoy, who, as the French troops levelled their firearms at the motionless English ranks, stepped forward and exclaimed, 'For what we are about to receive may the Lord make us truly thankful.' Henry's men are 'taking no thought for raiment' for if God gives them victory they will have the coats off the Frenchmen's backs, and if not He will otherwise provide robes for them in Heaven.

Nobleman and common soldier alike are inspired by Henry's gay and gallant spirits. Among the English nobles there is a courteous loyalty to each other quite unlike the sparrow squabbling of the French nobles, their preoccupation with vain boasting and their lack of foresight and order. Salisbury, the 'winter lion' of *2 Henry VI*, goes 'joyfully' into battle, and Westmoreland unwishes five thousand of the men he had previously desired. Henry himself sums up the heart of the matter in the memorable words,

> We few, we happy few, we band of brothers,

words that have come to stand for so much that is English. Dover Wilson recalls Churchill's famous epitaph on those who 'left the vivid air signed with their honour' in the summer of 1940, 'Never in the field of human conflict was so much owed by so many to so few', as coming from the same national mint. But it is older than Shakespeare, it is pure Hall. Listen to his last words on Henry V:

yet neither fyre, rust, nor frettying time shall amongest Englishmen ether appall his honoure or obliterate his glorye whiche in so fewe yeres and brief daies achived so high adventures and made so great a conquest.

The words are English but the mood is older and universal, it is the note of epic heroism that sounded at Thermophylae, at Maldon, and in a pass by Rouncesvalles.

While Henry infuses courage into his men, he is not without unease of soul. The conversation with Bates, Court and Williams forces him to examine his conscience on his responsibility for those who are to die in the coming battle, and to complain how little his subjects understand the hard duties of a king in their interests. Militarily his position is desperate: his enemy has selected the time and place for battle, his men are heavily out-numbered, tired and weakened by disease and lack of food. His faith in the righteousness of his cause is strained to the uttermost, and in prayer he pleads that his father's sin of usurpation may not be remembered against him. His courage is magnificent, and his extraordinary self-control has not always been acknowledged. He does not unpack his heart and curse like a drab, nor flutter Volscian dovecots, nor unseam his enemies from the nave to the chaps, he is no tragic warrior hero, he is the epic leader strong and serene, the architect of victory.

For all his self-control he is moved to rage by the treacherous attack on the boys and lackeys in his tents, and, fearing for the safety of his army, gives the harsh order to kill the prisoners. Dover Wilson's comment is valuable:

> The attack is historical; and Fluellen's exclamation, 'Tis expressly against the law of arms, 'tis as arrant a piece of knavery, mark you now, as can be offert!', is in accordance with much contemporary comment on the battle, which shows that the treacherous assault left a deep stain upon the chivalry of France. Thus any lingering doubt about Henry's action is blotted from the minds of even the most squeamish in the audience ...

Gower's remark, 'the king most worthily hath caused every soldier to cut his prisoner's throat. O! 'tis a gallant king', shows wholehearted approval of Henry's promptness in decision and his resolute determination. The rage of the epic hero leading to the slaughter of the enemy within his power is not without Virgilian precedent (see *Aeneid*, x and xii).

Exeter's account of the deaths of York and Suffolk also touches Henry to tears. The purpose of the description, for which there is no warrant in any of the sources of the play, seems to have been overlooked. It is not, as has been supposed, an imitation of the moving and presumably successful description of the heroic deaths of Talbot and his son in *1 Henry VI*, iv vi and vii. York and Suffolk die in the right epic way, their love 'passing the love of women' is fulfilled in death. The surviving heroes, in epic style, mourn their death at once so fitting, so sadly beautiful, so 'pretty and sweet', a phrase recalling at once that other pair of heroes who 'were lovely and pleasant in their lives, and in their death they were not divided'.

The Henry of Act v is to many a disappointment, indeed the whole act, it is suggested, is an anticlimax. Dover Wilson defends it rather unconvincingly as a good mixture, and, following Hudson, praises Henry's overflowing spirits and frankness in the wooing scene as a convincing picture of the humorous-heroic man in love. This is so, but the truth lies deeper. The Christian prince to complete his virtues must be married. Bouvaisteau, following Aegidius Romanus, is most emphatic on this point. Erasmus agrees, though he discounts the value of alliances secured by marriage; in this he differs from other theorists. The brisk and joyous wooing promises a happy marriage, though both Henry and Katharine have themselves well under control. In fact, Henry's remark that the eloquence of Kate's lips moves him more than the eloquence of the French Council may be a glance at what some chroniclers openly stated, that Katharine's beauty was used to try to make Henry lessen his demands. Henry's earlier proverbial reference to himself as the king of good fellows may show that he fully appreciates this point that Katharine proverbially is the queen of beggars.

This marriage in particular seals the union of two Christian countries with momentous possibilities for Christendom then divided by schism. Henry's letter to Charles as related by Hall puts the matter clearly:

Sometymes the noble realmes of Englande & of Fraunce were united, which nowe be separated and deuided, and as then they were accustomed to be exalted through the vniversall worlde by their glorious victories, and it was to theim a notable vertue to decore and beautifye the house of God . . . and to set a concorde in Christes religion.

The Treaty of Troyes saw Henry as the most powerful monarch in Europe, he had built unity by force of arms, by his inspiring military genius, and by the grace of God. He was now the complete Christian monarch, 'the mirror of christendom'. It is this completion that necessitated Act v, it was not implicit in Agincourt.

The character of Henry has not, of course, been 'deduced' from the writings of Erasmus, Chelidonius and others, but it is significant that where Shakespeare adds to his historical sources, the intruding passage or episode has an apt parallel with passages from these writers. Even some of his omissions, notably the absence of reference to the English archers to whom the victory was mainly due, can be construed as helping to enlarge the stature of Henry. It is also not without significance that the Henry of *Henry V* is a complete and balanced contrast in character and appearance with Richard II in the first play of the tetralogy.

If Henry has proved less interesting a man than Richard, it is because his problems are mainly external. The virtuous man has no obvious strife within the soul, his faith is simple and direct, he has no frailties to suffer in exposure. It is just this rectitude and uprightness, this stoicism, this unswerving obedience to the Divine Will that links both Aeneas and Henry, and has laid them both open to charges of priggishness and inhumanity. Both are complete in soul:

> omnia praecepi atque animo mecum ante peregi.

Of Henry as of Aenas can it truly be said,

> rex erat ... quo iustior alter
> nec pietate fuit, nec bello maior et armis.
>
> (*Aeneid*, 1 554–5).

Fluellen

Although Hotson has praised Pistol highly (in the *Yale Review*, 1948) the only other character of any significance is Fluellen.

Fluellen, whatever his origin, whether he is a gentle caricature of Sir Roger Williams as Dover Wilson thinks (though Hotson has pointed out that he is on the wrong side in the ancients versus moderns dispute), or whether, as seems more likely, he owes a great deal to Ludovic Lloyd,[7] is a well-conceived and endearing figure. The description of Parolles, 'the gallant militarist ... that had the whole theorick of war in the knot of his scarf, and the practice in the chape of his dagger' (*All's Well*, IV iii 162–5) fits Fluellen admirably. His quaint pedantry and self-conscious dignity link him at once with his fellow-countrymen Glendower and Sir Hugh Evans, in what may have been national traits, but his essential manliness and love for Henry shine through his oddities. Indeed, he underlines Henry's virtues, and if the ancestry of Falstaff be Riot as has been suspected, Fluellen in the uncensored version of *Henry V* may have performed with his cudgel a service that in earlier plays would have required a dagger of lath.

The Spiritual Significance of the Play

As for the play itself it has been roundly condemned as lacking spiritually significant ideas. This is curious. In hardly any other play of Shakespeare is there such interweaving of themes of the highest value to an Elizabethan. References, explicit and implicit, to 'breed', 'unity', 'honour' (fame), 'piety' abound throughout the play. It is noteworthy that the French display degenerate breeding, disunity, dishonour and impiety in waging a 'bellum impium' against Henry the rightful inheritor. Shakespeare's description of the evils and devastation of war as having befallen or as likely to befall the French, it should be observed, is part of his insistence that war is God's scourge for securing justice among the nations: defeat and despoiling is the portion of those nations whose cause is unrighteous.

What does seem to have escaped notice is the unfolding of Henry's character. At the outset of the play his virtue after his conversion, complete though it may be, is yet cloistered, it has not sallied forth into the dust and heat. Though he makes decisions, he is dependent on the advice of others, and in spite of his self-control, the treachery of Scroop, his bedfellow, obviously hurts him and he finds it necessary to ease his mind in speech. At Harfleur his speech is an incitement to battle, very skilfully done, but with no deeper note. By Agincourt he no longer seeks advice, he acts, he directs. His physical courage, long since proved on Shrewsbury field, is again apparent but not stressed. Shakespeare might have shown the famous combat with Alençon, but he did not; physical prowess in Henry was not at this point the most important quality. It is Henry's spiritual strength, his faith and moral courage which inspire and uphold his whole army. By sheer exaltation and power of spirit he compels his men to achieve the impossible. And this inspired mood does not leave him again, it carries him exuberantly through v ii to the union of England and France. No spiritual significance? Surely,

> The gods approve
> The depth, and not the tumult, of the soul.

SOURCE: Introduction to the New Arden edition of *King Henry V* (1954).

NOTES

1. For convenience the translation of the *Institutio*, by L. K. Born, *The Education of a Christian Prince* (New York, 1936) has been used.
2. This part of the *Institution* was added by Bouvaisteau.
3. Quotations taken from the translation of G. Lewis (Oxford, 1908), pp. 130–7.
4. Christopher Watson, *The Victorious actes of Henry the fift*, 'coarcted out of Hall' goes further than Hall. He refers to the 'panch-plying porkheads' who to divert Henry's attention from the bill seek to 'obnebulate his sences with some glistering vaile'.
5. John Strype, *Life and Acts of Archbishop Whitgift*, 1 434. See L. B. Campbell, *Shakespeare's Histories* (San Marino, Cal., 1947) p. 268.
6. Quoted without reference, P. Alexander, *Shakespeare's Punctuation* (British Academy, 1945), p. 1.
7. See E. Owen, *Ludovic Lloyd* (Wrexham, 1931).

Derek A. Traversi

THE CONFLICT OF PASSION AND
CONTROL IN *HENRY V* (1956)

THE political success aimed at by Henry IV is finally achieved, in the last play of the series, by his son. The general theme of *Henry V*, already approached in its predecessors, is the establishment in England of an order based on consecrated authority and crowned successfully by action against France. The conditions of this order are, again in accordance with the main conception, moral as well as political. The crime of regicide which had stood between Bolingbroke and the attainment of peace no longer hangs over Henry V – unless as a disturbing memory – and the crusading purpose which had run as an unfulfilled aspiration through the father's life is replaced by the reality, at once brilliant and ruthless, of the son's victorious campaign.

This, as critics have not always realized, is less a conclusion than a point of departure for the understanding of *Henry V*. It was the conditions of kingship, rather than its results, that really interested Shakespeare in these plays; and those conditions are viewed, by the time the last of them came to be conceived, in a light definitely akin to the tragic. The problem of political unity and that of personal order have been brought in the course of these historical studies into the closest relationship. Just as the state, already in *Henry IV, Part II*, is regarded in its divisions as a diseased body ravaged by a consuming fever, so is the individual seen increasingly as torn between the violence of his passions and the direction of reason; and just as the political remedy lies in unquestioned allegiance to an authority divinely constituted, so does personal coherence depend upon the submission of our uncontrolled desires to reason. The link between the two states, political and personal, is provided in these plays by concentration upon the figure of the king. The problem of the state becomes, in a very real sense, that of the individual at its head. The king, who rightly demands unquestioning allegiance from his subjects, is first called upon to show, through the perfection of his self-control, a complete and selfless devotion to his office. The personal implications of that devotion are considered, together with the patriotic triumph to which it leads, in *Henry V*.

It demands, in the first place, an absolute measure of self-domination. Called upon to exercise justice and shape policies for the common good, the king can allow no trace of selfishness or frailty to affect his decisions. He must continually examine his motives, subdue them in the light of reason; and this means that he is engaged in a continual struggle against his share of human weakness. As the play proceeds, we become increasingly aware that there is in Henry an uneasy balance between violent passion, in certain of its forms, and cold self-control. The control is, indeed, an essential part of his political capacity, but it has behind it an unmistakable sense of constraint which makes itself felt in his greeting to the French ambassador:

> We are no tyrant, but a Christian king;
> Unto whose grace our passion is as subject
> As are our wretches fettered in our prisons.   (I ii)

The harshness of the comparison is, to say the least, remarkable. Such self-control is necessarily precarious. The passions, 'fettered', treated with a disdain similar to that which, as Prince Hal, he had already displayed to normal human feelings when his success as monarch depended upon the renunciation of his past, may be expected to break out in forms not altogether creditable. Almost at once they do so. The French ambassadors, in fulfilling their mission by presenting him with the Dauphin's tennis balls, touch upon Henry's most noticeable weakness; they expose him to ridicule and, worse still, they refer – by the observation that 'You cannot revel into dukedoms here' – to the abjured but not forgotten past. Henry's reaction, in spite of an opening affirmation of self-control, takes the form of one of those outbursts which are habitual with him whenever his will is crossed:

> ... *I* will rise there with so full a glory
> That *I* will dazzle all the eyes of France,
> Yea, strike the Dauphin blind to look on us.
> And tell the pleasant prince this mock of his
> Hath turned his balls to gun-stones; and his soul
> Shall stand sore charged for the wasteful vengeance
> That shall fly with them: for many a thousand widows
> Shall this his mock mock out of their dear husbands;
> Mock mothers from their sons, mock castles down;
> And some are yet ungotten and unborn
> That shall have cause to curse the Dauphin's scorn.   (1 ii)

'*I* will rise there'; '*I* will dazzle all the eyes of France.' The Dauphin's gibe has set free Henry's 'fettered' passions and they express themselves frankly in a cumulative vision of destruction. The tone of the utterance – the impact of 'strike', the harsh reference to the balls which have been turned to gun-*stones*, the sense of irresistible, ruinous force behind 'mock castles down' – reflects the new feeling and already recalls the later, more masterly picture of Coriolanus in action (*Coriolanus*, II ii). The sense of power, inhuman and destructive, has at last been unleashed in the king. The responsibility for coming events, already assumed in the same scene by the Archbishop, has now been further fastened upon the Dauphin, and Henry is in a position to announce his coming descent upon France with a phrase that incorporates into his new vehemence the convenient certainty of righteousness:

> But all this lies within the will of God,
> To whom I do appeal.

No doubt the conviction is, as far as it goes, sincere, for the will of God and the will of Henry, now fused in the egoistic passion released by the Dauphin's jest, have become identical.

It is not until the opening of the French campaign that Henry's utterances and preparations are openly translated into action. The poetry of war in this play deserves careful attention, for much of it is unmistakably associated with the element of constraint already noted in his character. The rhetoric with which he incites his men to battle before the walls of Harfleur has about it a strong flavour of artificiality and strain:

> ... then imitate the action of the tiger;
> Stiffen the sinews, summon up the blood,
> Disguise fair nature with hard-favour'd rage;
> Then lend the eye a terrible aspect;
> Let it pry through the portage of the head
> Like the brass cannon; let the brow o'erwhelm it
> As fearfully as doth a galled rock
> O'erhang and jutty his confounded base,
> Swill'd with the wild and wasteful ocean.
> Now set the teeth and stretch the nostril wide,
> Hold hard the breath and bend up every spirit
> To his full height.   (III i)

There is about this incitation something forced, incongruous, even slightly absurd. The action of the warrior is an imitation, and an imitation of a wild beast at that, carried out by a deliberate exclusion of 'fair nature'. The blood is to be summoned up, the sinews stiffened to the necessary degree of artificial bestiality, while the involved rhetorical comparisons which follow the references to the 'brass cannon' and the 'galled rock' strengthen the impression of unreality. In stressing this note of inhumanity Shakespeare does not intend to deny the poetry of war which he expresses most fully in certain passages from the various prologues of this play (see especially the Prologues to Acts III and IV); but, as later in *Coriolanus*, he balances the conception of the warrior in his triumphant energy as a 'greyhound straining at the leash' against that, not less forcible, of a ruthless and inhuman engine of destruction. Both ruthlessness and splendour are inseparable aspects of the complete picture.

Henry's treatment of the governor and citizens of Harfleur, which immediately follows (III iii), relates this conception of the warrior to tensions already apparent in the king's own character. Not for the first time, Shakespeare places the two scenes together to enforce a contrast. The words in which Henry presents his ultimatum are full of that sense of conflict between control and passion which is so repeatedly stressed in his earlier utterances. The grotesque inhumanity of his words, however, is balanced by a suggestion of tragic destiny. Beneath his callousness there is a sense that the horrors of war, once unloosed, once freed from the sternest self-control, are irresistible. His soldiers, he warns the governor, are still held uneasily in check. 'The cool and temperate wind of grace', whose control over passion has already been indicated as the mark of a Christian soldier, still exercises its authority; but 'licentious wickedness' and 'the filthy and contagious clouds' of *'heady* murder' threaten to break out at any moment. In his catalogue of the horrors of unbridled war stress is laid continually upon rape and the crimes of 'blood'. The 'fresh-fair virgins' of Harfleur will become the victims of the soldiery, whose destructive atrocities are significantly referred to in terms of 'liberty':

> What rein can hold licentious wickedness
> When down the hill he holds his fierce career?

The processes of evil, once unleashed, move along courses fatally determined; but Henry, as usual, having described them in words which emphasize their horror, disclaims all responsibility for them, just as he had once disclaimed all responsibility for the outbreak of the war. The whole matter, thus taken out of his hands, becomes indifferent to him:

> What is't to me, *when you yourselves are cause,*
> If your pure maidens fall into the hand
> Of hot and forcing violation?   (III iii)

Yet this very assertion of indifference implies, at bottom, a sense of the tragedy of the royal position. Only this denial of responsibility, Shakespeare would seem to say, only the exclusion of humanity and the acceptance of a complete dualism between controlling 'grace' and the promptings of irresponsible passion, make possible that success in war which is, for the purposes of this play, the crown of kingship.

For it would be wrong to suppose that Shakespeare, in portray-traying Henry, intends to stress a note of hypocrisy. His purpose is rather to bring out certain contradictions, human and moral, which seem to be inherent in the notion of a successful king. As the play proceeds, Henry seems increasingly to be, at least in the

moral sense, the victim of his position. The cunning calculations
of the Archbishop, with which the play opens, have already given
some hint of the world in which he moves and which, as king, he
has to mould to his own purposes; and the treasonable activities
of Cambridge, Grey, and Scroop are further indications of the
duplicity with which monarchs are fated by their position to deal.
Somewhere at the heart of this court there is a fundamental
fault which must constantly be allowed for by a successful ruler.
It appears to Henry, in his dealings with the conspirators, as
something deep-rooted enough to be associated with the original
fall of man:

> Seem they religious?
> Why, so did'st thou: or are they spare in diet,
> Free from gross passion or of mirth or anger,
> Constant in spirit, not swerving with the blood,
> Garnish'd and decked in modest complement,
> Not working with the eye without the ear,
> And but in purged judgement trusting neither?
> Such and so finely bolted did'st thou seem:
> And thus thy fall hath left a kind of blot,
> To mark the full-fraught man and best indued
> With some suspicion. I will weep for thee;
> For this revolt of thine, methinks, is like
> Another fall of man.   (II ii)

It is remarkable that Henry, in meditating on this betrayal, should
return once more to that theme of control, of freedom from passion, which is so prominent in his own nature. By concentrating
on the functioning of the body, and on the sense of mutual diver-
gence between eye, ear, and judgement in the infinitely difficult
balance of the personality, Shakespeare sets spiritual control in
contrast with a sense of anarchy which proceeds, most typically,
from his contemplation of physical processes. 'Gross passion' –
the adjective is significant – is associated with the irrational
'swerving of the blood', and the judgement which controls it
needs to be 'purged' by fasting ('spare in diet') before it can attain
a scarely human freedom from 'mirth or anger'. By emphasizing
the difficult and even unnatural nature of such control, Shake-

speare casts a shadow, at least by implication, over that of Henry himself; but it is also seen to be necessary, inseparable from his office. The administration of justice, upon which depends order within the kingdom and success in its foreign wars, demands from the monarch an impersonality which borders on the inhuman. The state must be purged of 'treason lurking in its way' before it can be led, with that single-mindedness of purpose which is both Henry's strength and his limitation, to the victorious enterprise in France.

It is clear, indeed, that *Henry V* represents, however tentatively, a step in the realization of themes fully developed only in the tragedies. Inheriting from his sources a conception of Henry as the victorious king, perfectly aware of his responsibilities and religiously devoted to the idea of duty, Shakespeare emphasizes the difficulties of the conception, the obstacles, both personal and political, which lie between it and fulfilment. When he discusses, during his debate with Williams and Bates on the eve of Agincourt (IV i), the implications of his power, he approaches closely the spirit in which the great tragedies were to be conceived: 'The king is but a man as I am; the violet smells to him as it doth to me; . . . all his senses have but human conditions: his ceremonies laid by, in his nakedness he appears but a man; and though his affections are higher mounted than ours, yet when they stoop they stoop with the like wing.' The universality of the argument, in the true tragic fashion, transcends the royal situation. Men, differentiated by vain 'ceremony', are united in their common weakness, and the most notable feature of human behaviour seems to the speaker to be its domination by impulse, its helplessness before the stooping of the affections. In this respect, at least, the king is one with his men; and just because he is so like them, because his senses too 'have but human conditions', are constantly liable to break through the guard of rigid self-control imposed upon him by his vocation, there is something precarious and disproportionate in his absolute claim upon the allegiance of his followers.

The royal isolation is further underlined by Williams when he points out the spiritual consequences of a conflict for which the

king, as unquestioned head of his army, is alone responsible: 'For
how can they [his soldiers] charitably dispose of anything when
blood is their argument? Now, if these men do not die well, it
will be a black matter for the king that led them to it.' These
words repeat once more, but with a greater urgency, a preoccupation with the horrors of war which Henry has already expressed,
even if he succeeded in shaking off responsibility for them, to the
French ambassadors and to the governor of Harfleur. They imply, beyond the religious sense of responsibility which derives
from the traditional conception of Henry's character, a contrast –
already familiar – between the Christian law of 'charity' and the
'blood'-spurred impulse to destruction that threatens it in the
acts of war with the consequences of unleashed brutality. The
connection between this conflict of flesh and spirit and the tendency of human societies, states and families alike, to dissolve by
the questioning of 'degree' into individual anarchy is not established in this play as it is in the tragedies which followed. But
Hamlet himself might have reflected like Henry on the precarious
basis of human pretensions, and Angelo defined in similar terms
the catastrophic realization of it brought about by his fatal
encounter with Isabella. Had Henry once followed his line of
speculation far enough to doubt the validity of his motives for
action, or – on the other hand – had he given free play to the
sinister impulses dimly recognized in himself, the resemblance
would have been complete; as it is, there is only a premonition,
a first indication of possibilities brought more fully to light in
later plays.

For the moment, Henry counters the implications of Williams's
argument by pointing out that soldiers 'purpose not their death,
when they purpose their services'. His sombre view of human
nature, however, impresses itself upon the king, attaches itself
to his own meditations, and is profoundly echoed in his own
words. Connecting war with sin, and in particular with over-
riding passion, he repeats the tone of earlier statements: 'Besides,
there is no king, be his cause never so spotless, if it come to
the arbitrament of swords, can try it out with all unspotted
soldiers: some peradventure have on them the guilt of pre-

meditated and contrived murder; some, of beguiling virgins with the broken seals of perjury.' The result is, in part, a fresh emphasis upon meticulous self-examination as a means of conserving spiritual health – 'therefore should every soldier in the wars do as every sick man in his bed, wash every mote out of his conscience' – and in the soliloquy which brings the scene to an end, one of those outbursts of nostalgic craving for release which have appeared already in the *Second Part of Henry IV* and which will be repeated more urgently, with a more directly *physical* apprehension of existence, in Hamlet's meditations and in the Duke's incitations to Claudio in *Measure for Measure*:

> What infinite heart's ease
> Must kings neglect, that private men enjoy! (IV i)

The craving for 'heart's ease' in this long speech is still, generally speaking, that of *Henry IV*: a desire to be freed from the burden of an office in which human purposes seem fatally divorced from human achievement. The development of the verse is still painstaking, leisurely in the expansion of its long periods, and a little rhetorical; but there are moments which anticipate the association in *Hamlet* of this familiar nostalgia with a desire to be freed from the incumbrances, the 'fardels', the 'things rank and gross in nature', by which the flesh persistently seems to obstruct the unimpeded workings of the spirit. Greatness is a 'fiery fever' which consumes its royal victim like a bodily disease, and the contrasted peace of the humble subject is described with a curious ambiguity of tone:

> Not all these, laid in bed majestical,
> Can sleep so soundly as the wretched slave,
> Who with a body fill'd and vacant mind
> Gets him to rest, cramm'd with distressful bread.
>
> (IV i)

In the association of peace with bodily fulness and vacancy of mind, in the impression, harshly and directly physical, behind 'fill'd' and 'cramm'd,' there is a distinct suggestion of certain descriptions of satiated, idle contentment in plays as far apart as

Troilus and Cressida and *Coriolanus*. Here already such imagery represents a kind of residue, intractable and irreducible, in direct contrast to the king's unceasing emphasis on the need for spiritual discipline. It is no more than a suggestion, unabsorbed as yet into the main imaginative design of the play; but, tentative as it is, it does stand in a certain relationship to the clash of flesh and spirit, 'passion' and 'grace' which exacts continual vigilance from Henry, and which is slowly moving through these developments of imagery to more open dramatic realization.

A similar potential cleavage can be traced in the treatment of the two sides drawn up in battle at Agincourt. Shakespeare differentiates between the French and English forces in a way which dimly foreshadows the balance held in *Troilus and Cressida* between Greeks and Trojans, though here it is true that the unfavourable estimate of the English, which is scarcely compatible with the spirit of the play, is expressed only in the words of their enemies. The English are still morally worthy of their victory, but the French account of them at least anticipates the possibility of criticism. The French, combining a touch of the unsubstantial chivalry of Troilus with a more than Trojan emptiness, are, like the Trojans, defeated; the English, represented by them as gross and dull-witted, are as undeniably successful as the Greeks. Shakespeare's handling of the battle itself carries on this conception. The French, trusting in a thin and rhetorical belief in their own aristocratic superiority, rush hastily and incompetently to their deaths; the English, deriving their spirit from their king, win the day by their perseverance and self-control. Self-control, however, which is – as in Henry himself – not without some suggestions of harshness and inhumanity. Henry's righteousness does not prevent him from inflicting merciless reprisals on his prisoners, and there is something sardonic about Gower's comment that the 'king, most worthily, hath caused every soldier to cut his prisoner's throat. O 'tis a gallant king' (IV vii). By such excellence, Shakespeare would seem to say, must wars be won.

There is, indeed, a good deal of throat-cutting in this play. The king's ruthlessness, a logical consequence of his efficiency, needs to be seen against the human background which Shakespeare provided for it, most noticeably in the comic scenes which turn on the behaviour of the common soldiery. There is little room in *Henry V* for the distinctive note of comedy. Shakespeare's delineation of character is as clear-cut as ever, and his dialogue abundantly if discreetly flavoured with the sense of humanity; but there is about the humour of these scenes a certain dessicated flatness that contrasts sharply with the exuberance of earlier plays. Bardolph, Pistol, and the others, no longer enlivened by contact with Falstaff, quarrel like curs, and their jokes turn largely upon the bawdyhouses which will inevitably swallow them up when they return to England, and upon the cutting of throats. 'Men may sleep and they may have their throats about them at that time; and some say knives have edges' (II i). Nym's remark, itself dark and enigmatic, is prefaced by a sombre, fatalistic 'things must be as they may', which modifies the comic sententiousness of the speaker and implies a certain resigned acceptance of the ordering of things. The humorous conception of the character is toned down to fit in with a spirit no longer essentially humorous; and this applies not only to Nym but to his companions in arms. Fluellen and Gower, Williams and Bates are distinguished, not by comic vitality or by the penetration of their comments on men and events, but by their qualities of common sense, by a tough sense of loyalty and dedication to the work in hand; and it is by their devotion to the strictly practical virtues and by their definition of their various national idiosyncracies that they live. This is no longer the world of *Henry IV, Part I*. Falstaff himself, out of place in such company, is remembered only in his death,[1] serving as a kind of measure by contrast with which Shakespeare emphasizes his changing vision of humanity. This death – it is worth noting – is ascribed directly to the king, who 'has killed his heart'; and Nym, repeating that phrase of of resignation which conveys so much more than he realizes of the spirit of this new world, relates Henry's treatment of him to an obscure, inherent fatality: 'The king is a good king; but it must be as it may; he passes some humours and careers' (II i). His companions who remain must now accommodate themselves to the times. They do so by abandoning domestic crime to follow their king to France. War and its prospects of plunder are for them no more and no less than a means of livelihood and an alternative to preying upon one another. As Bardolph puts it: 'We must to France together; why the devil should we keep knives to cut one another's throats?' (II i).

It is indeed significant, in making a final estimate of this play, that the account in it of the death of Falstaff is, by common consent, the most human and deeply felt thing in the entire action. In an action where the touchstone of conduct is success, and in which humanity has to accommodate itself to the claims of expediency, there is no place for Falstaff. Shakespeare had already recognized this, and prepared us for the necessary changes, in the 'rejection' scene and in the events leading up to it; and now his end affects us tragically as the last glimpse of another and less sombre world. No doubt there is a patriotic purpose, not irrelevant to the play, and no doubt Shakespeare drew the character of his successful monarch with that purpose in mind. One aim does not, in Shakespeare, exclude another; and the fact remains that as we consider the uncompromising study of achieved success which rounds off this trilogy, a certain coldness takes possession of us, as it took possession of the limbs of the dying Falstaff, so that we find ourselves in a mood that already anticipates the great tragedies.[2]

SOURCE: *An Approach to Shakespeare* (1956).

NOTES

1. It might be added that his posthumous appearance, so to call it, in *The Merry Wives of Windsor* does not affect our main argument. The Falstaff of this comedy, as has been often observed, is no more than the halfhearted revival of a character originally conceived in a very different spirit.

2. The interpretation of *Henry V* here suggested receives some corroboration from H. Granville-Barker's *From Henry V to Hamlet* (British Academy Lecture, 1925). See above, pp. 62–4.

Rose A. Zimbardo

THE FORMALISM OF *HENRY V* (1964)

Henry V, a seemingly lucid play, presents an odd problem to criticism. It is full of warfare, yet empty of conflict. It centers upon adventure, yet is not, in the Aristotelian sense, an action. It embraces a courtship but never exploits the tensions inherent in love. Indeed, it is less a drama than a celebration. Before the play begins, its central conflict has already been resolved. If there are some ripples in the calm, like the pathos of Falstaff's death, they exist merely as reminders of a battle long since fought and won. The response of critics has been to classify rather than criticize. Traversi, for example, invests the play with a conflict that it does not have—'an uneasy balance between unbridled passion and cold control'[1] in the character of Henry — in the hope of writing it off as historical tragedy or tragical history. J. H. Walter [see above, p. 131] comes nearer the mark in describing the play as Shakespeare's attempt to render epic in the dramatic mode. However, classification can be dangerous in that, focusing upon the abstract, elusive problem of genre, it often obscures immediate problems raised by the particular work under consideration. For example, the strange comparison between Alexander's murder of Cleitus and Henry's 'murder' of Falstaff is not explained when we simply label it epic simile. More crucial, however, are the errors in perception that are likely to follow upon generic classification. For instance, the movement of *Henry V* is not the narrative progression of epic. Rather, the design and movement of the play are better understood when we think of them in rhetorical than when we think of them in generic terms.

Henry V is an almost perfect realization of meaning in form. Its thematic essence is to be found in the formalism of its style and architecture. In movement the play resembles a stately, ceremonial dance, each figure of which calls to life a different aspect of the hero's excellence. These figures, each retaining a degree of independence, each preserving its own boundaries, move in measured order to complete the design of the whole. The effect is of a universal harmony wherein each planet, exactly placed, has its proper movement and function. The thematic relevance of such a structure is obvious: the ideal king embodies in himself and projects upon his state the ideal metaphysical order. A harmonious operation of parts in an ordered whole is the design of the cosmos, of the state, of the perfect king,

> For government, though high and low and lower
> Put into parts, doth keep in one consent
> Congreeing in a full and natural close,
> Like music.   (I ii 180–3)[2]

And, as the object of art is to imitate such ideal forms as 'nature often erring yet shewes she would faine make,'[3] this is the design too of the imitative rhetorical construct, the play itself.

The first figure lays the groundwork for the whole: it is comparable in function to the first epistle of Pope's *Essay on Man*. Henry's recourse to religious authority to test the justice of his cause, his careful blend of wisdom, courage and temperance in exercising power, and the nice balance in his character of reason with passion outline the cosmic architecture of ideal kingship. The ideal kingdom realizes the kingdom of God on earth; the ideal king is the instrument and his own soul the medium through which that realization takes place. There is a confluence here of three planes of existence, the metaphysical, the political and the moral. In the world this can occur only when nature is tempered by an ordered formalism. Henry defines the relation of his office to his nature in terms of temperance.

> We are no tyrant [i.e. self-willed] but a Christian king
> [i.e. God-willed]
> Unto whose grace our passion is as subject
> As is our wretches fett'red in our prisons.   (I ii 241–3)

The interrelation of Christianity, kingship and personal morality is ordered and ordering.

Each of the succeeding figures displays in detail a facet of the kingly perfection outlined in the first. The second figure shows Henry's achievement in government of a golden mean between justice and clemency. The third measures the extent to which even his heroic valor is controlled by his perfect understanding of himself and his office (we might contrast here the irregular, Herculean heroism of Hotspur wherein the lust for glory overrules judgment). The last figure shows at once the simplicity and self-control of the hero in love.

The trappings of war that deck the play function as ornament, heroic conceit. There is no warlike clamor in the play; there is indeed no motion at all that is not controlled and measured. No moral tension is created by the war, for one knows from the beginning that God is with Henry. One knows before the battle that the English will win and would be no less confident had he never heard of Agincourt. Even the conspiracy, so quietly discovered and handled, on Henry's part with control and on the conspirators' with an almost grateful admission of guilt, creates no impression of faction. The army is displayed only that the comparison may be struck between its harmonious order and the disorder of the French army. The characters in the scene are types; like all the characters in the play they have no existence in themselves but serve only to illustrate some grace of Henry's. For example, the captains in Henry's army, Jamy, the Scot, Macmorris, the Irishman, and Fluellen, the Welshman, are by design exaggerated almost into music-hall types. Their function is to illustrate the *concors discordia* which the ideal king makes of his state, and which is comparable to the *concors discordia* of the natural universe under God.

The battle is over before it has begun. There is no presentation here, as there is, for example, in *Henry IV*, of actual fighting. The only battle scene, in which the dying York kisses the dead Suffolk, is a conceit, an emblem of heroic conduct that invests the war with courtly formality. Yet even this scene does not occur before our eyes, but is related as action past. Shakespeare uses this device throughout the play. The chorus, for instance, in addition to bridging gaps in time and place and enlarging the scene to epic proportion, also translates action into description; movement related becomes static. The effect, however, is not of lifelessness but of motion arrested. We envision the English sailing to France, or the camp on the eve of battle as we see a huge canvas, all at once and with the figures caught, frozen in the midde of action. That they are as figures in a tapestry, almost moving yet still, enhances the formality of the scene.

Just as action is fitted to the careful, measured order of the design, so is style. In Henry's speech reviling the treason of Lord Scroop there is not the slightest suggestion of personal anger. Henry's emotions are not his own but are in the control of an order larger than his limited human self. That his emotion is enlarged and controlled is manifested in the formality of his rhetoric:

> ... Show me men dutiful?
> Why, so did'st thou. Seem they grave and learned?
> Why, so did'st thou. Come they of noble family?
> Why, so did'st thou. Seem they religious?
> Why, so did'st thou. ...   (II ii 127–31)

The stylistic devices – rhetorical question, repetition, parison, paramoron, symmetry – might have come straight from a Renaissance book of rhetoric. They are purposely exaggerated to emphasize the control of passion by an ordered, ordering judgment in the character of the king. The speech of the ideal king, like every other of his attributes, is measured and controlled. At every juncture in the play where action or passion might threaten to disturb measured order, the agitating force is brought under control by a highly formal rhetorical style. Henry's exhortation to the troops ('Once more unto the breach . . .' etc.), for example, arrests and formalizes movement. His challenge to the governor of Harfleur (which, as Walter notes, echoes precisely the *rules* of warfare) is framed in such exaggerated rhetoric that it becomes Senecan – i.e. horrible subject matter is rendered as still as statuary by stylistic formality.

> [He] bids you, in the bowels of the Lord
> Deliver up the crown and to take mercy
> On the poor souls for whom this hungry war

Opens his vasty jaws and on your head
Turning the widow's tears, the orphan's cries
The dead men's blood, the pining maidens' groans
For husbands, fathers and betrothed lovers
That shall be swallow'd in this controversy.
This is his claim, his threatening, and my message.

(II iv 102–10)

Here the formal measure achieved in such devices as balance, the use of triplets ('husbands', 'fathers', 'lovers', 'claim', 'threatening', 'message'), and paramoron is enhanced by elevation and conventionality of diction ('vasty jaws', 'bowels of the Lord', 'widows' tears', 'dead men's blood', 'pining maidens'). The threat has nothing of passion in it. It cannot be mistaken for the personal threat of Henry or a reflection of his own feelings or desires, because its formalism marks it as part of a controlling order of which Henry himself is merely the instrument.

When we have recognized that formalism is at once the structure, style and meaning of the play, the relation of Act v to the whole becomes apparent. The tone of the last figure is quite different from that of the others, but since each episode in some measure retains its independence, the shift in mood does not disturb, but rather completes the whole design. One cannot ignore Johnson's objection that Act v presents a break in the character of Henry, that here Shakespeare invests his hero with the very social awkwardness that he had so effectively ridiculed in Hotspur [see above, p. 33]. How could a prince who once did 'Shine so brisk, and smell so sweet/ And talk so like a waiting gentlewoman' (*1 Henry IV*, I iii 54–5) grow into such a cloddish king? What would be a flaw in character development in a linear scheme, however, is perfectly consistent with the design of this play. The point to be considered is that character development has no place in such a design. Henry's character is fully developed when the play begins; the object here is to explore the operation of that character, to reveal the nature of its harmony and the harmony which grows out of it to control the state. For the sake of setting another balance for creating still another reconciliation of opposites, Shakespeare chooses here to make Henry a blunt

English soldier, that he may the better contrast with the sprightly, Gallic Katherine. It is true that to do this he had to sacrifice altogether the facile, witty Hal, but he had made that sacrifice long ago. The function of Act v, as of the rest of the play, is to exhibit harmonious order, the reconciliation of contrasting elements that would be opposing forces were they not brought into harmony by formalism. In the exchanges between Henry and Katherine the courtly dance shows a lighter side, but it remains nonetheless courtly and still a part of the stately, ceremonial whole.

Considering the play itself, then, we find it to be a system of contrasts and balances that are brought into order by stylistic and structural formalism. When we consider it in relation to the rest of the tetralogy it assumes still greater significance. Once again a contrast is being struck – here between Richard II and Henry V. In *Richard II* order was torn down not by Bolingbroke, who was merely an instrument, but by Richard himself, for it is Richard who is ultimately responsible for his deposition. In *Henry V* order is restored and again the king alone is responsible.

Richard's fatal error is in judgment. He believes that kingship can remain holy and God-protected when the man who fills the office is sinful. Throughout the play he projects his kingship against the background of history and tradition. Whatever he says about kingship is true, but in projecting his office into the realm of abstraction he divorces it from himself. He never measures himself against his office. The irony of such a statement as

> The breath of wordly men cannot depose
> The deputy elected by the Lord
> > (*Richard II*, iii ii 56–7)

is that while Richard can see the relation between God and kingship, he cannot see the relationship between God and himself, or kingship and himself. From the beginning of *Richard II* there is a confusion in Richard's mind between 'king' and 'self'. As the play progresses, the gap widens; while he is always aware of what kingship is, he does not know what he himself is. He confesses that he plays 'many people/ And none contentedly', and at last completely reveals his ignorance of self when, after his deposition, he asks, if an unkinged king is not a king, what is he.

Bolingbroke in office is deceitful rather than ignorant. Knowing himself criminal, he always uses trickery to make himself appear fair where he is foul. But he plays a quite minor role in this larger comparison because he is not a king but an usurper.

Henry V has from the beginning been aware that a virtuous king must be a virtuous man. So much is he the superior of his father that he has recognized his sins and vowed to reform them at the time when his father is merely urging that he put a good appearance on his behavior. His development in the *Henry IV* plays is a progress toward the attainment of virtue; before the beginning of *Henry V* he has reached his goal.

> Consideration like an angel came
> And whipped the offending Adam out of him
> Leaving his body as a paradise.   (1 i 28–30)

He has whipped sin out of his body in preparation for the sacrament of kingship. This does not, as Traversi maintains, make him less human, unless we equate humanity with sin. So human is Henry that his achievement of virtue has cost him great pain and sacrifice. He knows by experience what it is to be king, 'what infinite heartsease/ Must kings reject that private men enjoy' (IV i 240–1). He knows too that mere ceremony would be an empty reward for such sacrifice. The only real reward of the true king is the harmony of self and state within the all-embracing harmony of God's order. Rather than lapsing, as Richard does, into the excuse of being human, Henry screws his humanity to the highest pitch of virtue to realize the perfection that 'king' implies.

The critics argue that Falstaff dies because he has no place in the new order and that his death makes the final accusation of Henry's and the play's inhumanity. It is true that Falstaff (whose character is derived from the carnival figure The Lord of Misrule) has no place in the new order. But he is allowed to die only after his character has degenerated to the lowest ebb of venery and mean parasitism. Falstaff is one's warm, lively, much-loved self, but the path of self-indulgence can lead ultimately only to meanness and death. His death (which, significantly, does not 'happen' but is merely reported) can be pathetic in this play because its necessity has been established before the play begins. Falstaff is the old Adam who has had to be whipped out before Prince Hal could become King Henry. In this play he is a memory, just as Henry's recollection of his father's guilt is a memory. Both recall the struggle that had to be undergone that right order might be achieved.

Henry V is a study in order and harmony; it does not record, but rather it celebrates the victory of form over disorder and chaos. As form governs every attribute of the king, so does it every aspect of the play that celebrates him – structure, characterization, style. Finally, it reaches beyond the limits of the play to invest the tetralogy with new meaning and to draw the circle closed.

SOURCE: *Shakespeare Encomium*, ed. Anne Paolucci (City College Papers 1: New York, 1964).

NOTES

1. Derek Traversi, *Shakespeare from Richard II to Henry V* (Stanford, 1957) p. 172.

2. All references are to *The Life of Henry V* ed. R. J. Dorius (The Yale Shakespeare: New Haven, 1955).

3. Philip Sidney, *Arcadia*, in *Works*, ed. Feuillerat (Cambridge, 1922) II xi.

Zdeněk Střibrný

HENRY V AND HISTORY (1964)

The Life of Henry V is hardly the greatest play in Shakespeare's cycle of ten dramas of English history. Yet it may certainly be considered as central, or at least helpful in revealing his artistic approach to politics, politicians, world-order, kingship, the people, the Elizabethan nation-state, and more generally to war and peace – in a word, to history. It has the unquestioned distinction of crowning the second, and more mature, group of his 'histories' which stretch from the very beginnings to the actual close of his writing career.

For a clearer understanding of its place among these national historical plays a list of all of them, in the order in which they were probably written, may be useful:[1]

3 Parts of *Henry VI* (written about 1590–2) ⎫
Richard III (written about 1592–3) ⎬ The first historical tetralogy

King John (about 1595–6)
Richard II (about 1595–6)
2 Parts of *Henry IV* (about 1597–8) ⎫ The second historical tetralogy
Henry V (1599)
Henry VIII (about 1612–13),

There is no need to suppose that Shakespeare had such an extensive and neat pattern in his mind when he decided to try his hand at the English chronicle play. Nevertheless, the outcome of his endeavours was commanding enough. With the exception of *King John* and the late *Henry VIII*, all his histories are grouped in two tetralogies, culminating respectively in *Richard III* and *Henry V*. This gives these two plays a special position and perhaps a special appeal, even in our day: they are so far the only histories that have been filmed and thus brought to millions

of modern spectators. Laurence Olivier's choice may also have
been due to the fact that they present, in mutual contrast, supreme
examples of a bad and a good king, of a tyrant, as the humanist
thinkers of the Renaissance conceived and condemned him, and
of an ideal ruler, aspiring to the high place awarded by Thomas
More to his King Utopus, or by Thomas Elyot to his Governor.

It is a commonplace that it has always been easier for an
author to create a negative character, ranging up to a thorough-
going villain, than an accomplished hero. This applies even to
Shakespeare who, of all the world's great writers is only the
nearer to us for his normal share in our common frailties.
Nobody has any doubts about the crushing impact of his *Richard
III*. But his *Henry V* has been subjected to much discussion
and has been both extolled and execrated with considerable
vehemence. . . .

How are we to deal with these clashing critical contradictions?

There can be no doubt that Shakespeare wanted his *Henry V*
to become a triumphal account of the English victory against
overwhelming odds at Agincourt in 1415. As the historical
events, described in chronicles and sung about in ballads,
afforded, apart from the battle itself, rather little dramatic matter,
he was both forced and inspired to create a new dramatic genre,
what we might almost call an epic drama, certainly the most epic
of all his plays. Accordingly, he introduced every act by an epic
prologue and closed the whole piece by an epilogue in the form
of a narrative sonnet. In the opening lines of the play he invoked
his Muse to 'ascend the brightest heaven of invention': the final
play of his two historical cycles was to be a lavish parade of
mellow poetry both epic and dramatic, of richly varied prose and
of good-humoured parody on affected and outmoded dramatic
styles, not excepting the 'mighty line' of Marlowe.

Stylistic analysis certainly suggests that Shakespeare was
anxious to marshal and display all the formal resources he had
thus far mastered. The blank verse in *Henry V* reaches the highest
standard of his middle phase. Far from confining every idea to a
single line, as is the tendency in the early plays, the verse runs
majestically on, yet within a firm discipline and without breaking

under the pressure of heavy thought or overflowing into the
freedom of the later tragedies and final romances. It makes use
of all the bold images and ornamental devices of Renaissance
poetry, without piling them up or showing them off. Youthful
exuberance gives way to measure, balance and harmony:

> Suppose within the girdle of these walls
> Are now confin'd two mighty monarchies,
> Whose high upreared and abutting fronts
> The perilous narrow ocean parts asunder.
> Piece out our imperfections with your thoughts:
> Into a thousand parts divide one man,
> And make imaginary puissance;
> Think, when we talk of horses, that you see them
> Printing their proud hoofs i' th' receiving earth; ...
>
> (1 Prologue 19–27)

The prose presents an even greater fullness. It ranges from
passages highly rhetorical and refined in the manner of the
university and court wit John Lyly (most of the speeches of the
French courtiers) to passages almost naturally colloquial (e.g.
Henry's discourse with the good soldiers Bates, Court and
Williams) and to pieces still more homsepun and spiced with
farcical gags. Perhaps the best example of the latter type of prose
comes up in the scene where our hostess Pistol, *quondam*
Quickly, tells about the death of Sir John Falstaff. Already at
the beginning of the second act she has prepared us for the worst
by her announcement that 'he'll yield the crow a pudding one
of these days' because 'the King has killed his heart'. After the
contrasting effect of the ensuing scene in the King's council-
chamber at Southampton, full of solemn poetry, she comes again,
this time to deliver her famous comic dirge on Falstaff's end:

Nay, sure, he's not in hell: he's in Arthur's bosom, if ever man
went to Arthur's bosom. 'A made a finer end, and went away
an it had been any christom child; 'a parted ev'n just between
twelve and one, ev'n at the turning o' th' tide; for after I saw him
fumble with the sheets, and play with flowers, and smile upon his
finger's end, I knew there was but one way; for his nose was as
sharp as a pen, and 'a babbl'd of green fields. 'How now, Sir

John!' quoth I. 'What, man, be o' good cheer'. So 'a cried out
'God, God, God!' three or four times. Now I, to comfort him,
bid him 'a should not think of God; I hop'd there was no need to
trouble himself with any such thoughts yet. So 'a bade me lay
more clothes on his feet; I put my hand into the bed and felt
them, and they were as cold as any stone; then I felt to his knees,
and so upward and upward, and all was as cold as any stone.

(II iii 9–26)

This old wife's tale is typical of the way Shakespeare transformed
the farcical prose of his dramatic predecessors. He retained something of the clownish fooling which was expected from characters
of low life when they appeared on the pre-Shakespearian stage,
yet at the same time he permeated their speech with genuine
popular idiom and imagination, with sharply observed comparisons, with strong epic narrative and pithy dramatic dialogue,
as well as with pungent humour. Mistress Quickly's high-
explosive style, compounded of convention and originality, of
old cliché and realistic vision, of broad farce and unaffected feeling, was bound to give her an even stronger appeal than that of
her older relative, the Nurse in *Romeo and Juliet.*

The great variety of style, climbing from the depth of London
taverns up to the flights of court poetry, is in full accord with the
basic idea-content of the play. No pains are spared to present an
imposing panorama of Britain's unity in arms, including every
'kind and natural' citizen, whatever his rank and his nationality,
English, Welsh, Irish, or Scottish. *All* the sons of Mother England are called upon to do their duty, which is apportioned
according to their social 'degree', yet is in each case important
and responsible. Moreover, when it comes to the decisive battle,
everybody who sheds his blood is gentled in his condition while
any gentlemen who shun fighting must 'hold their manhood
cheap'.

The English nobility of action stands in sharp contrast to the
nobility of blood among the French who look down upon the
English 'beggared host' as well as on their own 'superfluous
lackeys' and 'peasants'. Even after their defeat they send their
herald Montjoy to ask King Henry to allow them

> To sort our nobles from our common men;
> For many of our princes – woe the while! –
> Lie drown'd and soak'd in mercenary blood;
> So do our vulgar drench their peasant limbs
> In blood of princes; ...   (IV vii 71–5)

The essential difference between the two nations is perhaps best reflected in their different conceptions of honour. The French conceive of honour in the old feudal sense as an aristocratic virtue *par excellence*, based on class superiority and hereditary privilege. For the English, on the contrary, honour is much more of a national ideal, attainable by all those who deserve it by their deeds. Here again the progressive social thinking of Thomas More and his humanistic circle comes to full flowering. Thus the whole conflict between France and England is presented as an encounter between the surviving feudal order and the English nation-state as it developed in Shakespeare's own time, especially during the years of struggle against the repressive power of Catholic Spain. Shakespeare lays special stress on the fact that the French lords at Agincourt refuse to lean upon their own people and rely solely on their own chivalric bravery. Whereas in the English host gentlemen fight side by side with their yeomen as one compact national army.

The leader of this 'band of brothers', King Henry, quite naturally assumes the place of a real father of his country and grows into a symbol of British unity and glory. Quantitatively speaking, he is the most voluminous of all Shakespeare's characters. As early as in *Richard II* he is spoken of as a young loafer who, despite his recklessness, harbours 'a spark of hope' in his bosom. The spark is fanned (not without tricky moments) in the next two plays in the cycle until, in *Henry V,* it bursts out into festive fireworks. We may therefore illuminate the whole play by centring our critical attention on Henry's character and career as well as on his relations both to his friends and his enemies.

One of the essential virtues of an ideal ruler, according to Thomas Elyot and other humanist thinkers, was concern for justice. Consequently, Shakespeare did not spare place or poetry to show right from the start that Henry's war against France was just and justifiable. Already at the end of *Henry IV* we saw him repudiate the wild company of Falstaff and choose the Lord Chief Justice for his main counsellor. In the exposition of our play another grave man, the Archbishop of Canterbury, is invited by the King to unfold 'justly and religiously', without fashioning or bowing his reading, whether the English claim to the French crown and territory is lawful. The Archbishop's answer is certainly too long-winded for our modern taste in tempo; however, Dover Wilson is probably right in assuming that not only Henry but also Shakespeare's audiences, being rhetorically minded and litigious, loved to hear a good pleader proving that France belonged to them.[2] Only when the Archbishop and all the English peers unanimously persuade the King of the righteousness of his action, does he give the final signal for the French expedition.

At the same time he insists, and keeps on insisting during the whole campaign, that he does not forget God as the supreme judge in whose name he puts forth his 'rightful hand in a well-hallowed cause'. On the eve of the Agincourt battle he prays the Lord not to remember the sin committed by his father in compassing the English crown, and repeats for himself, and for his audience, what he has done in the way of penitence. After the miraculous victory, when he hears about the French holocaust, while English losses are only some thirty, he ascribes it all to the arm of God and forbids anybody under threat of death to boast and so to take the praise from the only One to whom it is due. Taken in all, Henry may well claim the epithet of 'the complete Christian monarch' attributed to him by J. H. Walter, since piety appears as his second cardinal virtue.

We might go on pointing out Henry's virtues for a good while longer. Most of them have been extolled by his sympathetic critics: his magnanimity, modesty, bravery, coolness and high spirits in the face of danger. His sense of humour is what every Englishman likes to think of as typically English: he can even enjoy a joke or two against his own anointed person.

To close this part of our analysis, let us consider for a moment one trait in Henry's character which has not always been fully appreciated. I mean his plainness, his soldier-like bluntness, his dislike of social pretence and his striving for simple and honest relations between himself and all his subjects. Some American scholars[3] have observed how the blunt soldier had come to be a striking type in life and on the stage by the end of the Elizabethan period and how he was often placed in opposition to courtly fops or intriguers. Shakespeare developed and enriched this type in many of his characters, starting with the Bastard in *King John* and culminating tragically in *Coriolanus*. Surely the warlike Harry deserves to be admitted to this military brotherhood. Already his wild youth in the company of Jack Falstaff may be explained, at least in part, by his instinctive dislike of courtly falsity and foppery, because every court breeds flattery and dissimulation, and the court of Henry IV, the 'king of smiles', had been full of it. On this basis we are permitted to sympathize with Prince Hal's escapades in the less decorous yet more wholesome air of the London world, or underworld. What he learns there stands him in good stead later. Hardly any other kind would be able to mix with his common soldiers as freely as Henry does the night before Agincourt. Not only does he have a reassuring chat with them. He shows himself as eager to cut through the official hierarchy by means of his disguise and to learn the plain, even bitter, truth directly from their rank-and-file point of view, without trimmings. Moreover he thinks it proper to stress right at the beginning of his discussion that 'the king is but a man' to whom the violet smells the same as it does to anybody else. The ideal monarch of the sixteenth century must base his position on some sort of sense of essential human equality.

A similar candour informs his attitude to the woman of his heart. When he comes to woo the French Princess Katharine, he does not choose to speak in the vein of a mighty conqueror, however much he would be entitled to the pomps of a Tamburlaine. Nor does he 'mince it in love' like so many sonneteering and capering courtiers. Although his courting speeches are stylistically much more deliberate and cultivated than they may seem at first sight, essentially he remains true to himself as a 'plain soldier' and a 'plain king'. Many critics[4] have felt rather

baffled, if not disgusted, when Henry playfully suggests, instead
of love-lorn rhyming and dancing, that he buffet for his love,
or bound his horse for her favours and 'lay on like a butcher, and
sit like a jack-an-apes, never off'. However inelegant such words
may sound, we should not close our eyes to the simple truth and
beauty of what they really imply and lead up to:

... What! a speaker is but a prater: a rhyme is but a ballad. A
good leg will fall; a straight back will stoop; a blackbeard will
turn white; a curl'd pate will grow bald; a fair face will wither; a
full eye will wax hollow. But a good heart, Kate, is the sun and
the moon; or, rather, the sun, and not the moon – for it shines
bright and never changes, but keeps his course truly. If thou
would have such a one take me; and take me, take a soldier; take
a soldier, take a king.   (v ii 158–66)

It is certainly to Henry's credit that he keeps his course
throughout the whole play as 'the best king of all good fellows'.
He detests the courtly 'fellows of infinite tongue, that can rhyme
themselves into ladies' favours' only to 'reason themselves out
again'. Instead, he prefers quickly to 'leap into a wife' whom he
likes in the rough but honest manner of a real soldier-king. Only
such a soldier could win the sympathy and support of *all the
people* in his national army, as well as in Shakespeare's national
theatre. Only such a king could gain victory over the terrifying
odds commanded by the French princes and, to cap it all, get the
French princess.

So far so good. Yet there are more things in *Henry V* than are
dreamt of in the kind of philosophy most of his eulogists go in
for. However fervently Henry's ideal qualities are hammered
home, they represent only half of the poet's whole truth about
the King and his holy war. A deeper analysis, probing under the
shining surface, will find that the highlights in Henry's portrait
are thrown into relief by dark shades.

We need not take back anything that has been said and quoted
so far in Henry's favour. There is no doubt, first of all, that he *is*
shown as a just ruler and defender of the faith and international
law. At other moments, however, we may discover in his character quite different features and motives. For the first hint we

may look again at the end of *Henry IV* where the hidden motive
of his French campaign shows up. 'Therefore, my Harry, / Be it
thy course to busy giddy minds / With foreign quarrels' (*2 Henry
IV*, IV v 213–15): thus does the dying king, anxious to divert
the attention of his subjects from the drops of Richard's blood
which stain his crown, advise his son. And the young Harry
faithfully follows this course from the very beginning of our
play, being only too loyal to his dead father and his lion-and-fox
policy. After all, a foreign war, as every Renaissance politician
knew, has always certain advantages for rulers in difficulties at
home. To camouflage his aims, Henry leaves the Archbishop of
Canterbury to do most of the propaganda and goes so far as to
exhort him before God to take heed how he awakes the 'sleeping
sword of war'. And yet he knows better than anyone that the
Archbishop has his own urgent reason for advising foreign
quarrels if he is to save the better part of the Church's property
from the attacks of the Commons who are striving to pass a bill
against it.

It should be remembered that Shakespeare, in his usual way,
based the Archbishop's warlike speech on the Elizabethan
chronicler Raphael Holinshed who, in his turn, took it over
from the anti-Catholic chronicle of Edward Hall, where any
sign of corruption in the old unreformed Church was seized
upon with great gusto. However, the remarkable fact remains
that Shakespeare, in his fanfare introducing the glorious Henry,
did not suppress but gave full vent to the bass tones of his French
policy. When Henry succeeds in manœuvering the Archbishop
into a willing enough oath 'The sin upon my head, dread sovereign!', his typical knack of policy is completed. He always proves
extremely ingenious in putting the blame for his actions on
somebody else: on Falstaff, on the Archbishop, on the Dauphin,
on the besieged citizens of Harfleur, on whoever comes in handy,
not excluding God himself.

In this light, the second of Henry's cardinal virtues, his piety,
does not emerge untarnished. The more devout the words on his
lips, the more humble his glances towards Heaven, the more he
falls under suspicion of hiding the bad conscience of an aggressor

under constant references to God, as so many of his historical
predecessors and successors were in the habit of doing. If we
judge his piety not only by his words but also by his works, the
result is more disquieting. It is true that he does ostentatious
penance for the crime committed by his father upon Richard II.
Nevertheless, the fruit of this crime, the English crown, rests
firmly in his hands and is being stained by much more blood in
the war against France. Now nobody would expect Henry to give
up his crown in a fit of belated penitence. Such things seldom
happen in practical politics and, moreover, Shakespeare had his
Holinshed and the main historical facts, not to mention the
position of the Tudors, to consider. Yet would it not have been
much better for Henry, then, simply to leave Richard, as well
as God, at rest, without taking their names repeatedly in vain?
As it is, it would seem as though the poet had penetrated too
deeply into the King's soul not to see there an incessant strife
between political exigencies and human feelings, between the
call of power and glory and the urge towards genuine simplicity
and piety.[5]

Let us recall, in this connection what a really pious king,
Henry's successor Henry VI, created by Shakespeare some eight
years earlier, had to say about his father's actions:

> But, Clifford, tell me, didst thou never hear
> That things ill got had ever bad success?
> And happy always was it for that son
> Whose father for his hoarding went to hell?
> I'll leave my son my virtuous deeds behind;
> And would my father had left me no more!
> (3 Henry VI, ii ii 45–50)

Shakespeare must have kept these considerations in his mind
and imagination throughout both his historical cycles. Otherwise
he would not have closed his fervently patriotic *Henry V* with an
epilogue summing up unobtrusively, yet firmly, the whole
historical frame and outcome of Henry's famous victories:

> Henry the Sixth, in infant bands crown'd king
> Of France and England, did this king succeed;

> Whose state so many had the managing
> That they lost France and made his England bleed; . . .
>
> (Epilogue, 9–12)

After these apprehensions, there remains the image of Henry as a hearty soldier-king to be re-examined. Again his qualities as a good mixer and blunt wooer need not be denied. Only they need to be qualified and supplemented by some less engaging features. Henry, as we know from both parts of *Henry IV*, had acquired the art of free-and-easy intercourse with all sorts of people while playing truant from the court and painting London red in the company of Jack Falstaff. He was well aware all that time that as soon as he ascended the throne he would have to cut out the Falstaff side of his life, including Falstaff himself. This is quite understandable, and we cannot criticize it, without blaming Henry for doing what was, for a king, politically inevitable. What we do find hard to swallow, though, is the coldly self-righteous way he chooses to reject his former boon companion and win the approval of respectable society; and it is hard to believe that an Elizabethan audience, however ardently monarchist, would not also have had divided feelings at this point. We should not be too much surprised, therefore, to find similar streaks of hypocrisy and opportunism in Henry's character during his French expedition. However friendly, even brotherly, he appears during his incognito conversation with his common soldiers, as soon as he is alone again, he complains of his 'hard condition . . . subject to the breath of every fool'. And he goes on philosophizing plaintively until he finds that his wretched subjects enjoy their simple pastoral lives much better than he his ceremony, because he must keep watch day and night 'to maintain the peace, whose hours the peasant best advantages'.

This does not come altogether convincingly from a king whose main aim and occupation we have seen to be the waging of war and is bound to raise some doubts about the arguments he has used to convince the soldiers of the righteousness of his cause. Coming from the home of the good soldier Schweik, I appreciate with immense relish the spirit of deflated heroism and ironic common sense entertained by Court, Bates and Williams in the

face of war hysteria shared by both the English and the French
aristocrats. Not that the soldiers are afraid of fighting. They go
to it lustily enough when they see no other way of defending
themselves and their country. But before that they give the disguised king a gruelling time, asking him some really sticky questions about the welfare, both physical and spiritual, of soldiers
who die in an unjust war. Even when in the end they seem reason-
ably pacified, it is not difficult to perceive that the King's answers
leave much to be desired. Above all, they avoid any direct answer
to the most delicate point: whether the war against France is
really just or not. The contradictions within this telling scene are,
in fact, not resolved by Shakespeare, only stated.

Nor are the implications of Henry's courtship of Katharine
beyond criticism. Although we have clarified his offending bluff-
ness as behaviour fit for a soldier, there is a seamy side to his
wooing that cannot be so easily explained away. I mean the fact
that Katharine is regarded by everybody (including herself), and
by Henry in the first place, as part of the war spoils resulting
from the Agincourt victory. Henry puts it again quite bluntly
when Katharine coyly expresses her doubts whether it is possible
for her to love the enemy of France. Says Henry in a cock-sure
tone: 'No, it is not possible you should love the enemy of France,
Kate, but in loving me you should love the friend of France; for
I love France so well that I will not part with a village of it; I will
have it all mine. And, Kate, when France is mine and I am yours,
then yours is France and you are mine' (v ii 169–75).

It would not be fair to take Henry's humorous love-making
too seriously. His lady-killing attitude somewhat resembles the
cracking of a good-humoured Petruchio's whip over another
Kate. More clearly than in the early comedy we can see here the
amorous play of a pair of Renaissance lovers who use the old
crude farce of the taming of a shrew as a background for both
concealing and surprisingly revealing their own feelings, abounding in passionate intensity and new human dignity. Also we should
bear in mind the often very practical and businesslike character
of Elizabethan marriages in general. But for all that it has to be
conceded that Henry's marriage is essentially political, with all

the implications such marriages bring as their dowry, and that Shakespeare sees it as such with all his penetrating truthfulness.

Henry, in fact, unlike his creator, is often content with half-truths. He uses them with so much readiness and rhetorical convincingness that he often succeeds in persuading both his friends and his enemies, as well as, one suspects, himself. That is perhaps why he is also able to persuade so large a proportion of his modern audience.

But to less idealistic interpreters Henry reveals a less comforting but perhaps more rewarding dramatic character of a conquering king who has to pay a heavy human toll for his success. His good qualities are seen as reaching their richest and most interesting point by being both contrasted with, and dynamized by, equally potent qualities of the opposite tendency. The result is a double triumph: that of Henry and of truth. In the very act of apotheosis Shakespeare tears down Henry's godlike aureole and shows that 'in his nakedness he appears but a man'. A man with victorious laurels – and bleeding wounds.

A similar polarization may be observed in Shakespeare's vision of the French war as a whole. The most poignant contradiction here is that between the glory and the horror of war. To get an insight into the contradictory structure of the play, it is enough to compare the fiery, school-room-resounding poetry of the King before Harfleur

> Once more unto the breach, dear friends, once more;
> Or close the wall up with our English dead.   (III i 1–2)

with the chilling prose of Private Bates commenting upon the King's bravery on the eve of Agincourt:

He may show what outward courage he will; but I believe, as cold a night as 'tis, he could wish himself in Thames up to the neck; and so I would he were, and I by him, at all adventures, so we were quit here.   (IV i 112–16)

Still more chilling are the comments of Private Williams who reminds the King of 'all those legs and arms and heads, chopp'd off in a battle' that are going to 'join together at the latter day, and

cry all "We died at such a place" – some swearing, some crying
for a surgeon, some upon their wives left poor behind them, some
upon the debts they owe, some upon their children rawly left'
(IV i 134–40).

The contrasting of war heroics with suffering human beings
is only one of Shakespeare's strands in his realistic panorama of
war. He goes further to introduce into it, against all the patriotic
fervour, some very unflattering portraits of the English gentle-
men-rankers out on a French spree. Lieutenant Bardolph,
Ancient Pistol, and Corporal Nym, all three the brightest buds
of London brothels, do very little fighting, except in their bom-
bastic words. They are experts in quite another branch of soldier-
ing, that of looting. Their actual leader is Pistol and their
war-cry is his fustian on their leave-taking:

> Let us to France, like horse-leeches, my boys,
> To suck, to suck, the very blood to suck.
>
> (II iii 55–6)

Of course, they are not as bloodthirsty as all that. They know
easier methods by which their 'profits will accrue'. They are
extremely lightfingered with regard to all kinds of 'chattels and
movables', not excepting Church sacraments. And even though
Bardolph and Nym do not get away with their 'Loo! loo! Lulu!
Loot!' and are hanged in the end, Pistol survives all calamities
and steals back to England to steal there anew with added experience.

Finally, one more contrast appears in the complex unity of the
play, being displayed again not so much perhaps out of pre-
meditated purpose as out of true observation of reality. This is the
different approach to war by the statesmen and generals, both
English and French, and by the common soldiers. The statesmen,
and King Henry above all, start war in great style primarily to
divert internal dissension and to acquire new corners in foreign
lands. The Courts, Bateses and Williamses go to war nilly-nilly,
with a good deal of grumbling. Yet once they are in it, they fight
tooth and nail for their country and their king. To them war is
not an arena for winning honour, or profit, but an altar before

which they confess their love for England. And the king saves his soul and human face only when he comes to know and accept their standpoint, when he leads them as the brother and father of the whole nation.

Thus one of the essential features of Shakespeare's humanism emerges. It consists in the fusion, both in form and content, of the advanced social thinking of the sixteenth-century European humanists, who had set up the example of an ideal, though utopian governor, with the attitudes and feelings of the English people, particularly their moral integrity and sharp sense of reality. This fusion represents one of Shakespeare's greatest achievements.

The contradictions, contrasts and fusion that we have noticed within *Henry V* can be understood still better if we see the play not only in the context of the tetralogy of which it is the climax but in the light of (and indeed as the expression of) Shakespeare's whole vision of history.

Professor Jan Kott has recently remarked that Shakespeare's Histories are all concerned with the struggle for power and 'always, with Shakespeare, the struggle for power is divested of all mythology, presented in its purest form', and he goes on to suggest that the image of history that merges from the plays is one of an unchanging mechanism, a great stairway leading to an abyss.

It has a powerful impact on us, this image of history, repeated so often by Shakespeare. History is a great staircase which a line of kings endlessly ascends. Each step, each pace towards the summit, is marked by murder, perjury and treason. . . . The kings change. But the staircase remains the same.[6]

There is much that is true and telling in such an analysis, yet it surely leaves out something essential, perhaps because Kott, in his chapter on the Histories, concentrates on the Richards to the virtual exclusion of the Henries. What is left out is Shakespeare's acute realization of the emergence of the national monarchy of the Tudors as a new force which in some way or other resolves the contradictions of the English historical past.

The tetralogy consisting of *Richard II*, *Henry IV* and *Henry V*
is the nearest thing in Elizabethan literature to a realistic national
epic. It is set in the past, yet more than any other group of
Shakespeare's plays, it tells us what Tudor England was actually
like. We watch the events of late fourteenth- and early fifteenth-
century England and we see the England of Shakespeare's own
time coming to life before our eyes.

In *Richard II* we witness the passing of the medieval world,
a world of stable values and ceremonial actions. The structure of
the play, the very language of it, reflects, not without sympathy
and even a lyrical nostalgia, a past world, whose tone is set by
the formal challenges and decorums of the opening scene. One
might almost say that whereas the episode of the tennis balls in
Henry V already points towards the modern world of popular
international sport – test matches and Davis cups – the gages in
Richard II look back to the sport of the medieval tournament,
or even beyond. And when Richard II is deposed and conducted
to prison we know in our bones that the new men are indeed new,
different in some fundamental way. Bolingbroke, though a feudal
baron among feudal barons, belongs to a different world from
Richard and will be a different king.

Henry IV, in its two marvellous parts, is in this sense a transi-
tion play. The old world, reincarnated for a moment in the
chivalric Hotspur, is on the way out; but the new world has yet
to be born. The crown he has usurped sits very uneasily on
Bolingbroke's head: he is tormented by the past (Richard) and
fears the future (Hal). And *Henry IV*, amidst so much else, tells
us, almost in the terms of a Morality, of the making – the education and testing – of the new king who is to replace the transitional
figure of Bolingbroke. Hal must defeat Hotspur (the knightly
past) and understand – even, up to a point, identify himself with –
Falstaff and his cronies (the Commons). Like Elizabeth herself he
must get a whiff of the people, not as they ought to be but as
they are.

The contradiction which Henry IV cannot solve is that he has
seen the necessity of doing away with Richard, yet feels at the
same time that he himself is a usurper. It is not a contradiction

that can be resolved in abstract terms within the ideology and sanctities of the old world which Henry IV still accepts. Yet it has to be resolved, historically by England and the Tudors, artistically by Shakespeare the Elizabethan dramatist. And it is resolved by Henry V, though not, as we have seen, without human cost.

The sin of usurpation is forgotten and the bona fides of the new monarchy established by the act that links Henry most firmly with the future, with the Tudor state in general and in particular with the Elizabeth who has defeated the Spanish Armada. The sin which has tormented Henry IV is exorcized, not by time or argument, but by his son's victory over the French at Agincourt. Hal's education has not been in vain. Henry V is the hero of the tetralogy and able to settle its haunting problems for one reason above all – he is the new *national* king, the herald of the Tudor monarchy which is no longer a monarchy of the old type, but something different and necessary.

It adds to Shakespeare's greatness that he can divine, at the very moment of reaching his historical synthesis, the destructive and ultimately self-destructive nature of the new men and their new ways. This divining glimpse in *Henry V* points forward to some of the conflicts in the great tragedies.

SOURCE: *Shakespeare in a Changing World* ed. Arnold Kettle (1964).

NOTES

1. The list can only be tentative because the chronology of Shakespeare's plays is a vexed problem of long standing. For our purposes, however, there is no need to go into the innumerable discussions of Shakespearian scholars. Two important and sound views are presented in E. K. Chambers's *William Shakespeare: a study of facts and problems* (Oxford, 1930), 1 243–74, and in James G. McManaway's 'Recent Studies in Shakespeare's Chronology', in *Shakespeare Survey 3* (1950) 22–33.

2. New Cambridge *Henry V*, ed. J. Dover Wilson (Cambridge, 1947) p. xxiv.

3. This observation already appears in the classic book of the American historian, E. P. Cheyney, *A History of England from the Defeat of the Armada to the Death of Elizabeth*, 2 vols (1914, 1926). It has been developed by the literary historians, notably by Lily B. Campbell, *Shakespeare's Histories: mirrors of Elizabethan policy* (San Marino, 1947), P. A. Jorgensen, *Shakespeare's Military World* (Berkeley and Los Angeles, 1956), and H. J. Webb.

4. e.g. Samuel Johnson, or, to give a modern instance, E. M. W. Tillyard, *Shakespeare's History Plays* (1944). Dr Tillyard considers Henry's speech to Katharine to be 'a piece of sheer writing down to the populace' (309). Later on he adds a highly sophisticated speculation: 'The coarseness of Henry's courtship of Katharine is curiously exaggerated; one can almost say hectic: as if Shakespeare took a perverse delight in writing up something he had begun to hate' (p. 313).

5. Derek Traversi, in his recent monograph, *Shakespeare from Richard II to Henry V* (Stanford, University Press, 1957), arrives at somewhat similar conclusions: 'The inspiration of *Henry V* is, in its deeper moments (which do not represent the whole play), critical, analytic, exploratory ...' (pp. 197–8).

6. Jan Kott, *Shakespeare Notre Contemporain* (Paris, 1962) p. 17. [*Editor's note*. English edition, *Shakespeare Our Contemporary*, tr. B. Taborski (1964; 2nd ed. 1967).]

A. C. Sprague

SHAKESPEARE'S *HENRY V*:
A PLAY FOR THE STAGE (1964)

Henry V, first acted in wartime before a popular audience, was written in praise of an English national hero and soldier king. Though by no means without shadows, it is on the whole a clear, straight-forward history, and certain subtleties of interpretation, as that Henry was tricked by selfish ecclesiastics into fighting what was in fact a war of pure aggression, seem out of keeping with its occasion and purpose. Shakespeare was not tactless. Nor does it appear likely that a play so busily occupied as this one is with a single military event should prove at last to be an exposition of Renaissance thought on the nature of kingship. *Henry V* is no more a scholar's play than it is a giddy one.

Revived in 1738, it was acted rather often during the remainder of the century, sometimes with the Chorus omitted and sometimes with coronation pageantry added. 'Gentleman' Smith and the handsome Spranger Barry were liked as Henry. The French wars gave point to many speeches. On 7 February 1804, when the play was performed in Manchester, threats of invasion from across the Channel were being met with defiance. The appropriateness of Shakespeare's history, 'abounding, as it does, with loyal sentiments, and being descriptive of one of our greatest victories over the French', was commented upon by the critic of the Manchester *Townsman*. He noticed, too, that the local Henry, Mr Huddard, had slightly altered the text. In 'addressing the soldiers before the battle, in that speech, ending "Cry God for Harry, England, and St George!" he had read, "Cry God for Harry, England, and *King George*!" whether this was a *lapsus linguae*, or whether his *loyalty* provoked the expression, I must leave to Mr Huddard to determine.'

Meanwhile, John Kemble, who was good at defying the Corsican tyrant (witness his Rolla in Sheridan's *Pizarro*), had resumed the part of Henry, after an interval, at Drury Lane. Although Kemble liked pomp and was certainly not uninterested in detail, he paid little heed to historical propriety, and A.A., in the *Monthly Mirror* for December 1801, had grounds for complaint. His description of what might be termed a 'pre-archaeological production' is of curious interest. King Henry's throne consisted of a 'few steps' and a 'modern arm chair'. The Boar's Head, of which traces including the 'stone sign' were extant as recently as 1788, was a 'modern country inn for drovers'; Southampton, as represented by the scene painter, had 'modern ships, a lighthouse, &c.'; and before Agincourt the English camp was 'an extensive view of a modern camp arrangement, from the general's marquee to the common soldier's tent'. In describing the costumes, A.A. is equally observant, equally censorious. Kemble's tailor had, he admits, 'gone a century or so back for some sort of rayment' for the King, but it failed to match: 'he has picked up a jerken, cloak, boots, and high-topped gloves of Charles I's reign; but the neckband, is of your Oliverian trim; a cap of Elizabeth's time, and an odd sort of a crown stuck round its brims, a ribband, and the George', assigned only in Henry VIII's time. Of the other characters, Fluellen had on 'a petit maitre's small laced cocked hat' and Pistol, who bore a cudgel – 'an odd weapon for a soldier' – wore 'a modern enormous parade cocked hat'. The two bishops were austerely got up in 'the present Protestant black gown and lawn sleeves, wigs, square caps, &c. &c.!' and no one wore any armour.

For a generation the play's history becomes less cheerful than it had been. This was the time of Edmund Kean's shocking breakdown as King Henry and of the prejudiced criticism of Hazlitt and Leigh Hunt. Oxberry, in 1823, was satisfied that *Henry V* had 'rarely been very attractive in representation', lacking as it did 'exciting bustle', in its plot, and 'female interest'. The charms of the new archaeological staging were needed to restore the piece to popularity. Macready's celebrated production, in 1839, was the first in a line which continued with Charles Kean's, in 1859, and Charles Calvert's, at the Prince's Theatre, Manchester, in 1872. Calvert's production was exported to America, where it flourished, returning to England, and at last London, only in 1879. It supplemented Shakespeare by means of an interpolated tableau, 'The Battle of Agincourt', and an 'historical episode', the 'Reception of King Henry the Fifth on Entering London'. As described in the Manchester press, some three hundred persons appeared in this last scene, including not only women looking anxiously for their loved ones among the returning soldiers, but also, 'a group of girls, attired to represent angels ... with golden trumpets and fitting music'.[1] Much use was made of incidental music, with 'no idea, of course, of converting the play into a melodrama' but merely to accompany the action, as at Harfleur with 'the march from "Tancredi" ', or at Agincourt with passages from Verdi's *Macbeth*. But the chief emphasis, thanks to Calvert himself and the architect Alfred Darbyshire, was on the recreation of a particular period, even to its heraldry and the actual banners and shields used. Only, as was pointed out a little tactlessly at the time, 'the armour and appointments of the English army at Agincourt' looked rather 'too fresh and bright'.[2] (The theatre, in such matters, had its own sense of decorum.) It remained for Henry James, when the Calvert production was brought to New York, to expose the 'fallacy' upon which its 'scenic splendours' rested.

Illusion, as such an enterprise proposes to produce it, is absolutely beyond the compass of the stage. The compromise with verisimilitude is not materially slighter than in the simple days before 'revivals' had come into fashion. To assent to this you have only to look at the grotesqueness of the hobby-horses on the field of Agincourt and at the uncovered rear of King Harry's troops, when they have occasion to retire under range of your opera-glass.[3]

James liked young George Rignold as the King. 'He was "worth looking at and listening to".' And Rignold, along with the white horse, 'Crispin', which he rode on the stage each night, was long associated with the play. Dutton Cook pictures this actor at Drury Lane in 1879:

As, falchion in hand, clothed in complete steel, with a richly emblazoned tabard, he stands in that spot so prized by the histrionic mind, the exact centre of the stage, the limelight pouring upon him from the flies its most dazzling rays, and declaims speech after speech to his devoted followers, he presents as striking a stage figure as I think I ever saw.

Cook speaks of the extraordinary enthusiasm which Rignold's performance aroused, adding, perhaps a little drily: 'Of course subtlety of interpretation was not required; *Henry V* is not an intellectual character.'[4]

The treatment of Shakespeare's history on the stage remained much as it had been. Of three productions in 1900 (Benson and Waller both gave *Henry V* in London), that of Richard Mansfield in New York, 3 October, was most completely in the upholstered, heroic manner. In the preface to his acting edition, Mansfield refers to the usual conception of Henry as a part requiring strong lungs rather than intelligence. This he deplores. Among the inducements which had led him to choose the play were 'a consideration of its healthy and virile tone (so diametrically in contrast to many of the performances now current); . . . the lesson it teaches of Godliness, honour, loyalty, courage, cheerfulness and perseverance; its beneficial influence upon young and old;' and, inevitably, 'the opportunity it affords for a pictorial representation of the costumes and armour, manners and customs, of that interesting period'. Mansfield introduced, accordingly, the now familiar tableau of the Battle of Agincourt, with painted soldiers reinforcing the live ones, and the equally trite return of the victorious army to London, with Henry once more on a white horse and, as extraordinary members of the procession, 'six English prophets and six English kings'.[5]

Change, a change in the whole approach to Shakespeare's history, came at last with the work of William Poel. Poel produced *Henry V* for Ben Greet's company at the Memorial Theatre, as a special matinée, 23 October 1901. Aiming at Elizabethan simplicity, he used no scenery – merely curtains and a small gallery at the back. The costumes, too, were Elizabethan.[6] Stratford seems not to have been much interested; nor, I am sorry to say, was Boston when Ben Greet's players gave a performance at Jordan Hall four years later. H. T. Parker, newly come to *The Transcript* and not yet the oracle he became for many of us in later years, wrote grumblingly of the 'pseudo-Elizabethan' mounting, and in a company which included Sybil and Russell Thorndike, Fritz Leiber, and Dudley Digges, praised only Greet himself, as Pistol.[7]

Poel's influence, in part personal, for with all his eccentricity there was a touch of genius in the man, in part the influence of an idea, shows more and more clearly from the time of the First World War. Martin-Harvey in special performances of *Henry V* at His Majesty's in 1916 had only two intermissions and avoided pausing between scenes by playing many of them well forward before closed curtains.[8] In 1930 Bridges-Adams and, at the Old Vic in 1921, Robert Atkins gave the play in full, or nearly so, the former with unpretentious scenery and Mr Atkins (a follower of Poel) with none at all.[9]

Poel and the earlier advocates of a return to Elizabethan staging for Elizabethan plays worked under the gravest disadvantages. They had a stage, or more accurately, perhaps, the idea of a stage, but no theatre to go with it. Existing theatres when obtainable were wholly unsuited to their purposes: better some obscure hall; better, as Atkins was to discover in 1936, the 'cheerless and unpromising surroundings' of the prize ring at Blackfriars! Their experiments remained always incomplete. With time, indeed, the character of the movement changed. Its antiquarian phase has largely passed. What is now known, with broad comprehensiveness, as 'the open stage' is sometimes criticized as an eccentric departure from tradition. It is no longer abused as an offence against progress.

In 1956 *Henry V* was twice given excitingly on open stages. Douglas Seale produced it in Sanders Theatre (Harvard), early in the summer, and the Stratford Ontario Festival Company brought their production of it to the Assembly Hall, Edinburgh, at the end of August. Seale's stage had a towering structure built at the back, with visible stairs on each side, a gallery, and high above this a platform. During the assault on Harfleur, vividly

simulated, both these upper levels were used by the French, who
flung down from the higher one a scaling ladder momentarily
raised by the attackers. The English, who had rushed down the
aisles of the theatre to gain the stage, now retreated, leaving
Henry exactly where he could address them, and us, to best
advantage. The illusion approached, though it did not equal, that
of the storm-swept decks of a ship at sea in Bernard Miles's
Elizabethan *Tempest* in 1952, and in each case brevity was an
important factor. There was no time in which to inquire how the
spell had been cast. The Canadian company did well by Harfleur,
too, as by much else in the play, and their performance was swift
and vigorous. It was, I thought, shabbily dealt with by some of
the English reviewers, as if out of hostility towards any successful
production on the open stage.

In the long debate on how Shakespeare's plays should be given,
the choruses in *Henry V* have often been cited. In them, it is
generally agreed, Shakespeare's own voice is heard, not that of
any one of his characters. The very anonymity of 'Chorus' – he
is not even Gower, not even Time or Rumour – makes the
identification all but certain. And he speaks, Shakespeare speaks,
of the impossibility of doing justice to his play's great theme 'on
this unworthy scaffold', and of the few

> most vile and ragged foils
> Right ill-dispos'd in brawl ridiculous,

who must disgrace, in attempting to represent, the Battle of Agincourt. That Shakespeare was experiencing a sense of the inadequacy of drama as a form seems clear. What must be questioned
is the cheerful assumption that if only he could have seen his play
mounted by Charles Kean, say, or Richard Mansfield, he would
then have been perfectly satisfied. The choruses, it is noteworthy,
rarely fulfil a utilitarian purpose. Either they expatiate on matters
sufficiently set forth in the dialogue, as in the great Fourth Act
nocturnal, or they go out of their way to describe what a novelist
might describe, or a narrative poet – the splendour, for instance
of the English fleet sailing towards Harfleur. Their appeal, many
times repeated, is not the conventional one for attentive silence.

More was expected of the audience, this time: a sustained participation; the full exertion of just those powers of the imagination which the Elizabethan stage had taught them to use.

Henry the Fifth is 'the mirror of all Christian kings' and 'this grace of kings ... this Star of England'. The seriousness of the choruses is as remarkable as their eloquence. For Shakespeare in this most commemorative, most epic of the histories is taking sides. He is not in the least detached, nor even momentarily ironic.[10] *Henry V* in its way is almost as damaging to stock generalizations about the dramatist as *Troilus and Cressida*.

Earlier I suggested that the hostility expressed towards Henry by many critics was in part a reaction against the manner in which the character had come to be expounded. In the schoolroom the morals of Shakespeare's works loomed even larger than their syntax. Thus the introduction to the play in the Oxford and Cambridge Series – an influential edition many times reprinted – contains a three-fold comparison between Richard II, who is treated as a thoroughly reprehensible sort of king, Henry IV, and Henry V. The last-named was 'a practical man' (Richard, by the same token, was a dreamer) 'combining strength of character with a joyous humour, justice with bravery, dignity with simplicity, piety with martial enthusiasm; in a word, an ideal king in whom all the good national qualities are seen in their highest perfection'. The French in this play were to the English about what Richard was to Henry. 'Not the least shallow of these vain, supercilious, and contemptuous braggarts is the Dauphin. ... What a contrast to this frivolity and bombast is the pious humility and fear of God of King Henry!'[11] (Were there boys, I wonder, who from that moment tried very hard to *like* the 'Dolphin'?)

Criticism of Henry, during the last years of Victoria's reign and after, has concentrated on a few episodes and speeches. There was his entering upon the war with France, encouraged by bishops, and the order he gives his soldiers, under attack, to cut the throats of their prisoners. There was the mention he makes in his prayer of having had masses said for the soul of Richard II, and there was his alleged want of interest in the anonymous

private soldiers slain in battle. Finally, as a grim background for
these misdoings, there was his 'betrayal', as it has often been
called, of friendly Jack Falstaff at the end of *Henry IV, Part 2*, an
episode, already discussed, which prejudiced many critics against
him. He has been denounced, accordingly, as hypocritical, cruel,
superstitious, sanctimonious, snobbish, and in the *Athenaeum*
soon after the First World War, as 'this fearful cockerel'.[12]

The identity of the person thus denounced is not always clear.
At times, he seems more like the Henry of the chronicles than like
Shakespeare's hero. In Holinshed we are left with few illusions
as to the origin of the war with France. Beginning with the insult
of the tennis balls, Holinshed tells us next of the bill to curb
ecclesiastical abuses and of the attempt by the clergy to 'mooue
the kings mood with some sharpe inuention, that he should not
regard the importunate petitions of the commons'.[13] The device
hit upon is the Archbishop's exposition – 'his prepared tale', as
it is described here – of the workings of the Salic Law, accompanied by an offer of the money voted by Convocation. (As
Michael Drayton wrote of the Archbishop, in *The Battaile of
Agincourt*, 1609,

> He found a warre with *France*, must be the way
> To dash this Bill,

and the speech he made subsequently was prompted by 'the
Clergies feare'.[14]) In Shakespeare's play, the effect is different.
The Dauphin's insult, shifted to the end of the sequence, gives it
a rousing climax. The speech on the Salic Law is dissociated from
the reform bill. It is the King who takes the initiative, adjuring
the Archbishop to state whether or not the English claim is a just
one. Far from being 'trapped' into declaring war by 'a group of
men whose sole and quite explicit motive is to preserve their
own revenues'[15] – or, worse still, from turning to the Archbishop
for what he knows very well the Archbishop will tell him out of
self-interest[16] – he insists passionately that he be told the truth.[17]
And the Archbishop, as we recognize at once in the theatre,
exists simply to inform us; is as authoritative in what he says as

one of Shakespeare's doctors, whose word, in the theatre again, we accept without hesitation.

The determination of the King to be satisfied, even while his nobles were already clamouring for war, and his joy when Canterbury at length assured him of the justness of his title, were admirably brought out by Christopher Plummer in the Canadian production. Except, indeed, for the passing aberration of representing one or both of the bishops as comic characters, a grotesque expedient to make their long speeches more palatable,[18] the scene has not to my knowledge been falsified in performance, though it has often been greatly abridged.

The slaughter of Henry's French prisoners, who if a new battle had begun in earnest might have been the source of grave danger to their captors, is all too graphically described by Holinshed. It has been urged by Kittredge, Dover Wilson, and others that the drastic order issued by the King was a necessary one, though even the chronicler speaks of it as 'contrarie to his accustomed gentlenes'.[19] Shakespeare, at this point, has the King leave the stage, to return deeply angered by what he has seen at his camp, where the defenceless boys and lackeys had been put to death by a group of the enemy. In several recent productions, business has been interpolated here, usually with the omission of a fair number of lines. The Boy, whom we know and like, once Falstaff's page, is shown being set upon by Frenchmen, or his limp body is borne in by Fluellen.

> I was not angry since I came to France
> Until this instant,

the King says; and the savageness of his order to cut the throats of the prisoners no longer offends us.

Too much, surely, has been made of Henry's comment as he lays down the paper containing the list of English dead,

> None else of name; and of all other men
> But five-and-twenty,

as if the words were a betrayal, somehow, of his protestation of brotherhood with his soldiers. The anonymity is no necessary mark of contempt.[20] It is Montjoy, the French herald who comes, in his own words,

> To sort our nobles from our common men;
> For many of our princes (woe the while!)
> Lie drown'd and soak'd in mercenary blood;
> So do our vulgar drench their peasant limbs
> In blood of princes.

Nor will Montjoy himself, a lonely, desolate figure, be found undeserving of pity when the scene is played with understanding.[21]

As for Henry's prayer before battle, many malicious things have been written about it by critics who appear vexed that Shakespeare did not choose to make this mediaeval king a Protestant before his time. The speech in question begins, it is noticeable, with concern for his soldiers. Then for the last time in this sequence of histories Richard is named, and the sin of Bolingbroke. Bolingbroke's son speaks of 'good works' he has performed in seeking pardon. He has been accused of bargaining with the Almighty here, but the close of the speech forbids this interpretation.

> More will I do!
> *Though all that I can do is nothing worth,*
> Since that my penitence comes after all,
> Imploring pardon.[22]

Henry's humility at this moment, and indeed his modesty throughout are an individualizing trait, but one which seems more in keeping with his own time than that of Shakespeare. The flamboyant Elizabethans of Yeats's essay on Edmund Spenser, or those strange beings imagined by Lytton Strachey and Virginia Woolf, were not, one is sure, among his contemporaries.

On the stage, Henry has come to be played in a different manner from that of Rignold and Mansfield. Even before 1914, *The Times* called attention to Benson's 'grave and thoughtful King'.[23] Olivier and Clunes, Richard Burton and Christopher Plummer, each has struck this note. In contrasting Olivier's thoughtful King with Waller's hearty one, Gordon Crosse referred to the 'low, anxious tone' in which the later Henry answered Fluellen's

'As long as your majesty is an honest man', 'God keep me so.'[24]
Clunes one associates with the searchingly analytical soliloquy,
'Upon the King', in the first scene of Act IV; Plummer, with the
quietly perceptive, almost wistful line at its close,

> The day, my friends, and all things stay for me;

and Burton with the moment when he heard the name of the
man just executed: 'one Bardolph, if your Majesty know the man.
...' To some conservatives, this new Henry of the actors has
seemed a little tame. He has remained human still, and likeable,
and to that extent is more Shakespearian than the monstrous
being sometimes conjured up in the study.

> O, now, who will behold
> The royal captain of this ruin'd band
> Walking from watch to watch, from tent to tent,
> Let him cry 'Praise and glory on his head'. . . .

Words like these, addressed as they were to an English popular
audience, cannot be disregarded in arriving at a soundly conceived interpretation of the character – and their import is clear.
Shakespeare, on occasion, can be his own best interpreter.

SOURCE: *Shakespeare's Histories: plays for the stage* (Society for
Theatre Research, 1964).

NOTES

1. *Shakespeare's Historical Play of Henry the Fifth, As Produced
under the Direction of Charles Calvert at the Prince's Theatre, Manchester, September, 1872. Opinions of the Press* (Manchester, *1872*) pp.
11, 21.

2. Ibid. p. 24. Darbyshire writes eloquently of the production in his
book, *The Art of the Victorian Stage* (London and Manchester, 1907)
pp. 41 ff.

3 *The Scenic Art*, ed. Allan Wade (New Brunswick, 1948) pp. 26,
27. Some 1200 lines, or a little over one-third of the play, are cut in the

acting edition, based on this production, published by French in 1875. Promptbooks, I fancy, might show that in actual performance many more went by the board.

4. *Nights at the Play* (1883) II 230, 231. On Rignold's Henry see also *Opinions of the English Speaking Press on George Rignold as Henry V* (c. 1880); G. C. D. Odell's *Annals of the New York Stage* (1927–49) IX 528 ff, X 10, 122; J. J. Chapman, *A Glance Towards Shakespeare* (Boston, 1922) p. 52; and, for the popularity of 'Crispin', L. J. Davidson, 'Shakespeare in the Rockies', in *Shakespeare Quarterly*, IV (1953) 45.

5. *The Richard Mansfield Acting Version of King Henry V* (New York, 1901). See also Norman Hapgood, *The Stage in America 1897–1900* (New York and London, 1901) pp. 174–9. Hapgood praises the picture of Henry's wedding, which concluded the play. Here, too, Mansfield had been anticipated by Calvert.

6. M. C. Day and J. C. Trewin, *The Shakespeare Memorial Theatre* (London and Toronto, 1932) pp. 137, 138; Ruth Ellis, *The Shakespeare Memorial Theatre* (1948) p. 28. See also Robert Speaight, *William Poel and the Elizabethan Revival* (Melbourne, London, and Toronto, 1954) p. 282.

7. *Boston Evening Transcript*, 6 Dec 1905 (in Blinn Shakespeare Scrapbooks, Harvard Theatre Collection).

8. *Autobiography* (1933) pp. 461 ff.

9. Archibald Haddon, *Green Room Gossip* (1922) p. 63; *Athenaeum*, 22 Oct 1920, and Royal Shakespeare Theatre cuttings; Carroll scrapbooks in the Victoria and Albert Museum.

Tyrone Guthrie's production in 1937 is remarkable for the imaginative use of massed banners, red, and blue and silver – as setting. (For the manner in which flags on the stage were formerly 'displayed by means of a scythe-like curve of cane at the top, to prevent their drooping in natural folds', see Godfrey Turner, 'Show and its Value', in *Theatre*, 1 May 1884.)

10. That the unusual method followed by Shakespeare in this play, his insistence on 'telling us', is responsible for the dislike felt by many readers, who do not enjoy being told, is suggested by Professor Peter Alexander in his edition of Shakespeare's histories (London and Glasgow, 1955), pp. 273 ff; cf also R. M. Alden, *Shakespeare* (New York, 1922) p. 181. A warning against accepting the Chorus 'without qualification' as 'the author's voice' is sounded by Clifford Leech, 'Shakespeare's Prologues and Epilogues', in *Studies in Honor of T. W. Baldwin* (1958).

11. *Henry V*, ed. F. Marshall and Stanley Wood (1900, 1930) pp. xvi, xvii. *Henry V* and *Richard II* were two of the plays most frequently studied in English schools of the period (John D. Jones, 'Shakespeare

in English Schools', in *Shakespeare Jahrbuch*, XLII (1906). I am indebted to Professor Terence Spencer for this reference.

12. D. L. M., reviewing Bridges-Adams's production at the Strand, 22 Oct 1920 (he was answered at a number of points by William Poel a week later). For the abusive treatment of Henry at this time, see also Gerald Gould, above, pp. 81–94.

13. 1587 Edition, III 545, 546.

14. *The Battaile of Agincourt*, in *Works*, ed. J. W. Hebel (Oxford, 1931–41) lines 71, 72, 179.

15. Charlton, *Shakespeare, Politics and Politicians* (1929) p. 16; cf Harbage, *As They Liked It* (New York, 1947) pp. 12, 13.

16. Bradley, *Oxford Lectures on Poetry* (1909) p. 257.

17. See Lily Campbell, *Shakespeare's 'Histories': mirrors of Elizabethan policy* (San Marino, California, 1947) p. 260, Irving Ribner, *The English History Play in the Age of Shakespeare* (Princeton, 1957) p. 189, and especially Dover Wilson's Introduction to the play.

18. A comic Canterbury (played by Harcourt Williams) was introduced in Tyrone Guthrie's Old Vic production in 1937; Ely was still made ridiculous at the same theatre in 1955 when, under Michael Benthall, the first scene in the play was omitted altogether.

19. 1587 Edition, III 554.

20. Cf Paul Jorgensen, *Shakespeare's Military World* (Berkeley and Los Angeles, 1956) p. 121, who cites also the Messenger's account of the casualties, at the beginning of *Much Ado About Nothing*,

> But few of any sort, and none of name.

Ivor Brown calls the King's words 'ugly to our ears' (*Theatre 1955–6*, p. 50) but distinguishes between a reader's Henry and 'the Happy Warrior' we accept in the theatre.

21. See *The Times*, 1 Dec 1931, 13 Feb 1957; and for an unmercifully chauvinistic interpretation of the episode, cf Mrs Inchbald's introduction to *Henry V* (1808).

22. IV i 319–21 (the second 'do' is emphatic, according to Kittredge). See Una Ellis-Fermor, *Frontiers of Drama* (1945) pp. 43 ff, and for the defence H. N. Hudson, *Shakespeare: his life, art, and characters* (Boston, 1872), II 129 ff.

23. 14 Sept 1911 (cutting in Blinn scrapbooks).

24. *Shakespearean Playgoing* (1953) p. 105.

Honor Matthews

THE USURPED THRONE AND
THE AMBIGUOUS HERO (1962)

IT is pleasant to imagine that Shakespeare at the age of eleven
actually witnessed the performance of the Coventry Cycle which
took place at Kenilworth in 1575.[1]

> *Lucifer*. I wyl go sythen in Goddes seat
>   Above sunne and mone and starres or sky
>   I am now set as ye may see
>   Now worship me for most mighty
>   And for your lord honour now me
>   Syttyng in my seat.
> *Deus*. Thou Lucyfer ffor thi mekyl pride
>   I byode thee fall from heaven to hell ...
>   At my commandment anoon down thou slyde
>   With mirth and joy never more to mell.
> *Lucifer*. At thy bidding this syl I werke
>   And pas from joy to peyne smerte
>   Now I am a devil full darke
>   That was an angelle bryht.[2]

If he had never heard similar words on a stage, there is no
doubt of the power of their story over his imagination, for he
dramatised such blind and arrogant rebellion against the divine
purpose, not once but many times, in terms of the illicit assumption of a throne. Apparently this symbol was already burning in
his imagination at the end of *3 Henry VI*, but it was too late
then to incorporate it as the centre of interest, for this was already
fixed elsewhere. The mind of the king-killer is never more vividly
revealed than it is in Richard of Gloucester, but his murder of
Henry VI is only one incident in the pattern of civil strife and
does not appear as more important to Richard himself than his

other murders. The later plays, however, show that it *was* more
important to Shakespeare . . .

In *Richard II* the divine pattern is so suggested as to win our
acceptance of its fitness, but this is done principally by the poetry
which describes it or alludes to it, for we never see in existence
the ordered Kingdom ruled with justice and mercy in accord
with the purposes of God. The chorus-like figures of the gardeners, who are related to this play as the equally anonymous
Father and Son are to *Henry VI*, make the comparison of state
and garden in a style as formal as that of the Elizabethan knot
and herb gardens which they praise.

> *Gardener.* Cut off the heads of too fast growing sprays,
>   That look too lofty in our commonwealth:
>   All must be even in our government. . . .
> *Servant.* Why should we in the compass of a pale
>   Keep law and form and due proportion,
>   Showing, as in a model, our firm estate,
>   When our sea-walled garden, the whole land,
>   Is full of weeds . . .
>   Her knots disordered and her wholesome herbs
>   Swarming with caterpillars?   (III iv 34–47)

Richard himself does not conform to the pattern; that is both
his sin and his tragedy, and the divine purpose is once again
thwarted as it had been in that earlier garden of our first parents.
The Commonwealth, thus first betrayed from within by the
man who frivolously left empty the place he had been divinely
deputed to fill, was defenceless before the external attack of
Bolingbroke, who by fraud and force defeated and murdered
his anointed sovereign.

It is true that it was Piers Exton's hands that actually shed
Richard's blood, and that Bolingbroke allowed Northumberland,
that 'haught insulting man', to do much of his bullying for him,
but he is none the more acceptable for that, and this 'silent king',
who was clever enough to wait while his rival walked into the
net spread for him, is clearly himself responsible for the 'trenching
war' and 'the intestine shock and furious close of civil butchery',
which he laments at the beginning of the next play. It is not long

before we are reminded of his victim, for the forceful dissyllable of
his name occurs three times in thirty lines of Act I, scene iii.

> *Worcester.* I cannot blame him: was not he proclaim'd
>   By Richard that dead is the next of blood? . . .
> *Hotspur.* But, soft, I pray you; did King Richard then
>   Proclaim my brother Edmund Mortimer
>   Heir to the crown? . . .
>   Shall it for shame be spoken in these days, . . .
>   That men of your nobility and power
>   Did gage them both in an unjust behalf, . . .
>   To put down Richard, that sweet lovely rose,
>   And plant this thorn, this canker, Bolingbroke?
>   (*1 Henry IV*, I iii 145–76)

It is accompanied by the name of the rightful heir which is hammered into the ear fourteen times before the scene ends. We hear
of noble Mortimer, revolted Mortimer, foolish Mortimer, down-
trod Mortimer, until Hotspur seems to have become the very
starling he would have taught to 'speak nothing but "Mortimer" ',
to keep the king's 'anger still in motion'.

The crime of the first play is thus brought right to the centre
of the attention and nailed there firmly at the start of the second.
This is important, for the origin of the rebellion of the northern
lords soon loses its prominence. If it were clearly developed the
rebels would inevitably become the heroes of the play, and this
no dramatist could afford to allow in the 1590s. Yet it is the logic
of the situation. It was potent in Shakespeare's imagination and it
leads to a curious and increasing ambivalence in his work which
reaches its peak in the character of Henry V.

We have already noticed Shakespeare's surprising ability to be
a voice for a discredited minority, but in his first presentation of
the rebels he does not emphasise the legitimacy of their cause.
When Hotspur and his allies define their aims (*1 Henry IV*, III i)
they do not mention the restoration of the Yorkist line but only
the division of England into three estates for themselves. In this
they commit a fault close to Richard's own when he leased his
revenues and turned his realm into a 'tenement or pelting farm'.
Later indeed Hotspur does put forward their claims as representa-

tives of the disinherited Earl of March, and vividly recapitulates
Henry's treachery to Richard, but here again Shakespeare does
not leave the rebels' cause unsmeared. The Earl of Worcester
warns Hotspur:

> ... stop all sight-holes, every loop from whence
> The eye of reason may pry in upon us:
> This absence of your father's draws a curtain,
> That shows the ignorant a kind of fear
> Before not dreamt of.   (IV i 71–5)

The imagery here is as threatening and dark as Lady Macbeth's
when she faces for a moment the full implications of her fell
purpose:

> Come, thick night,
> And pall thee in the dunnest smoke of hell,
> That my keen knife see not the wound it makes,
> Nor heaven peep through the blanket of the dark,
> To cry 'Hold, hold.'   (*Macbeth*, I v 51–5)

The extreme vividness and superficial incongruity of the images
of the peepholes in the blanket and the curtain hanging limply
from its rings show that for Shakespeare the association of hanging drapery with secret evil must have been very strong and
reinforces the suggestion that in Worcester's words the rebels
themselves are made to suggest the wrongness of their action.
Facing the Northern lords, Prince John voices the claims of the
reigning family with force and dignity:

> You have ta'en up,
> Under the counterfeited zeal of God,
> The subjects of his substitute, my father,
> And both against the peace of heaven and him
> Have here up-swarm'd them.
>   (*2 Henry IV*, IV ii 26–30)

But the substitute of this substitute of God shortly afterwards
perpetrates the most cold-blooded treachery in Gaultree Forest,
and Shakespeare adapts his source in order to give the treachery

to a member of the royal house itself. In spite of Worcester's
words the balance of sympathy here is clearly with the rebels, not
with the prince. Something seems to be compelling Shakespeare
to cloud the issue, and indeed the Tudor horror of rebellion is
obviously at work in the play, muddying the clarity of its design.
Shakespeare never forgets, however, the origin of these dilemmas and this is clear from the fact that he never allows Henry
himself to forget that the primary cause of all his misfortunes –
and ironically of other men's sins if rebellion against him be a sin
– is his own action. He says to his son:

> I know not whether God will have it so . . .
> But thou dost in thy passages of life
> Make me believe that thou art only mark'd
> For the hot vengeance and the rod of heaven
> To punish my mistreadings.
>
> (*1 Henry IV*, III ii 4–11)

He is haunted by the memory of the past; indeed there is no play
where more brilliant vignettes of past scenes are conjured up,
often by Henry, although sometimes by the rebels too. Again and
again the past intrudes on the present. Henry makes for himself
the excuse of necessity, but he always sees himself and his past in
terms of a guilt the Dead-Sea fruits of which he finally admits:

> . . . But which of you was by? –
> You, cousin Nevil, as I may remember –
> When Richard, with his eye brimful of tears,
> Then check'd and rated by Northumberland,
> Did speak these words, now proved a prophecy!
> 'Northumberland, thou ladder by the which
> My cousin Bolingbroke ascends my throne,'
> Though then, God knows, I had no such intent,
> But that necessity so bow'd the state
> That I and greatness were compelled to kiss;
> 'The time shall come, that foul sin, gathering head,
> Shall break into corruption': so went on,
> Foretelling this same time's condition,
> And the division of our amity.
>
> (*2 Henry IV*, III i 65–79)

He winces at a hint of his past by others, as when, in his hasty interruption of Northumberland he covers his pain by an outburst of temper.

> *Worcester.* Our house, my sovereign liege, little deserves
>   The scourge of greatness to be used on it;
>   And that same greatness too which our own hands
>   Have holp to make so portly.
> *North.* My lord, –
> *K. Henry.* Worcester, get thee gone; . . .
>   You have good leave to leave us: when we need
>   Your use and counsel, we shall send for you.
>   (*1 Henry IV*, I iii 10–21)

In case it be felt that the unity suggested by these continuous references to the past extends only to the first three plays, it should be remembered that the last of them occurs in the mouth of Henry V on the eve of Agincourt. It is the force with which the plays present the passage of time during which a single evil deed prolongs its influence and proliferates in unforeseen directions that makes this tetralogy so impressive as a whole, for the space it provides is used dramatically in working out to the full the implications of its theme.

At the opening of *1 Henry IV* we see the loyalty of men like Blunt beginning to attach itself sincerely to the new king, but the pattern is continually flawed or broken by the old evil, and there is a curiously moving scene at Shrewsbury when the Douglas dispatches one simulacrum after another and finds no certainly true king, even when he at last encounters Henry himself.

> *Douglas.*   . . . what art thou,
>   That counterfeit'st the person of a king?
> *Henry.* The king himself; who, Douglas, grieves at heart,
>   So many of his shadows thou hast met
>   And not the very king . . .
> *Douglas.* I fear thou art another counterfeit.   (v iv 27–35)

But can it finally be claimed that the theme of regicide and its consequences unfolded in the first three plays does in fact inform *Henry V*? I believe that it can, although the pattern is obscured by an ambiguity at the heart of the fourth play, which has led to different opinions about the basic design of the tetralogy. In his Festival production of 1951, Anthony Quayle sought its unity in the gradual 'grooming' of the Prince of Wales into England's ideal king. This attempt failed because it involved transmogrifying three characters – Richard and Bolingbroke as well as Hal himself – by frequent playing against the sense of Shakespeare's lines. We saw in Bolingbroke a modest and serene young rebel, facing a degenerate and ultimately worthless king, and this is not an accurate presentation of the relationship Shakespeare created between Richard and his successor. The play's pattern does not show Hal's development into Shakespeare's ideal monarch: it shows rather the impossibility that the murdered Richard could ever be forgotten or peace and prosperity ever arise out of blood-shed.

This interpretation is enforced by the closest of the links between the plots of *2 Henry IV* and *Henry V*. The last speech of the first play is Prince John's, and contains the lines:

> I will lay odds that, ere this year expire,
> We bear our civil swords and native fire
> As far as France.   (v v 111–13)

To distract men's thoughts from his doubtful title by foreign conquest was Henry IV's dying advice to his son, and to follow this advice is the son's first major decision of policy after ascending the throne. It seems impossible not to believe that Shakespeare was deliberately ambiguous here. When *Henry V* is performed by itself it is possible to interpret Henry as sincerely anxious to establish his rightful title to the French crown before declaring war and as genuinely convinced by the archbishop's deliberately tendentious reasoning. But when the earlier play is remembered his motives must be suspect. We know his father had considered even the re-winning of the Holy Sepulchre as a means of securing his own usurped throne. He admits he

> had a purpose now
> To lead out many to the Holy Land,
> Lest rest and lying still might make them look

> Too near unto my state. Therefore, my Harry,
> Be it thy course to busy giddy minds
> With foreign quarrels.   (*2 Henry IV*, IV v 210–15)

Such 'machiavellism' cannot possibly have been intended to win approval, yet it is in principle identical with Henry V's later conduct. The audience forgets happily enough their hero's hidden motive, and probably Shakespeare intended that they should, but he himself when writing the play can hardly have done so, and his knowledge throws an additional irony into the famous lines of Michael Williams:

> *Bates*. We know enough, if we know we are the king's subjects: if his cause be wrong, our obedience to the king wipes the crime of it out of us.
> *Williams*. But if the cause be not good, the king himself hath a heavy reckoning to make, when all those legs and arms and heads, chopped off in a battle, shall join together at the latter day and cry all 'We died at such a place'; some swearing, some crying for a surgeon, some upon their wives left poor behind them, some upon the debts they owe, some upon their children rawly left. I am afeared there are few die well that die in a battle; for how can they charitably dispose of any thing, when blood is their argument? Now, if these men do not die well, it will be a black matter for the king that led them to it; whom to disobey were against all proportion of subjection.   (IV i 130–46)

Richard's murder followed by the wars in France is really as clear an example of violence breeding violence as any that *Macbeth* itself can show, and by Henry's agonised prayer before the battle, Agincourt is indissolubly linked to Pomfret.

> Not to-day, O Lord,
> O, not to-day, think not upon the fault
> My father made in compassing the crown!
>
> (IV i 310–12)

Henry V fails as completely as do his father and his son to give his people the peace which is the intended and decorous pattern

of social life, and the direct reason of the failure of all three men
lies in their wrongful title to the throne, which accounts for the
foreign wars in the one reign as completely as it does for the civil
wars in the next.

Like his father, like Claudius, like Macbeth even, Henry V
succeeded in establishing a temporary order on an unsound
foundation, but in spite of its glamour it was as spurious as the
ceremonial of Claudius' stately court or Macbeth's ghost-
haunted banquet – a mere mockery of the god-given order which
had been violated. The price of Henry IV's rebellion was paid in
full not by himself or his son but by his grandson and the people
of his realm, and this Shakespeare must have remembered when
he wrote of the wooing of Katharine.

Shall not thou and I, between Saint Denis and Saint George,
compound a boy, half French, half English, that shall go to
Constantinople and take the Turk by the beard? shall we not?
what sayest thou, my fair flower-de-luce?   (v ii 219–24)

It was a hope that was soon to be belied.

Before the embarkation for France there is a similar though
smaller example of the equivocal treatment of historical material
to which Shakespeare was driven in this play. Considered only
in the setting of *Henry V* the motive for the treachery of Cambridge, Scroop and Grey is quite without importance, at least
for the normal playgoer whose whole attention is focused on the
heroic figure of the threatened king, while the traitors themselves
are made peculiarly repulsive by their hypocritical calls for vengeance on the drunkard whom the king forgives. But in the light
of the plays of *Henry VI* – already written by Shakespeare – it
is evident that the three men represent the cause of the murdered
Richard. The dramatist himself cannot conceivably have been
unaware of the fact, for in his own – or at the very least his company's – earlier play, these words are spoken by Earl Mortimer
to Richard of York:

Long after this, when Henry the Fifth,
Succeeding his father Bolingbroke did reign,
Thy father, Earl of Cambridge, then derived

> From famous Edmund Langley, Duke of York . . .
> Levied an army, weening to redeem
> And have install'd me in the diadem:
> But, as the rest, so fell that noble earl
> And was beheaded.   (*1 Henry VI*, II v 82–91)

In as recent a play as *1 Henry IV* Shakespeare had made the
Archbishop of York send a sealed letter (*1 Henry IV*, IV iv) 'to
my cousin Scroop' to summon him to the Yorkist forces.[3] This
man also was sent to his death by Henry for his support of the
Earl of Cambridge, whose son successfully asserted his claim to
the throne against Henry's son in the Parliament House some
thirty years later. No word of all this is uttered in defence of the
rebels in *Henry V*, but that they *had* a defence, the dramatist
very well knew; it was, however, one which no patriotic Elizabethan, lost in admiration of the usurper's son, would care to
hear.

Although the two historical tetralogies were created indepen-
dently of each other this does not mean that Shakespeare was
oblivious of Bosworth as he wrote of earlier happenings; on the
contrary he appears, very naturally, to have been increasingly
aware of the shadow of coming events as he approached the end
of *Henry V*, and this awareness must have brought him a measure
of satisfaction. It perhaps appeared to him that if the original
hubris could ever be forgiven it would be in the case of the modest
victor of Agincourt. But he allows no escape; the wages could
only be postponed not remitted, and it is possible that in the
dramatist's view the child of Henry and Katharine fulfilled his
destiny when, instead of taking the Turk by the beard at Constantinople as his father had hoped, he died in the Tower, a
vicarious sacrifice, that the sins of his grandfather might be
atoned.

Shakespeare's material dictated to him a triumph for Henry V
which should include not only military victory but a full measure
of admiring affection for this 'star of England'. Equally his
material dictated – in his view – condemnation and failure for the
archetypal rebel, the king-murderer. Within the framework of
the second tetralogy these two purposes are mutually exclusive,

but the history of their own land assured both dramatist and
audience that, while they could love their hero-king, yet they
were assured of the fulfilment of the pattern of justice which
they had been long taught to expect in the events of the world.

It is clear that, although considerable licence to tamper with
his sources, particularly by omission, evidently existed for the
Elizabethan dramatist, the material of English history became
increasingly unmalleable for Shakespeare's purposes. Rich in
themes he seized on as fertile, these stories of the kings of England could not be exploited so as to externalise what was to the
dramatist their full significance. The implications of this come
increasingly from imagery and comment, such as Michael
Williams's description of death in battle, rather than from the
structure of outward events, which may indeed be in contradiction to them, as when Henry's guilt-ridden memories of Richard's
murder occur just before the apparently 'crowning mercy' of
Agincourt. To fulfil his imaginative purpose Shakespeare needed
material which he could handle more freely; he soon found it. . . .

At the centre of Shakespeare's portrait of the Elizabethans' hero
king is the prayer before Agincourt:

> Not to-day, O Lord,
> O, not to-day, think not upon the fault
> My father made in compassing the crown!
> I Richard's body have interred new;
> And on it have bestow'd more contrite tears
> Than from it issued forced drops of blood:
> . . . More will I do.
>   (IV i 309–19)

These lines are of crucial importance; they are among the few
given to Henry that sing and do not shout or orate or merely
talk, and they occur at a critical moment, one of those points of
rest, where into the stillness words drop with a maximum of
significance. It is at such a moment and with such verse that
Shakespeare reminds us that Henry's crown is stained with blood.

Having, for whatever reason, chosen to write a play about
Henry V, for a London audience in about the year 1599, Shake-

speare had no alternative but to write of a hero – valiant, modest
and successful in war as in love. He apparently does so, recreating
the contemporary historical myth with complete success. Yet the
central figure is unaccountably difficult of assessment. This, it is
suggested, is owing to a division in the author's mind. Shakespeare respected – and very possibly in a measure shared – the
popular estimate of Henry. The country was living through a
prolonged period of crisis; men were fighting and dying in
France. Many modern critics who find the patriotism of the play
chauvinistic today responded to it wholeheartedly in the atmosphere of 1945, appreciating Sir Laurence Olivier's film at the
same level as the original audience appreciated the play. But the
dissatisfaction, the nagging doubts, returned with calmer days,
and it is difficult not to believe that Shakespeare shared them. To
him Henry's place in the historical sequence was that of successor
to the man who killed a king and one moreover who had repeatedly been presented as the direct and visible symbol of God
himself.

> Yet I well remember
> The favours of these men: were they not mine?
> Did they not sometime cry, 'all hail!' to me?
> So Judas did to Christ:
>
> *(Richard II*, IV i 167–70)

It is true that many such references are in Richard's own mouth,
and in a realistic drama their value as evidence of the dramatist's
intention would be weakened by Richard's own weaknesses, but
in a poetic play the music and rhythm of the lines are decisive in
determining an audience's response. The quality of the writing
ensures that we are ready to remember the broken looking-glass
and the shadow of a sorrow which destroyed the shadow of a
face, even on the field of Agincourt, and the dramatist cannot
have been unaware of this.

Henry V accepted his crown from his usurping father with his
eyes open.

> *King Henry.*　　　　　God knows my son,
> By what by-paths and indirect crook'd ways
> I met this crown; and I myself know well

> How troublesome it sat upon my head.
> To thee it shall descend with better quiet, . . .
> For all the soil of the achievement goes
> With me into the earth. . . .

The Prince, however, does not hesitate –

> My gracious liege,
> You won it, wore it, kept it, gave it me;
> Then plain and right must my possession be.

The casuistry could not be better emphasised, and the next couplet implies that no price is thought too high:

> Which I with more than with a common pain
> 'Gainst all the world will rightfully maintain.
> (*2 Henry IV*, IV v 184–225)

'You won it, wore it, kept it, gave it me.' It is significant that the harsh monosyllables awake in the memory echoes of a gentler voice, heard when, with unaccustomed cynicism, Richard watching the same impassive face as Hal did, remarked:

> they well deserve to have,
> That know the strong'st and surest way to get.
> (*Richard II*, III iii 200–1)

This is the perfect statement of Henry IV's claim, a claim which exists in the realm of 'Realpolitik' and nowhere else. In other words, Hal knew what his inheritance was and accepted it in that knowledge. The *non sequitur* of 'Then plain and right must my possession be', serves only to emphasise the original jibe from Richard.

Hal claims the crown by descent but knows he must be prepared to defend it by force.

> Lo, here it sits,
> Which God shall guard; and put the world's whole strength
> Into one giant arm, it shall not force
> This lineal honour from me: this from thee
> Will I to mine leave as 'tis left to me.
> (*2 Henry IV*, IV v 43–7)

'As 'tis left to me': that means doubtfully and only to be held by force ruthlessly applied. Henry's son proved an unsuitable recipient of such a sinister legacy. It is true but irrelevant that in this historical situation it is inconceivable that Henry should do other than accept and defend the crown, for a part of the present argument is that the very nature of the historical material is such as would inevitably produce such inconsistencies. These plays make two statements: the surface statement that Henry receives and defends what is his right, and below it – the clearer to read when the glitter of a public performance has faded – a second. This reports that Henry occupies, not by inheritance only but by conscious choice also, the throne of a murdered king. He 'repents', it is true, but Shakespeare shows through Claudius the petty value of such half-repentance and through Macbeth the emptiness of a stolen crown.

Henry V has many virtues which are of value in the body politic, but he 'retains the offence', and though during his reign stability is achieved, rebellion crushed in embryo and the nation united in a foreign war, yet the recovery is temporary, and the payment of the price of blood is only postponed. Apparently a very different man from his father, Hal shares with him one dominant characteristic: he deliberately chooses to emancipate himself from the bonds to which humanity should submit. Hal admits in words his bond to God, but like the other 'machiavels' he cultivates a deliberate 'non-attachment' to humanity, and Shakespeare reveals this both in his words and in his behaviour.

> I know you all, and will awhile uphold
> The unyoked humour of your idleness:
> Yet herein will I imitate the sun,
> Who doth permit the base contagious clouds
> To smother up his beauty from the world,
> That, when he please again to be himself,
> Being wanted, he may be more wonder'd at.
> *(1 Henry IV*, I ii 219–25)

This is the speech of a man who takes from others exactly what he wants – crown or companionship, love or amusement, the kingdom of England or the kingdom of France. He dismisses Falstaff,

forgets Poins, executes Bardolph, sends Cambridge, Scroop and
Grey to death, all with equal ease. Although one critic claims that
he dismisses Scroop 'with a sob', and the verse certainly takes
wing during this speech, the situation is essentially as remote
from emotion as the more famous dismissal of Falstaff. It is not
by coincidence that a special quality of music occurs in these
lines, the content of which is quite at variance with the character
of the speaker.

> What shall I say to thee, Lord Scroop? . . .
> Thou that didst bear the key of all my counsels,
> That knew'st the very bottom of my soul,
> That almost mightst have coin'd me into gold,
> Wouldst thou have practis'd on me for thy use,
> May it be possible, that foreign hire
> Could out of thee extract one spark of evil
> That might annoy my finger?   (II ii 94–102)

Henry was not a man with the right to condemn anyone for practising on another *for his use*; but Shakespeare could never stand
completely detached from a story of 'man's ingratitude' and perhaps these lines give us a fleeting glimpse not of Henry's mind
but of his creator's.

Henry's gaiety and ease of manner do not present any obstacles
to identifying him with the more obvious 'machiavels'. On the
contrary they are common elements in Shakespeare's picture of
the type. It seems as though he felt that only by exceptional charm
could such men hope to blind their fellows to their essentially predatory purposes. Even Falconbridge, from his ebullient first
entry to his temporary adoption of a machiavellian allegiance to
'commodity', has not a more delightful buoyancy than Edmund.
Richard III's animal spirits under the stimulus of danger are
infectious.

> Stir with the lark to-morrow, gentle Norfolk . . .
> Come, bustle, bustle; caparison my horse.
> . . . let us to't pell-mell.   (v iii 55, 289, 312)

Iago was apparently always popular; Desdemona herself enjoyed
his company, and with his songs and his jokes he was as welcome

to the gentle Cassio as to the foolish Roderigo. Even Macbeth is gifted with a winning graciousness, and it is only because actor and audience alike have such a plethora of riches to contend with that the fact is not always obvious in the theatre.

> Kind gentlemen, your pains
> Are register'd where every day I turn
> The leaf to read them,   (I iii 150–2)

he says, wringing the hands of Ross and Angus. And Duncan looks forward to visiting him with genuine pleasure:

> Let's after him,
> Whose care is gone before to bid us welcome:
> It is a peerless kinsman.   (I iv 56–8)

The graciousness that won those 'golden opinions' should be made clear in the opening scenes, for it is the same that he desperately strives to exercise after he is king, and which he knows deserts him. In Edmund, as in Falconbridge, this charm is closely related to a zest for life, as though the challenge of facing the universe untrammelled by scruples was intoxicatingly delightful. But if we have the slightest inclination to be fascinated by it, we need only remember Edmund leaving his father to the tender mercies of Cornwall, on the night of a storm which might well have shaken the complacency of the coolest heart.

How then, if by situation and character Henry V is clearly of the line of the 'machiavels', could Shakespeare adapt this child of his imagination to a play written to please an audience determined to admire and love their 'patriot king'? He succeeds in this apparently impossible task by creating a character which convincingly embodies the two apparently contradictory conceptions. In Henry V Shakespeare presents a man whose deliberately adopted machiavellian 'non-attachment' may fail him in a crisis, so that he becomes involved with humanity against his will and momentarily loses his defences. This quality of Hal's character, fully developed in the story of Agincourt, is indicated in *2 Henry IV*, where his relationship with his father is given unexpected overtones.

Prince. Shall I tell thee one thing, Poins?

Poins. Yes, faith, and let it be an excellent good thing. . . .

Prince. Marry, I tell thee, it is not meet that I should be sad,
now my father is sick: albeit I could tell to thee, as to
one it pleases me, for fault of a better to call my friend,
I could be sad, and sad indeed too.

Poins. Very hardly upon such a subject.

Prince. By this hand, thou thinkest me as far in the devil's book
as thou and Falstaff. . . . But I tell thee, my heart
bleeds inwardly that my father is so sick: and keeping
such vile company as thou art hath in reason taken
from me all ostentation of sorrow.

                                          (*2 Henry IV* II ii 37–55)

Very occasionally his creator allows a touch of sincere feeling to
find expression amid the formal rhetoric which usually characterises dialogue between Henry IV and his eldest son. The passionate, repetitive rhythm of:

> Do not think so; you shall not find it so:
>   (*1 Henry IV*, III ii 129)

rings true, and so does the last half line of:

> God witness with me, when I here came in,
> And found no course of breath within your majesty,
> How cold it struck my heart!   (*2 Henry IV*, IV 150–2)

But when we remember what Shakespeare sometimes makes of the
relationship between parent and child there seems little enough
warmth in this one.

The prince is shown, however, as genuinely stirred by his own
accession to the crown. Shakespeare appears to have realised with
peculiar intensity the crowding emotions which must sway a
young monarch mounting his father's throne. They add a quivering sensibility to the modest words of Malcolm after the death of
Macbeth, and he allows them to touch the usually cold heart of
Henry Plantagenet, giving him an unwonted gentleness.

> This new and gorgeous garment, majesty,
> Sits not so easy on me as you think.
> Brothers, you mix your sadness with some fear;

> This is the English, not the Turkish court.
> Not Amurath an Amurath succeeds,
> But Harry Harry. . . .
> I'll be your father and your brother too;
> Let me but bear your love, I'll bear your cares.
>   (*2 Henry IV*, v ii 44–58)

Such tenderness stirs in him again on the night before Agincourt. In spite of the mordant jesting with Williams and Bates he was suddenly touched by the plight of the tiny army surrounded in the darkness by its enemies, by the pathos of his lonely, helpless soldiers, by his vision that the victory he hoped to win is not for himself alone but for them all, by his unexpected realisation of his responsibility for everyone there:

> The day, my friends and all things stay for me.
>   (*Henry V*, iv i 325)

The words convey a humble, wondering acceptance of the role of leadership.

The same sudden, and to Henry himself surprising, involvement partially redeems the wooing of Katharine from the coarse, political bluster which it is sometimes said to be, and as which it certainly begins.

> To say to thee that I shall die, is true; but for thy love, by the Lord, no; *yet I love thee too.*   (v ii 159–60)

One can feel the check, the pause, the change of rhythm which show the actor how he may capture the surprise with which the wooer realises the birth of a genuine emotion. The speech changes in quality, the excitement mounts as, his 'blood begins to flatter' him that he desires and is desired. There is real feeling as he takes her into his arms with the words: 'Therefore, patiently and yielding . . .' which prepares us for the wondering murmur after the silence of his kiss: 'You have witchcraft in your lips, Kate.' Only a few minutes later, however, he has escaped from his emotion and is driving his hard bargain and making his bawdy jokes with Burgundy and the king. Not an unusual change perhaps, but here it seems deeply characteristic of the man.

If Henry is indeed the individualist, the unscrupulous 'getter' whose allegiance to 'commodity' could nevertheless occasionally be pierced by an attack on his heart, the earlier scenes with Falstaff fall more easily into their place. We can understand that Shakespeare intended to show us Hal responding to Falstaff's wit and light-hearted iconoclasm – as the rhythm and vigour of the language insist that he did. Between those two the current leapt genuinely enough; for a time they were neither of them – as their very similar philosophies of life dictated – simply self-sufficient and self-seeking. But Henry, free of two worlds for a while, soon made his choice and had re-established his independence of his friend long before he publicly rejected him. The most highly charged scene between Hal and Falstaff is the first, and even here the emotional warmth springs from Falstaff, not from the prince. It may be only a coincidence that we hear Shakespeare at work with the magic he elicits from the use of a repeated Christian name. Coriolanus and Othello are both given this trick of speech when they appeal in desperate loneliness to a false friend, and so it is not without interest that Falstaff uses it with Hal, on an occasion apparently so different and so cheerful.

Thou hast done much harm upon me, Hal; God forgive thee for it! Before I knew thee, Hal, I knew nothing; and now am I, if a man should speak truly, little better than one of the wicked. . . . Why, Hal, 'tis my vocation, Hal; 'tis no sin for a man to labour in his vocation.[4]   (1 *Henry IV*, I ii 102–17)

This is tender chaffing indeed, and Hal must be relishing it and responding at least in part, but his own tone is very different:

> *Prince.* A purse of gold most resolutely snatched on Monday
>   night and most dissolutely spent on Tuesday morning;
>   got with swearing 'Lay by' and spent with crying
>   'Bring in'; now in as low an ebb as the foot of the
>   ladder and by and by in as high a flow as the ridge of
>   the gallows. . . .
> *Falstaff.* I prithee, sweet wag, shall there be gallows standing
>   in England when thou art king? . . . Do not thou,
>   when thou art king, hang a thief.
> *Prince.* No; thou shalt.

Falstaff. Shall I? O rare! By the Lord, I'll be a brave judge.
Prince. Thou judgest false already: I mean, thou shalt have the
hanging of the thieves and so become a rare hangman.
Falstaff. Well, Hal, well.   (I ii 39–77)

Falstaff bears no malice for the snub, but the greater refusal to
come gives poignancy to the naively eager speech-rhythms of
his question and exclamation. In the episode of 'excellent sport'
when first Falstaff and then the prince play the part of the king,
there can be no doubt whose fooling is the more gracious. The
prince's language has a flavour almost nauseous, which indicates
that any feeling he once had for Falstaff has been cast away.

> *Prince.* . . . . there is a devil haunts thee in the likeness of an old
> fat man; . . . Why dost thou converse with that trunk
> of humours, that bolting-hutch of beastliness, that
> swollen parcel of dropsies, that huge bombard of sack,
> that stuffed cloak-bag of guts, that roasted Manningtree
> ox with the pudding in his belly. . . .
> *Falstaff.* I would your grace would take me with you: whom
> means your grace? . . . for sweet Jack Falstaff, kind
> Jack Falstaff . . . and therefore more valiant, being, as
> he is, old Jack Falstaff, banish not him thy Harry's
> company: banish plump Jack, and banish all the world.
> *Prince.* I do, I will.   (II iv 492–528)

Again the warning sounds, but the act which it appears to foretell
has in reality already taken place. One feels inclined – Brabantio-
wise – to agree with Falstaff when he complains that he must have
'taken medicines' to make him love this cold-blooded young man,
particularly when one realises that at the very moment he makes
this protest he believes that the prince has hidden his horse. The
play-acting scene is the last intimate meeting between Falstaff and
the Prince, for at their later encounter at Mistress Quickly's Falstaff's attention is elsewhere, and he has in fact just given his
shrewdest summing-up of the prince's character:

A good shallow young fellow: a' would have made a good pantler,
a' would ha' chipped bread well.   (*2 Henry IV*, II iv 257–8)

There is no more talk of love philtres.

Falstaff's own attitude is of course a genuine and brilliant example of ambivalence. His conscious philosophy of life is as machiavellian as Hal's own, and his marauding expeditions to Gloucestershire show him as ruthless as ever his prince could be:

> if the young dace be a bait for the old pike, I see no reason in the law of nature but I may snap at him.   (III ii 355–7)

His allegiance is divided between the values of two distinct worlds. When news of Hal's accession reaches him his first reaction is utterly unscrupulous, though generous as well.

> Away, Bardolph! saddle my horse. Master Robert Shallow, choose what office thou wilt in the land, 'tis thine. Pistol, I will double-charge thee with dignities. . . . Let us take any man's horses; the laws of England are at my commandment.
>   (v iii 127–32)

It is easy to dismiss the excitement while he waits for the newly crowned king as selfish and the emotion of his greeting as merely histrionic, but the situation is not so simple. If it were, what is to account for the death scene in *Henry V*, and his followers' poignant explanation of it?

> *Nym.* The king hath run bad humours on the knight; that's
>   the even of it.
> *Pistol* Nym, thou hast spoke the right;
>   His heart is fracted and corroborate.   (II i 127–30)

Shakespeare has elsewhere written of a parallel situation in which a young friend, admired although criticised, betrays the love of an older man. There are certain lines in some of the sonnets between nos. 87 and 112 which are curiously relevant to his portrait of Henry. The lines

> That tongue that tells the story of thy days,
> Making lascivious comments on thy sport,
> Cannot dispraise but in a kind of praise;
> Naming thy name blesses an ill report,
>   (Sonnet 95, 5–8)

strongly suggest the ambivalent attitude to the royal hero which breaks the play apart. So does

> Thou makest faults graces that to thee resort.
> As on the finger of a throned queen
> The basest jewel will be well esteem'd,
> So are those errors that in thee are seen.
>
> (Sonnet 96, 4–7)

The best comment on the scene in which Falstaff is disowned is found in the famous lines concerning the men

> Who, moving others, are themselves as stone,
> Unmoved, cold, and to temptation slow.
> They rightly do inherit heaven's graces
> And husband nature's riches from expense;
> They are the lords and owners of their faces,
> Others but stewards of their excellence.
>
> (Sonnet 94, 3–8)

'Stone' and 'cold' have pejorative overtones which are reinforced by their uses elsewhere in Shakespeare's work,[5] and it is equally true that the possible parallels with Falstaff are all sympathetic ones.

The friend who is in the time of life

> When yellow leaves, or none, or few, do hang
> Upon those boughs which shake against the cold,
>
> (Sonnet 73, 2–3)

pleads that for his conduct Fortune should be blamed:

> The guilty goddess of my harmful deeds,
> That did not better for my life provide
> Than public means which public manners breeds.
>
> (Sonnet 111, 2–4)

He too hopes his friendship may be preserved if he is content to hide it:

> I will acquaintance strangle and look strange,
> Be absent from thy walks,[6] and in my tongue
> Thy sweet beloved name[7] no more shall dwell.
>
> (Sonnet 89, 8–10)

Finally, the poet foresees for himself the death which he allotted to Falstaff:

> But do thy worst to steal thyself away,
> For term of life thou art assured mine,
> And life no longer than thy love will stay,
> For it depends upon that love of thine.
>
> (Sonnet 92, 1–4)

The truth appears on the lips of simple men:

> The king hath run bad humours on the knight . . .
> Nym, thou hast spoke the right.

Whatever his historical material made necessary in the plotting of his play, the poems make plain where, according to Shakespeare, the true values lay. When the king's voice cuts the air with the words 'I know thee not, old man,' all the glittering panoply of the coronation procession is torn aside for a moment to show the abyss where human beings betray each other's trust and where a young man may break an old man's heart. The love so deliberately rejected was real, and it is the manner of Falstaff's death which proves it. There had been a warning: 'Banish plump Jack and banish all the world.' 'I do. I will.' The world which Hal banished with such easy assurance contained more than he knew.

The interpretation of Henry as a man deeply divided within himself is reinforced by a consideration of the abnormally violent and unpleasant emotionalism of some of the young king's speeches on war, which is stressed by Mr Traversi in his recent book.[8] He notices particularly the speech before Harfleur and remarks on its gratuitous threats of sexual outrage:

> If I begin the battery once again,
> I will not leave the half-achieved Harfleur
> Till in her ashes she lie buried.
> The gates of mercy shall be all shut up,
> And the flesh'd soldier, rough and hard of heart,
> In liberty of bloody hand shall range
> With conscience wide as hell, mowing like grass
> Your fresh-fair virgins and your flowering infants.
> What is it then to me, if impious war,

> Array'd in flames like to the prince of fiends,
> Do, with his smirched complexion, all fell feats
> Enlink'd to waste and desolation?
> What is't to me, when you yourselves are cause,
> If your pure maidens fall into the hand
> Of hot and forcing violation?
> What rein can hold licentious wickedness
> When down the hill he holds his fierce career?
>
> (III iii 7–23)

All this is horrible and Shakespeare of course knew it to be so.
The nature of his own response to physical violence is proved by
the trembling awareness shown in much of his animal imagery:

> And as the butcher bears away the calf
> And binds the wretch and beats it when it strays,
> Bearing it to the bloody slaughter-house,
> Even so remorseless have they borne him hence;
> And as the dam runs lowing up and down,
> Looking the way her harmless young one went,
> And can do nought but wail her darling's loss,
> Even so myself bewails good Gloucester's case.
>
> (*2 Henry VI*, III i 210–17)

'The hot scent-snuffing hounds', though the musician in Shakespeare could enjoy the sound of their baying, particularly 'in the
distant valley', could not swing his sympathy from hunted to
hunter:

> By this, poor Wat, far off upon a hill,
> Stands on his hinder legs with listening ear,
> To hearken if his foes pursue him still . . .
> Then shalt thou see the dew-bedabbled wretch
> Turn and return, indenting with the way;
> Each envious brier his weary legs doth scratch,
> Each shadow makes him stop, each murmur stay.
>
> (*Venus and Adonis* 697–708)

Since the dumb victims of man's violence present themselves to
his mind in these colours it is impossible that Shakespeare wrote
such words as Henry's without being aware of their implications.

The only man who rivals Henry in the violence of his language about the ravages of war is Timon, who in the desperation of his misanthropy urges Alcibiades to ravish Athens in words hardly stronger than Henry's own.

> *Timon.* If Alcibiades kill my countrymen,
> Let Alcibiades know this of Timon,
> That Timon cares not. But if he sack fair Athens,
> And take our goodly aged men by the beards,
> Giving our holy virgins to the stain
> Of contumelious, beastly, mad-brain'd war,
> Then let him know, and tell him Timon speaks it,
> In pity of our aged and our youth,
> I cannot choose but tell him, that I care not.
>   (*Timon of Athens*, v i 172–80)

The parallel is sufficiently startling to suggest that Shakespeare thought things about his hero king that could not be openly proclaimed in the play of his victories but which could be insinuated so as to make the judicious grieve. Moreover it is certain that such hysterical over-emphasis and obsession with the horrors of what he was doing would be a likely element of a guilt-ridden and divided mind. Mr Traversi also points out Henry's habit of endeavouring to put the responsibility of his own acts of violence on to others, as he does at Harfleur and also before declaring war on France – another realistic touch in the portrait of a neurotic who has deliberately suppressed his more honest and generous qualities but has by no means inhibited them entirely.

SOURCE: *Character and Symbol in Shakespeare's Plays* (1962).

NOTES

1. Civic records show that the Coventry plays were 'laid down' in 1580.

2. This is the text of the *Ludus Coventriae* play. The MS of the Coventry Guild play is of course lost.

3. The Scroop executed by Henry was in fact the nephew of the archbishop. There is no reference to him in Holinshed in connection with the rebels, and he is not known to have been implicated in the northern rebellion. I can find no other historical character to whom Shakespeare could have been referring however, and his choice of the name is therefore significant.

4. But yet the pity of it, Iago! O Iago, the pity of it, Iago! (*Othello*, IV I 206–7)

> Aufidius, though I cannot make true wars,
> I'll frame convenient peace. Now, good Aufidius,
> Were you in my stead, would you have heard
> A mother less? or granted less, Aufidius? (*Coriolanus*, V iii 190–3)

5. e.g. Toad, that under cold stone
Days and nights has thirty-one. (*Macbeth*, IV i 6–7)

6. Cf. I shall be sent for soon at night. (*2 Henry IV*, V v 94).

7. Cf. above, p. 220.

8. Derek Traversi, *Shakespeare from 'Richard II' to 'Henry V'* (1958) pp. 182–3. See above, pp. 154–5, 158.

L. C. Knights

SHAKESPEARE'S POLITICS (1957)

WHEN we speak of Shakespeare's politics there are possibilities of misunderstanding to guard against. 'Policy', 'politic', and 'politician' are words that occur in Shakespeare, sometimes with a pejorative implication – 'a scurvy politician', 'base and rotten policy' – that might tempt us to suppose a context like that of the modern political platform. The supposition would of course be wrong. 'Politics' (which Shakespeare does not use) only acquired its most frequent modern meanings – 'political affairs', 'political principles or opinions' – much later, with the rise of the parties. If you had said to Shakespeare, 'Do you take any part in politics?' or 'What are your politics?' he would probably have been puzzled. 'Politics' still implied systematic thought on the constitution of states and the art of government – a matter for philosophers: our 'politics', the conduct of internal affairs of state, together with the observation of 'who's in, who's out', and plans to reverse that order – these were matters for the men who did the work, of constant interest only to them, to those with special interests to press, and to a fringe of Politic Would-be's. Shakespeare, like the great majority of his fellow-countrymen, 'had no politics': he had too many other things to think about. The fact remains, however, that although he made no arbitrary separation between what is politics and what is not (and this, to anticipate, is a notable aspect of his political wisdom), he showed throughout his career a lively concern with men not only in their private and personal, but in their public and formal, relations. And this concern included questions of power and subordination, of mutual relations within a constituted society, of the ends and methods of public action, so that we may properly speak of Shakespeare's political philosophy – so long, that is, as we remember that this philosophy is not something ready formed once for all, and applied or exhibited in varying circumstances, but a part of that constant search for meanings that informs his work as a whole.

A recent writer on the history of political thought has called Shakespeare 'a superb interpreter of group psychology and an almost unrivalled observer of political behaviour'.[1] I doubt whether these phrases quite do justice to Shakespeare's political wisdom. They do, however, call attention to one element in it, namely its realism. Shakespeare's political realism is not of course Machiavellian or modern realism ('How realistic is the realist?' is a question that the plays force us to ask), but it is certainly based on a clear perception of the actualities of political situations. Consider for example the implicit comment made by the play *Richard II* on the wishful thinking of a king for whom words and dramatic postures take the place of action; the explicit comments of the Bastard on 'commodity' in *King John*, and the place his comments have within the larger political action; or the sombre demonstration in *King Henry IV* of what is involved in getting and keeping power: the recognition of inevitable consequences by the dying Bolingbroke

> – For all my reign hath been but as a scene
>   Acting that argument –

enforces the same political moral as Marvell's Horatian Ode

> – The same Arts that did gain
>   A Power must it maintain –

and enforces it with a similar effect of irony. But Shakespeare's realism goes further than this; fundamentally it is a refusal to allow the abstract and general to obscure the personal and specific. After the earliest plays on English history Shakespeare's political plays are not shaped by a predetermined pattern of ideas: like the rest of his work they are the result of a full exposure to experience. If they unavoidably raise moral issues it is because of the felt pressure of life itself.[2] If they clarify for us Clarendon's phrase about 'that fathomless abyss of Reason of State', it is because they insist on setting every 'political' action in the widest

possible human context and so – implicitly, if not always explicitly – assessing it in relation to that context. It is of especial
significance that the political action of *Henry IV* has for setting
scenes in which the actions of great ones take on a quite different
appearance, in which the assumptions of the dominant groups
are by no means taken for granted, and which therefore act as a
challenge to those assumptions.

In the two political plays that follow *Henry IV*, in *Henry V*
and *Julius Caesar*, Shakespeare continues the questioning of what
statesmen are likely to accept without question. It is one of the
curiosities of literature that *Henry V* should have been seen so
often as a simple glorification of the hero-king. I am not suggesting that we should merely reverse the conventional estimate. It
is simply that, on the evidence of the play itself, Shakespeare's
attitude towards the King is complex and critical. As M. Fluchère
has said, 'While making the necessary concessions to patriotic
feeling . . . Shakespeare lets us see . . . that the political problem,
linked with the moral problem, is far from being solved by a
victorious campaign and a marriage with happy consequences
for the country'.[3] In other words, the political problem, purely at
the level of politics and the political man, is insoluble. In *Julius
Caesar*, freed from the embarrassments of a patriotic theme, and
with the problem projected into a 'Roman' setting, Shakespeare
examines more closely the contradictions and illusions involved
in political action. The matter cannot be properly argued here,
but it seems to me undeniable that the play offers a deliberate
contrast between the person and the public persona, the face and
the mask; that tragic illusion and error are shown to spring from
the wrenching apart of the two worlds – the personal and the
public; and that Brutus, in particular, is a study in what Coleridge
was to describe as the politics of pure – or abstract – reason, with
the resulting sophistries and inevitable disappointments.[4]

I hope that even from so cursory a survey of some of the plays
preceding the great tragedies one point has become clear: that
even in plays where the political interest is most evident, it is
never exclusive or, as it were, self-contained. The implied question, What does this political action or attitude mean? is invari-

ably reduced to personal terms: How does this affect relations between men? What kind of man acts in this way? How does he further make himself by so acting? Swift says of the party man, 'when he is got near the walls of his assembly he assumes and affects an entire set of very different airs; he conceives himself a being of a superior nature to those without, and acting in a sphere, where the vulgar methods for the conduct of human life can be of no use.'[5] It is Shakespeare's distinction that, when dealing with rulers and matters of state, he constantly brings us back to 'the vulgar methods for the conduct of human life', that he refuses to accept a closed realm of the political. Indeed, it is only by a deliberate focusing of our interest for a particular purpose that we can separate 'political' from 'non-political' plays, the two kinds being in fact mixed by common themes and preoccupations. Thus in the Second Part of *Henry IV* Shakespeare's interests are plainly setting away from his ostensible subject towards a more fundamental exploration of the human condition that points towards the great tragedies; and *Julius Caesar* shares with later, non-political plays, a preoccupation with the ways in which men give themselves to illusion. So too, from *Julius Caesar* onwards, it is possible to trace Shakespeare's political themes only in plays that, with the exception of *Coriolanus*, are not primarily political plays.

Troilus and Cressida, King Lear, Macbeth – each of these, in one of its aspects, takes the political theme a stage further. *Troilus and Cressida* makes a simple but far-reaching discovery: it is that the sixteenth-century commonplace of the necessity for order and degree might mean much or little according as the reason that formulated it was, or was not, grounded in the responsiveness to life of the whole person. I refer especially to what might be called the dramatic status of Ulysses' well-known speech on 'degree'. In the context of the whole play – the clash of varied attitudes to life which forces us to a judgment – this speech appears as something other than the expression of an unquestioned standard: for the significant thing is that it is spoken by Ulysses, and Ulysses is the chief exponent of a reason and policy that do not, any more than Troilus' emotionalism, commend themselves to us. To put it simply, just as emotion, divorced from reason, is reduced to appetite ('And the will dotes that is inclinable To what infectiously itself affects . . .'), so reason, divorced from intuition, is reduced to cleverness: statecraft, for Ulysses, is the manipulation of men. Political order and authority – so the play as a whole forces us to conclude – are not concepts to be accepted without question, independent of some prior ground from which they draw their justification.

That ground is explored in *King Lear*; it is taken for granted in *Macbeth* and *Coriolanus*. What I mean is this. *King Lear* is not a political play; it is a play about the conditions of being human, and it seeks to answer the great question put by Lear as Everyman, 'Who is it that can tell me who I am?' But at the same time it has marked political implications. A play in which 'the king *is* but as the beggar' was bound to raise the social question, and to do rather more than hint that 'distribution should undo excess'. It was almost bound to raise the question of justice: why should the half-witted vagrant be whipped from tithing to tithing, or the farmer's dog be an image of authority? But the political implications go further than that. In a lecture on 'The Politics of *King Lear*' Edwin Muir has suggested that Goneril, Regan, and Edmund have in common a way of seeing people which lacks a dimension. For Edmund, as A. C. Bradley had remarked, men and women are 'divested of all quality except their relation to [his] end; as indifferent as mathematical quantities or mere physical agents'. So too, says Mr Muir, Goneril and Regan 'exist in this shallow present'; without memory, they are without responsibility, and their speech 'consists of a sequence of pitiless truisms. . . . Their shallowness is ultimately that of the Machiavellian view of life as it was understood in [Shakespeare's] age, of 'policy'. We need not shrink from regarding Edmund and his confederates as political types'.[6] This, if we do not push it too far, suggests one of the ways in which the group opposed to Lear may properly be regarded. And the converse also holds. *King Lear* establishes the grounds of any politics that claim to be more than a grammar of power. Behind hierarchy and authority, behind formal justice and public order, is a community of persons bound by 'holy cords. . . . Which are too intrinse t'unloose.' The basic political facts of this play are that men can feel for each other, and that this directness of relationship – expressing itself in the humblest of ways as well as in the most exalted forms of loyalty and sacrifice – is the only alternative to a predatory power-seeking whose necessary end is anarchy. Ulysses, it will be remembered, had foretold how chaos would follow the 'choking' of degree:

> Then everything includes itself in power,
> Power into will, will into appetite;
> And appetite, an universal wolf,
> So doubly seconded with will and power,
> Must make perforce an universal prey,
> And last eat up himself.

In *King Lear*, Albany, envisaging the same state of chaos, significantly shifts the argument:

> That nature, which contemns its origin,
> Cannot be border'd certain in itself;
> She that herself will sliver and disbranch
> From her material sap, perforce must wither
> And come to deadly use . . .
> If that the heavens do not their visible spirits
> Send quickly down to tame these vile offences,
> It will come,
> Humanity must perforce prey on itself,
> Like monsters of the deep.

We hardly need to put each passage back in its context to see that the later one draws on a far deeper sense of what it is that sanctions the human order.[7] Lear's discovery of his kinship with the naked poor is both a moral and a political discovery: it is a king who says, 'O! I have ta'en too little care of this.'

That is what I meant by saying that *Macbeth* takes for granted the ground established in *King Lear*. Evil in *Macbeth* is more than tyranny; but tyranny is part of the evil, and it is defined in terms of a violation of those bonds – the 'holy cords' – that are essential to the being of man as man. We cannot fail to be affected by the varied images of concord, of mutual service and relationship, through which we are made aware that behind the disintegration and dissolution of Macbeth's state – of his 'single state of man' and of the state at large – are contrasting possibilities of order. And it seems to me that the conception of order – as we are given it, in the play – draws on a different dimension of experience from that envisaged in the 'degree' speech of Ulysses. In *Macbeth* institutional life – all that is indicated and symbolized by churches, castles, 'humane statute' – guards and guarantees a living system of relationships ('honour, love, obedience . . .'), which in turn are related to more than human sanctions. Thus the evocation of the temple-haunting martlets, of the birds that securely build and breed, is an image of life delighting in life, and it subtly and powerfully contributes to our sense of the ideal presence of a life-bearing order in the human commonwealth – in what the play calls 'the gentle weal'.[8]

In *Coriolanus*, which is the last of the great tragedies and also the last overtly political play, Shakespeare takes up again from the earlier 'histories' the theme of the Governor. Those earlier plays were largely, though not exclusively, studies of rulers who failed because they were isolated within an arbitrary conception of power or privilege: and I think one could deduce from them that Shakespeare saw the good ruler as not merely set over the people whom he ruled (though rule is necessary), but linked with, and in some sense expressive of, the society for whose sake he performs his office.[9] In *Coriolanus* the main subject is the relation between a member of the ruling class, a Governor, and the political society to which he belongs; and the handling of it results in a breaking-down of any over-simple distinction we might be tempted to make between what is 'individual', on the one hand, and what is 'social' and 'political' on the other. It is clear that if individual qualities are partly the result of social pressures (behind Coriolanus is Volumnia, and behind Volumnia is the patrician class), the political crisis is, to say the least, exacerbated by the personal disorders that play into it. The isolation and over-development of one quality in the hero is not only analogous to the failure of connexion and integration in the social group ('Rome and her rats'), the one is shown as having a direct bearing on the other. The play thus draws on the same established affirmations as *Macbeth*: the state is not simply an embodiment of power, it is society in its political or public aspect; and society is a mutual relation of persons who, by and large, need each other if they are to come to anything like maturity. What the play emphasizes is the challenge of difference and diversity. There is no suggestion that the social distinctions between patricians and plebeians ought not to exist: it *is* suggested that the diversified social group, the body politic, is in danger of corruption to the extent that *what lies behind diversity* is lost sight of. 'What lies behind' is of course simple humanity. It is Coriolanus's defective humanity that makes him a defective governor.

If I have spoken as though these plays offered us a simple political moral or message, my excuse must be that the necessary qualifications are sufficiently obvious. Indeed it might be claimed that my simplifications have all been in the interest of a recognition of complexity. Shakespeare's political thought, I have insisted, is not a body of abstract principles to be applied and illustrated. It is part of a continuous exploration and assessment of experience: it grows and develops. And in any one play it is part of a complex organization whose very nature it is, as work of art, to challenge each individual reader to become imaginatively alive: the political meanings are only *there* to the extent that we do so respond. So long as we keep this clearly in mind, simplification may have its uses. What I most want to suggest, then, is that Shakespeare's political meanings – the things he tells us about politics – are inherent in and inseparable from his method, his way of presenting his political material. Aware as he is of the need for mutual relationships within society, he does not merely preach this: rather he explores – with a maximum of concreteness and immediacy – the nature of mutuality and its opposite. Thus the distrust that he shows, from first to last, for individualism – for the attitude expressed in Richard of Gloucester's 'I am myself alone' – is based on a sure grasp of the self-mutilation inherent in egotism and isolation, of the inevitable denaturing effect of an attitude that wilfully blinds itself to the fact that personal life only has its being in relationship; Macbeth as tyrant inevitably 'keeps alone'. The converse of this is the pervasive sense that we find in the plays that the foundations of political organization are in the realm 'beyond politics', in those varied relationships that are the necessary condition of individual growth: it is only a Caliban (and Caliban drunk at that) who can wish for an untrammelled 'freedom'. What we may call the idea of the state in Shakespeare is thus fundamentally opposed to the Renaissance conception of the state as a work of art.[10] Nor can it be adequately expressed by the conventional analogy of the bees,

> Creatures that by a rule in nature teach
> The act of order to a peopled kingdom.

Shakespeare probed further and more subtly than the political Archbishop of *Henry V*. What he went on to ask – what, I think, he was already asking when he wrote *Henry V* – was, what are the foundations of a living order? Both *Macbeth* and *Coriolanus* confirm the maxims,

> If a man have not order within him
> He can not spread order about him . . .
> And if the prince have not order within him
> He can not put order in his dominions:

the disordered man makes for disorder, not only in his more immediate circle but in his wider social relations.[11] And the contrasting positive values? Shakespeare does not sum things up for us, but I think that a few sentences from Boethius' *De Consolatione Philosophiae* (in the English of Chaucer) come close to the spirit of his political philosophy: '. . . al this accordaunce of thynges is bounde with love, that governeth erthe and see, and hath also commandement to the hevene. . . . This love halt togidres peples joyned with an holy boond, . . . and love enditeth lawes to trewe felawes.'[12] The love that is in question is not of course simply a matter of feeling; it includes a neighbourly tolerance of differences and a sense of mutual need; and in its openness to life, its willingness to *listen*, it is allied to that justice which gives each man his due, looking towards what he is, or can become; and there is delight superadded.[13] Shakespeare's abundance, his feeling for uniqueness and variety, his imaginative grasp of what makes for life – these qualities ensure that when political issues are handled in the plays we sense behind them a concern for the 'trewe felawes' (Boethius' *sodales*), for the living body politic in all its variety. We are inevitably prompted to a clearer recognition of the fact that a wholesome political order is not something arbitrary and imposed, but an expression of relationships between particular persons within an organic society. The 'concord' that Shakespeare invokes as the alternative to both tyranny and anarchy in *Macbeth* (IV iii 97–100) has this depth of meaning behind it.

SOURCE: 'Shakespeare's Politics: with some Reflections on the Nature of Tradition', Annual Shakespeare Lecture of the British Academy, 1957, in *Proceedings of the British Academy* Vol. XLIII.

NOTES

1. Christopher Morris, *Political Thought in England: Tyndale to Hooker* (Home University Library: Oxford, 1953) p. 103.
2. I have in mind the passage in Henry James's Preface to *The Portrait of a Lady*, where he speaks of 'the perfect dependence of the "moral" sense of a work of art on the amount of felt life concerned in producing it'.
3. Henri Fluchère, *Shakespeare*, tr. G. Hamilton (1953) p. 204. I also agree with Mr D. A. Traversi that the effect of the play is 'to bring out certain contradictions, moral and human, inherent in the notion of a successful king'. *Shakespeare: from 'Richard II' to 'Henry V'* (1957) p. 177.
4. See *The Friend*, First Section, 'On the Principles of Political Knowledge'.
5. Swift is speaking of 'those, who in a late reign began the distinction between the personal and politick capacity'. *A Discourse of the Contests . . . between the Nobles and the Commons in Athens and Rome* (1701) ch. v.
6. 'The Politics of *King Lear*', in *Essays in Literature and Society*, pp. 39–42. See also J. F. Danby's *Shakespeare's Doctrine of Nature: a study of 'King Lear'* (1949, repr. 1965) especially, in this connexion, p. 38.

7. In *The Allegory of Love* (1936) p. 110, C. S. Lewis translates some lines from the Latin *Architrenius* of Johannes de Altavilla which curiously sum up the central movement of *King Lear*, including its political meaning:

> This must I do – go exil'd through the world
> And seek for Nature till far hence I find
> Her secret dwelling-place; there drag to light
> The hidden cause of quarrel, and reknit,
> Haply reknit, the long-divided Love.

8. These values are of course positively present to our minds and imaginations even in the explicit denial of them by the protagonists – in Macbeth's great invocation of chaos in IV i, for example.

9. In the simple moralizing of the gardeners' scene in *Richard II* (III iv) the King's function is explicitly to 'trim and dress' his land, 'as we this garden': that is, not to impose his mere will, but to foster what is given in accordance with the laws of its nature. We may compare Burgundy's speech in *Henry V*, v ii. In *Measure for Measure* Escalus, unlike Angelo – and this helps to define the Deputy – has a side of himself open to the rather foolish Elbow: Angelo talks about abstract justice; Escalus patiently sifts the evidence in an apparently unimportant case.

10. See Burckhardt, *The Civilization of the Renaissance*, part I, 'The State as a Work of Art'.

11. Ezra Pound (Canto XIII) puts these words into the mouth of a Chinese sage. The idea, I suppose, is common in Western philosophy; my point is that Shakespeare does not merely invoke the idea, valuable as it is, he makes vividly present the kind of actuality from which the idea springs. Professor D. W. Harding, writing on the psychological aspects of war in *The Impulse to Dominate*, has reminded us that a mass phenomenon like war is not something that simply *happens* to a community, that in the last analysis it is rooted in individual habits that make part of the texture of normal 'peaceful' existence.

12. Book II, Metrum 8.

13. Paul Tillich's *Love, Power and Justice* (1954), describing the intrinsic and necessary relation between these three concepts, will be found to clarify the meaning of love in social – as well as in directly personal – relations. On listening as a function of creative justice see especially pp. 84–5.

SELECT BIBLIOGRAPHY

There are several good modern critical editions:

The New Cambridge, ed. J. Dover Wilson (Cambridge U.P.,
London and New York, 1947).
The New Arden, ed. J. H. Walter (Methuen, 1954).
The Yale, ed. R. J. Dorius (New Haven, 1955).

Some of them are now available in paperback editions.

E. M. W. Tillyard, *The Elizabethan World Picture* (Chatto &
Windus, 1943; Macmillan, New York, 1944, 1961; Peregrine
paperback, 1962).
A useful, though simplified account of the Elizabethan view of
the universe as an ordered and harmonious hierarchical struc-
ture.
E. M. W. Tillyard, *Shakespeare's History Plays* (Chatto &
Windus, 1944; Macmillan, New York, 1946; Barnes &
Noble, 1964; Peregrine paperback, 1962; Collier paperback).
Irving Ribner, *The English History Play in the Age of Shakespeare*
(Princeton U.P., 1957; Methuen, 1965; Barnes & Noble,
1965).
These studies by Tillyard and Ribner are essential reading if
the history-plays are to be placed in their literary and historical
contexts.
J. Dover Wilson, *The Fortunes of Falstaff* (Cambridge U.P.,
1943; Macmillan, New York, 1944; Cambridge paperback,
1964).
One of the classics of modern Shakespeare criticism; particularly important for the relationship of *Henry V* to the *Henry
IV* plays.

Lily B. Campbell, *Shakespeare's 'Histories': mirrors of Elizabethan policy* (Huntington Library, San Marino, Cal., 1947; Methuen, 1964).

Argues, with impressive force and massive detail, that the history-plays mirror contemporary Elizabethan situations.

J. W. Cunliffe, 'The Character of Henry V as Prince and King', in *Shakespearian Studies*, ed. B. Matthews and A. H. Thorndike (New York, 1916), pp. 311–31.

A good example of the uneasy marriage of admiration and distaste for Henry V found in the early twentieth century.

Narrative and Dramatic Sources of Shakespeare, ed. G. Bullough, vol. IV (Routledge & Kegan Paul, 1962; Columbia U.P., 1962).

Extensive extracts from Holinshed and other sources, the text of the anonymous play, *The Famous Victories of Henry V*, and a thorough examination of Shakespeare's use of his sources.

Allan Gilbert, 'Patriotism and Satire in *Henry V*', in *Shakespeare Studies*, ed. A. D. Matthews and C. M. Emery (University of Miami Press, 1953) pp. 40–64.

In discussing 'independent and even contradictory' elements in *Henry V*, Gilbert provides a valuable examination of Shakespeare's use of Holinshed.

John Palmer, *The Political Characters of Shakespeare* (Macmillan, 1945; reissued, with *The Comic Characters*, Macmillan, 1962).

A thorough Bradleyan study of the character of Henry V, shot through with a pleasant but often devastating irony.

M. M. Reese, *The Cease of Majesty* (Arnold, 1961).

A leisurely, well-written study of the history-plays that comprehends a great deal of the background material and the critical discussions.

H. E. Toliver, 'Falstaff, the Prince, and the History Play', in *Shakespeare Quarterly*, XVI (1965) 63–80.

A scholarly study of the relationship of *Henry V* to *Henry IV* and of the critical problem of genre.

C. B. Hogan, *Shakespeare in the Theatre 1701–1800*, 2 vols (Clarendon, 1952, 1957).

G. C. D. Odell, *Shakespeare from Betterton to Irving*, 2 vols
   (Constable, London and New York, 1920).
J. C. Trewin, *Shakespeare on the English Stage (1900–1964)*
   (Barrie & Rockliff, 1964).
   These three works, together with the 'Stage History' section
   in Wilson's New Cambridge Edition, supplement Sprague's
   essay on *Henry V* as 'a play for the stage'.

BIBLIOGRAPHICAL ADDENDUM, 1980

James L. Calderwood, *Metadrama in Shakespeare's Henriad: 'Richard
   II' to 'Henry V'* (University of California Press, 1979).
   A lively and original approach to the Histories; *Henry V* is
   discussed mainly in relation to Shakespeare's 'epic' technique
   and the play's 'popular' appeal.
Andrew Gurr, 'Henry V and the Bees' Commonwealth', in
   Shakespeare Survey, 30 (1977), 61–72.
   In a world where few are innocent, the King is under pressure
   to justify his claim to the throne.
Robert Ornstein, *A Kingdom for a Stage* (Harvard University Press,
   1972).
   An important challenge to the Tillyard-Campbell orthodoxy,
   with a cautiously ironic reading of *Henry V*.

NOTES ON CONTRIBUTORS

UNA ELLIS-FERMOR (1894–1958), Somerville College, Oxford; taught at Bedford College, London, 1918–47; Hildred Carlile Professor of English in the University of London from 1947; general editor of the New Arden Shakespeare; author of *The Jacobean Drama* (1936), *The Irish Dramatic Movement* (1939), *The Frontiers of Drama* (1945), etc.

GERALD GOULD (1885–1936), poet, essayist, journalist, lecturer; sometime Fellow of University College, London, and of Merton College, Oxford.

L. C. KNIGHTS (b. 1906), Member of the editorial board of *Scrutiny* 1932–53; Professor of English in Sheffield 1947–52 and in Bristol 1953–64; King Edward VII Professor of English in Cambridge 1965–73, subsequently Emeritus Professor and Hon. Fellow of Selwyn College; author of *Drama and Society in the Age of Jonson* (1937), *Explorations* (1946), *Some Shakespearean Themes* (1959), *Further Explorations* (1965), etc.

HONOR MATTHEWS, sometime Head of the Department of Speech and Drama, Goldsmiths' College, University of London.

E. E. STOLL (1874–1959), for many years professor of English at the University of Minnesota; one of the first exponents of the view that Shakespeare should be studied in terms of the conventions of Elizabethan drama; author of *Shakespeare Studies* (1927), *Poets and Playwrights* (1930), *Art and Artifice in Shakespeare* (1933), etc.

A. C. SPRAGUE (b. 1895), taught English at Bryn Mawr; author of *Shakespeare and the Audience* (1935), *Shakespeare and the Actors: the stage business* (1944), *Shakespearean Players and Performances* (1953), etc.

ZDENĚK STŘÍBRNÝ, Head of the Department of English, Charles University, Prague; author of *Shakespeare's History Plays* (1959), etc.

DEREK A. TRAVERSI (b. 1912), formerly Fellow of Merton College, Oxford and since 1970 Professor of English, Swarthmore College, Penn. author of *Approach to Shakespeare* (1938), *Shakespeare: the last phase* (1954), *Shakespeare; From 'Richard II' to 'Henry V'* (1957), *Shakespeare: the Roman Plays* (1963).

MARK VAN DOREN (1894–1972), poet, critic; universities of Illinois and Columbia; author of *John Dryden* (1920), *Shakespeare* (1938), etc.

J. H. WALTER, formerly headmaster of Minchenden School, Southgate, London; editor of the New Arden edition of *Henry V* and of schools editions of other Shakespeare plays.

CHARLES WILLIAMS (1886–1945), novelist, poet, playwright, critic; author of *Reason and Beauty in the Poetic Mind* (1933), *Selected Writings* (1961), etc.

ROSE A. ZIMBARDO (b. 1932), Brooklyn College and Yale; has taught at City College, New York, and in the State University of New York.

INDEX